D1613362

Victorian women were exhilarated by the authoritative voice and the professional opportunity that, uniquely, the theatre offered them. Victorian men, anxious to preserve their dominance in this as in every other sphere of life, sought to limit the theatre as being distinctively, irrevocably masculine. Actresses were represented as inhuman monstrosities, not women at all. Furthermore, the executive functions of theatre-manager and playwright were carefully defined as requiring supposedly masculine qualities of mind and personality. A woman playwright came to be seen as an impossibility, although their number actually increased toward the close of the nineteenth century. In this book Kerry Powell chronicles the development of women's participation in the theatre as playwrights, actresses, and managers and explores the making of the Victorian actress, gender, and playwriting of the period, and the contributions these made to developments in the following century.

WOMEN AND VICTORIAN THEATRE

WOMEN AND VICTORIAN THEATRE

KERRY POWELL

Miami University
Oxford, Ohio

CAMBRIDGE
UNIVERSITY PRESS

PUBLISHED BY THE PRESS SYNDICATE OF THE UNIVERSITY OF CAMBRIDGE
The Pitt Building, Trumpington Street, Cambridge CB2 1RP, United Kingdom

CAMBRIDGE UNIVERSITY PRESS
The Edinburgh Building, Cambridge CB2 2RU, United Kingdom
40 West 20th Street, New York, NY 10011-4211, USA
10 Stamford Road, Oakleigh, Melbourne 3166, Australia

First published 1997

Printed in the United Kingdom at the University Press, Cambridge

Typeset in Baskerville 11/12.5 pt. [VN]

A catalogue record for this book is available from the British Library

Library of Congress cataloguing in publication data
Powell, Kerry.
Women and Victorian theatre / Kerry Powell.
p.   cm.
ISBN 0 521 47167 2 (hardback)
1. Women in the theatre – Great Britain – History – 19th century.
2. Women dramatists, English – History – 19th century. I. Title
PN2582.W65P68 1997
792'.082'094109034 – dc21   97-5746   CIP

ISBN 0 521 471672 hardback

For Beth

"Two souls with but a single thought,
two hearts that beat as one."

Contents

Illustrations

Preface

This book argues that the Victorian theatre conspired in producing repressive codes of gender even as it provided women with a rare opportunity to experience independence and power. It revises the familiar narrative in which women of the theatre achieved social acceptance gradually over the Victorian period. But it also opposes the idea that such women were the helpless victims of tyranny, despite uncovering a Victorian discourse of the theatre that perpetuated social control where gender was concerned. This book demonstrates instead that the theatre was a battleground for competing ideologies of gender at the end of the Victorian era no less than at the beginning; indeed, that in certain ways this combat of the mind intensified over time.

Women were exhilarated, sometimes liberated, by the authoritative speaking voice and the professional opportunity that, uniquely, the theatre offered them. Men, at once attracted and repelled by female power on stage, reacted with speech of their own – a strategic rhetoric designed to ensure male dominance in their own personal lives, in the theatre, and in society as a whole. By formulating the actress as intrinsically different from other women, having little or nothing in common with their own wives and daughters, Victorian men defended themselves, and society at large, against the apocalyptic terrors which female power evoked for them.

Victorian rhetoric therefore worked to gender the theatre as being distinctively, irrevocably, masculine. Actresses, even the greatest, were absorbed in this formulation, for in their supposed excesses performing women were represented as diseased or inhuman monstrosities, not women at all. Furthermore, and crucially, the executive functions of theatre-manager and playwright were carefully defined as requiring supposedly masculine qualities of mind and personality. A woman playwright came to seem an impossibility, although the number of women playwrights actually increased near the close of the nineteenth century, and thereby a long record of difference and achievement by women writers for the stage was lost. A major aim of this book is to bring to light what was theorized as impossible by Victorian discourse on gender and the theatre, and has been unrecognized since – a tradition of women's playwriting, and the vision of a revolutionary, feminized theatre which it influenced.

This book has grown out of my earlier work on Oscar Wilde and popular late Victorian theatre. That project exposed the tip of an iceberg – a forgotten tradition of women's writing for the stage, and alongside it a pervasive rhetoric of the theatre – personal, journalistic, literary – whose purpose, I believe, was one of social control in matters of gender. The relationship between Wilde's theatrical career and the subject of the present book is particularly evident in the final chapter, portions of which have appeared in *Modern Drama* and *Nineteenth Century Theatre*. No matter the circumstances, however, it is difficult if not impossible for a male author to do justice to this subject. I have tried anyway, with the encouragement that women scholars, at my own university and elsewhere, have generously offered. They reassured me that *Women and Victorian Theatre* has an important story to tell, one that seemed unlikely to become known in the absence of this book.

Conversations with Nancy Armstrong and Regenia Gagnier helped to formulate the thesis of this work. Jane Marcus made me aware of the importance of Elizabeth Robins, the late-Victorian actress, novelist, and manager, and pointed me toward a little-known but invaluable archive of Robins documents at New York University. Robins's biographers, Angela John and Joanne Gates, have graciously shared their knowledge of the woman who, more than any other, resisted the masculinist theatre of the Victorian period and imagined a revolutionary alternative. Conversations with Sheila Stowell were important in providing an understanding of what a feminist critique of Victorian theatre could be. John Russell Stephens graciously shared the page proofs of his excellent book on the profession of playwriting, thus saving me the duplication of much time and effort. Mary Wetton helped me through the complexities of British copyright law in relation to drama.

Feminist scholars at Miami University – especially Susan Jarratt, Mary Jean Corbett, Frances Dolan, and Susan Morgan – have offered encouragement and perspective on this project over a long period of time. Ann Ardis helped to frame the book conceptually, and introduced me to the work of Netta Syrett, whose experience was crucial, I believe, to an understanding of the dilemma of women playwrights at the end of the Victorian era.

Among others whose encouragement and help have been especially important are Barry Chabot, Joseph Donohue, Sos Eltis, Russell Jackson, Joel Kaplan, Peter Raby, Ian Small, and John Stokes. I am grateful as well for grant support from the National Endowment for the Humanities, the American Council of Learned Societies, and Miami University. John Skillings of Miami University provided assistance with the illustrations for *Women and Victorian Theatre*. And without the research leaves awarded by Miami University, the completion of this book would have been long deferred.

Because much of the record of women in Victorian theatre remains unpublished or available only in rare books and periodicals, I owe an enormous debt to the staff members at the libraries where materials essential to this project are located. Frank Walker of the Fales Library, New York University, was always a helpful guide through the labyrinthine collection of materials by and about Elizabeth Robins. Mabel Smith, on behalf of the trustees of Backsettown, graciously gave permission for me to copy and quote from the papers of Robins. William Wortman of Miami University libraries went to great lengths to secure rare textual materials or microfilm copies of them whenever possible. The staffs of the Mander and Mitchenson Theatre Collection, the Ellen Terry Museum, the Fawcett Library, and the Humanities Research Center provided every possible assistance. And without the incomparable resources and timely assistance of the Theatre Museum, Covent Garden, and the British Library this project could never have been brought to a satisfactory conclusion.

Finally, for her love and care during the final stages of this project, I will be forever grateful to Beth Halvorsen Newton.

PART ONE

The making of the Victorian actress

CHAPTER I

"Think of the power—"

I don't care whether I make money or not. I want to sway people. Think of having a great audience hanging on the words that fall from your lips! Think of the power–

(John Strange Winter, *Connie the Actress*, London, 1902)

For women throughout the Victorian period the stage possessed a unique allure. It afforded the active, disciplined life and potentially the financial rewards of a profession, one of few then accessible to women. Even more importantly in some cases, a life in the theatre offered women a voice – the ability to speak compellingly while others, including men, sat in enforced silence, waiting in suspense for the next word. Actresses could be intoxicated by their control over audiences, and in particular over men, who in most other situations reserved power for themselves and compelled women to silence. Stunned and sometimes bewildered by the power of exceptional actresses, Victorian men often became infatuated on one hand while they felt imperiled by these exceptional women on the other.

To moderate the threat that actresses, by their very existence, posed to the masculine domination of women, many Victorians adopted a defensive and self-serving rhetoric that was used pervasively throughout the period – even late in the nineteenth century when actresses and actors often sought, and in some cases achieved, an enhanced social standing. This male-configured language reconstructed the performing woman as more than an actress – as a renegade female, one fundamentally different from normative wives and mothers, marginally "feminine" if feminine at all, quite possibly inhuman. In thus rhetorically dividing her from other women, their own wives and daughters, Victorian men could permit the actress a limited freedom and a certain power. They could do so, in large part, because of a tactical rhetoric that underwrote and even guaranteed the unequal distribution of

3

power by gender across society as a whole, and in their own personal relations.

The panic that Victorian men felt in the presence of actresses, and the varied and often ingenious ways in which they defended themselves against it, will be an important theme of this study. But to comprehend the scope and importance of this masculinist rhetoric, we must attend first to a competing discourse of the theatre, one emanating in large part from women themselves and representing the actress as being freed and empowered by her life on stage. At the end of the Victorian period, for example, Mary Elizabeth Braddon depicts in *A Lost Eden* (1904) a heroine who rejects the opportunity of becoming a governess, deciding to be an actress as a means of establishing herself in a profession and achieving independence. Unlike the starry-eyed heroines of many Victorian novels of the stage – especially those written by men – she has "thought it all out," realizing that her career will begin not with overnight success and wealth but as an "extra" with a nonspeaking part at 12 shillings a week. Although her salary would pay for little more than bus fare, the aspiring actress remains unshaken in her determination to go on stage. The hard work is what attracts her. "It lies," she says, "between burying oneself alive or having a career."[1] The actress Angela Clifton expresses a similar idea in Francis Gribble's novel *Sunlight and Limelight* (1898): "it's only on the stage, you know, that we poor girls are allowed to have careers."[2]

The stage-fever depicted more famously in Gwendolyn Harleth's ambition to embark on a professional life as an actress in George Eliot's novel *Daniel Deronda* (1876) was therefore no anomaly, but a phenomenon that could be discerned in other registers of Victorian culture, in popular thought and writing and in the lives of real Victorian women. Karl Marx's daughter Eleanor took acting lessons from Mrs. Herman Vezin in 1882 after her sister Jenny had been discouraged by their parents from going on stage herself. Although her work as a performer would be brief and undistinguished, Eleanor Marx persevered in preparing herself for what her sister called "the only free life a woman can live – the artistic one."[3] Helen Taylor, the stepdaughter of John Stuart Mill and daughter of Harriet Taylor Mill, had pursued acting for the same reasons in the 1850s, taking lessons from Fanny Stirling and then performing for low wages or none at all in touring companies and provincial theatres.[4] Marx and Taylor resemble one of the fictional characters of Mary Elizabeth Braddon: the title character and would-be actress of *The Doctor's Wife* (1890) – "so eager to be *something*," to rise above the "blank flat level" of domestic life "along which she was to creep to a nameless grave." Letting down her long black hair before the mirror, Isabel Sleaford could imagine herself an actress "dominating a terror-stricken pit" instead of being only a country surgeon's wife.[5]

Florence Nightingale draws attention in *Cassandra* to women's fascination for the stage, and accounts for it, not in terms of a desire for fame or wealth, but in the opportunity that acting provided for a truly professional life. Most women, in common with the daughters of Karl Marx, were brought up as amateurs, singing or drawing "as an amusement (a *pass*-time as it is called)," while any vocation of their own had to be sacrificed to the demands of others, in particular their husbands. The actress's life appealed to women, Nightingale writes, because:

> in the morning she studies, in the evening she embodies those studies: she has the means of testing and correcting them by practice, and of resuming her studies in the morning, to improve the weak parts, remedy the failures, and in the evening try the corrections again.[6]

An actress was different from other women, in Nightingale's view, because she was not compelled to "annihilate herself" by becoming merely the "complement" to her husband and his vocation.[7] She had a vocation of her own, and through it escaped the victimization of women generally by exercising an autonomy and sometimes a power which few others could share. Implied by the self-sufficiency of actresses was the possibility that women could live this way offstage – like the character in Mary Elizabeth Braddon's *Aurora Floyd* (1863), a former actress who, as a banker's wife in suburban London, keeps the imperious ways she learned as a performer. "How should she be abashed on entering the drawing-rooms of these Kentish mansions," writes Braddon, "when for nine years she had walked nightly on a stage to be the focus of every eye, and to entertain her guests the evening through. Was it likely she was to be overawed...?"[8]

While many women, like Mary Elizabeth Braddon herself, were at least partly motivated to try acting out of financial necessity, the perceived benefits of a theatrical career, where Victorian women were concerned, were not exclusively and probably not chiefly economic. Madge Kendal, writing her memoirs near the end of a long career as "Matron of the Drama," repeats the familiar theme that "I do not think there is a thing in the world that a woman could be better than an actress." She would earn less money than in any other line of work,

Kendal says, but the actress is fortunate above all in possessing "the blessedness of independence, and that is a great thing to a woman, and especially a single woman."[9] Geraldine Ensor Jewsbury describes in her novel of the theatre, *The Half Sisters* (1848), a heroine whose life on stage allows her to fill productively the long hours of idleness enforced upon ordinary women. In their lassitude and empty days can be found the chief impediment of leisured women's lives:

They want an object, they want a strong purpose, they want an adequate employment, – in exchange for a precious life. Days, months, years of perfect leisure run by, and leave nothing but a sediment of ennui: and at length they have all vitality choked out of them. This is the true evil of the condition of women.

As an actress, says the heroine Bianca, she has had "this one blessing" – a life of employment, so that "when I rose in the morning my work lay before me, and I had a clear, definite channel in which all my energies might flow." In their scope for demanding and productive work, actresses seem to the heroine of this early Victorian novel as unique as they are fortunate. "I have often wondered," she says, "how women, who were not actresses, contrived to pass their time; what they could find to do when they had their whole day free from any large occupation – no rehearsal for three hours in the morning, no long performance in the evening, – to say nothing of hard study between the times."[10]

In the same vein an anonymous writer for the *Englishwoman's Journal* in 1859 identifies the most significant benefit of actresses as their larger experience of life:

the way in which they have had to grapple with real, hard facts, to think and work and depend upon themselves...and the constant use of the higher faculties of taste and imagination, raise them far above those women who are absorbed by the petty vanities and trifles and anxieties of a woman's ordinary life.[11]

Actresses' work itself, more than any financial rewards that came from it, thus appealed to some Victorian women – perhaps to a great many, as Nightingale believed – as the greatest attraction of a career on stage. To spend one's days in productive work instead of leisure, to rely on oneself rather than a husband or any other person – these are the inducements which impel young women to become actresses in Florence Marryat's novel *Facing the Footlights* (1883):

To be independent...is the most glorious and ennobling feeling which we can experience, and women will never rise to the height of which they are capable until they are no longer contented to sit in an armchair and be fed like a set of Circassian slaves whose highest ambition is to grow fat, and keep their complexions fair.

Women do not go on the stage chiefly for money in Marryat's novel, nor is the life of an actress necessarily happier than that of any other woman. "But it has one great advantage," insists Marryat. "It is full of work and change."[12]

Acting was also, as Madge Kendal emphasized, a way to make money – as much, or more, as women could earn in any other endeavor, and economic independence was a necessary condition for independence of other kinds in a woman's life. Financially self-sufficient actresses could refuse to surrender themselves to a man, whether in mind, body, or possessions. "I earned the money myself," a provincial actress reminds her tight-fisted husband in George Moore's *A Mummer's Wife* (1885), "and if you think to rob me of what I earn you're mistaken. You shan't."[13] The successful actress in the novel *Connie, the Actress* (1902) is equally bold in dealing with her husband, whom she leaves for good with the announcement that she will not behave as a "mere domesticated animal" or "pussy-cat in the house."[14] But prosperity eluded most Victorian actresses. For women more than for men, as Tracy C. Davis has shown, acting was a competitive, overcrowded, and underpaid profession, with subsistence wages of £1 or £2 a week, if that much, being the rule rather than the exception even by the 1890s.[15] Even so, as Mrs. Patrick Campbell recalls in describing the meager beginnings of her own career, "you could get a nice room and board for 18s. a week; and many actresses lived on £1 a week."[16] From the rosier perspective of a leading lady, however, Ellaline Terriss writes with satisfaction of contracting with the Gaiety Theatre for the handsome sum of £25 a week, while her husband Seymour Hicks, who wrote as well as starred in Gaiety productions, earned only £15. "In our profession," she declares, "it is the woman who usually gets paid the most."[17]

Although the prospects for most actresses were not nearly as sanguine as Terriss's comment implies, many women were influenced by a desire for financial independence in deciding to go on the stage. Mrs. Campbell, famous for her portrayal of the title character in *The Second Mrs. Tanqueray*, traced the origin of her own career to the need for money – Mr. Campbell having gone to Australia, leaving her with children who "must be provided for."[18] Less successfully, Mary Elizabeth Braddon, before launching her career as a novelist, acted under the pseudonym of

Mary Seyton to support her mother and herself after her father deserted the family. Several of Braddon's fictional heroines are actresses as well, motivated sometimes by a desire for an independent life like Flora in *A Lost Eden*, at other times by the need for money, like Rosalie Morton in "Across the Footlights." The latter – with "no more power of earning money than if she had been a humming-bird" – decides out of desperation to try acting, wildly misinformed in her expectation of earning a handsome salary of £20 or £30 a week from the start.[19]

Overnight success of the kind for which Braddon's heroine wishes was fundamental to Victorian imaginings of the actress, who in fact belonged to a demanding profession in which women were underemployed and, if working, generally underpaid. This misreading of actresses, as one of them complained in a letter to the press in 1895, could be traced to novels of the theatre like William Black's *Macleod of Dare* (1878).[20] A long list of plays – also by men – might have been mentioned as well, including Tom Taylor and Charles Reade's *Masks and Faces* (1852), Dion Boucicault's *Grimaldi; or, The Life of an Actress* (1855), and Louis N. Parker's *A Buried Talent* (1890). In *Grimaldi*, a typical example, a young actress becomes the "new theatrical divinity" with astonishing ease and rapidity. "Riches, honours, coronets fall at her feet – who last year begged her bread in the streets of Nottingham," recounts one of the characters at the outset of Boucicault's play.[21] Wealth and fame acquired as if by magic were therefore integral to this popular rationale for the success of women on stage – a success which could be interpreted differently from the perspective of an actress. For example, Anna Cora Mowatt, the American star, describes the successful actress as possessing the talent, professionalism, and physical endurance that were usually associated with men. "Unless the actress in anticipation is willing to encounter disappointment in myriad unlooked-for shapes," she writes in her autobiography, "to study incessantly, and find that her closest study is insufficient; to endure a kind and amount of fatigue which she never dreamed of before...I would bid her shun the stage." The successful actress, Mowatt argues, is not the passive object of transfiguration, but prevails through hard work unknown to a type of woman who feels " 'the grasshopper a burden,' and the 'crumpled rose leaf' an inconvenience to her slumber."[22] And in his essay "Mummer-Worship" – for the most part scathingly critical of performers – George Moore characterizes the life of an actress as a Darwinian struggle in which only an exceptional woman can possibly "fight her way to the front."[23]

But even among the few actresses who prevail in what Moore terms the "battle of the footlights," perhaps a much smaller number knew the intoxication – so it was often termed – of absolutely dominating the men as well as women before whom they performed. Anna Mowatt's own satisfaction in acting was due less to the money she made than in the control that she exercised in performance. "The power of swaying the emotions of a crowd," she writes, "is one of the most thrilling sensations that I ever experienced."[24] Eleonora Duse was among this minority, commanding "almost slavish attention and admiration from her audience."[25] "The great actresses play the great parts, they rend the hearts and shatter the emotions of their audiences," writes Ellaline Terriss, looking back over a career in which she became famous as the heroine of Adelphi melodramas – "I never had that power and I never pretended to it."[26] Although Terriss was no ordinary Victorian woman, neither was she an Adelaide Ristori, the Italian actress who overwhelmed audiences at the Lyceum and Covent Garden with her Lady Macbeth. "It was delicious to me. . .to feel that I could move human souls at my will, and excite their gentlest as well as their strongest passion," Ristori writes in her autobiography. The ability to command the feelings of others transfigured her, or so she imagined – "to count, as I may say, the heart-throbs of the character which moved them, by their own – all this intoxicated me, made me feel as though I were endowed with superhuman powers."[27] Although not every actress could experience this intoxication, a mid-Victorian women's magazine distinguished actresses by the control they exercised over those who saw their performances. "Perhaps no greater pleasure can exist than that of awakening the sympathies and emotions of a large audience, and receiving their warm, living responses and acknowledgments," said an anonymous writer in the *Englishwoman's Journal* in 1859. "To no other artist does this intense enjoyment of actually beholding the effect of their powers, and accepting the result in person, belong."[28]

Victorian novels of the theatre, more numerous and more popular than has been recognized so far, similarly emphasize the motive of power where actresses are concerned. The actress-heroine of Geraldine Jewsbury's *Half Sisters* is attracted to the stage because of the "real power" that it allows her to exercise:

You do not know the sense of power there is in seeing hundreds of men and women congregated together and to know that I can make all that assembled multitude laugh, weep, or experience any emotion I please to excite: – there is positive intoxication in it, and I would not change that real power to become a queen, and have to work my will through the cumbrous machinery of a government. I act directly upon my subjects, and the EFFECT follows instantly upon my effort, I see all I produce...

Indeed, says the actress Bianca, a successful performance provides so "delirious" a sense of power that for a time it "elevates one above mortality."[29] This type of power, not money, is what motivates the heroine of *Connie, the Actress* to enter the profession. "I don't care whether I make money or not," she declares; "I want to sway people. Think of having a great audience hanging on the words that fall from your lips! Think of the power —"[30]

The actress's exhilaration at the sound of her own voice, and its powerful effect upon others, is easily understood. Unlike most Victorian women, who were told in advice literature to "suffer and be still," actresses were allowed the power of speech and often exercised it with results that could be measured by the profound silence of a crowded auditorium.[31] Thus in Louis N. Parker's hit play of 1886, *A Buried Talent*, one of the male characters describes the audience reaction to the "overwhelming" performance of a new prima donna: "We sat spellbound, white and wordless in our excitement."[32] This reversal of Victorian norms in the theatre, where women could vocalize powerfully while men fell mute, goes a long way toward explaining the fascination that reviewers themselves expressed for the *voices* of women performers. The speech of actresses beguiled them into a passivity that could be likened to the effects of witchcraft or narcotics. Sarah Bernhardt's voice, according to the theatrical trade newspaper, the *Era*, was "so exquisitely toned and modulated that it realised the fable of the Sirens. It acted on the hearer like some soothing, intoxicating Indian drug."[33] For Arthur Symons the voice of Bernhardt was like an electrical shock, "as if nerve touched nerve, or the mere 'contour subtil' of the voice were laid tinglingly on one's spinal cord."[34]

The "clear, pitiless voice" of Genevieve Ward had its own powerful effect on reviewers. "The actress last Saturday seemed to cast a spell over her audience," wrote a critic of her signature role in *Forget-Me-Not* (1879), noting that the "silence" of the audience "denoted awe as well as interest, and gave an unmistakable proof of the actress's power."[35] Ellen Terry, as Imogen in *Cymbeline*, was said to have spoken "in a voice that melted your bosom."[36] In Henry James's *The Tragic Muse* (1890) the voice of actress Miriam Rooth – "the richest sound to be heard on earth" – exercises a fascination which rivals the interest an audience could feel in any play in which she would appear. "Its richness," James writes, "was quite independent of the words she might pronounce or the poor fable they might subserve."[37] Not the play itself, but a voice rising above it, emancipated from the text, enthralls the male spectator and places him under subjection to the actress.

As Lord Henry Wotton expresses it in Wilde's novel, *The Picture of Dorian Gray* (1890), most women "never have anything to say" even when they are conversing "charmingly." In denying most women a voice, or rather a voice that communicates with meaning and depth, Wotton reiterates in his own distinctive voice one of the organizing ideas of Victorian culture as a whole. This lack of a voice in women – or the sound of a voice without significance, without effect – is a rule whose exception is the actress, or at least an actress such as Sybil Vane. She is beautiful, of course, "the loveliest thing I had ever seen in my life," but Dorian, as he explains to Lord Henry Wotton, is moved more by the sound of Sybil Vane than by what she actually says in *Romeo and Juliet*:

her voice – I never heard such a voice. It was very low at first, with deep mellow notes, that seemed to fall singly upon one's ear. Then it became a little louder, and sounded like a flute or a distant hautbois. In the garden-scene it had all the tremulous ecstasy that one hears just before dawn when nightingales are singing. There were moments, later on, when it had the wild passion of violins. You know how a voice can stir one. Your voice and the voice of Sybil Vane are two things that I shall never forget.[38]

In being stirred by a woman's voice, hearing in it something "different" from Lord Henry Wotton's misogynistic comments, Dorian Gray re-sembles many other Victorians who experienced the difference and power of an actress in her vocalizing. He also resembles other personae in Victorian novels of the theatre. In the forgotten *Life and Love of an Actress* (1888), for example, the voice of a young performer enacting the role of Juliet is as transfigurative as Sybil Vane's in the same role – "as to her voice, it was electric," writes the anonymous novelist; "the dingy, tawdry stage trappings faded away as if by magic, when she spoke."[39]

But Victorian men often considered actresses from a perspective determined by their own masculinity. Dorian Gray, for example, places emphasis on the "glamour" and "mystery" of Sybil Vane, her ability to enchant him. What the actress can do for the male spectator – the qualities which make her "the only thing worth loving" – are for Dorian Gray the distinguishing and indeed the only worthwhile features of the performing woman.[40] Lost in this male-centered analysis is what made acting seem particularly attractive to Victorian women as various as Marx's daughters, Florence Nightingale, Madge Kendal, and Geraldine Jewsbury. These women were less impressed by the "mystery" and "glamour" that seduce a masculine spectator than by the independence, professionalism, and hard work that were required of an actress, and by the power which enabled her to hold crowded assemblies of men as well as women in the palm of her hand.

CHAPTER 2

Masculine panic and the panthers of the stage

Rachel was the panther of the stage...she had little tenderness, no womanly caressing softness.

(G. H. Lewes, *On Actors and the Art of Acting*, 1875)

What have we to do with homes, and firesides? Have we not the theatre, its triumphs, and full-handed thunders of applause? Who looks for hearts beneath the masks we wear?

(Peg Woffington on actresses, *Masks and Faces*, 1854)

Victorian men, including the male coterie of drama critics, reacted with anxiety as well as admiration when they beheld displays of female control on stage. Captivated by the power of an exceptional actress, they experienced under her influence a sense of danger to themselves and an apprehension – often frankly expressed, sometimes covertly – that social codes of gender were being challenged before their eyes. Could women so commanding be women at all? Could their multiple assumed identities be reconciled with the narrow domesticity which ordinarily defined femininity? In exceeding the limits of what was thought proper to woman's nature, could actresses be considered healthy specimens of their gender in either a physical or mental sense? From such misgivings the Victorians constructed a rhetoric of the actress which functioned to monitor and control her excesses even as it allowed a space for her intimidating performances.

G. H. Lewes, for example, writes most confidently of the actress famed for her pathos-charged enactments of Phèdre when he metaphorizes her in nonhuman terms. Rachel, as Lewes sees her, is less a woman than a magnificent, but dangerous, animal:

Rachel was the panther of the stage; with a panther's terrible beauty and undulating grace she moved and stood, glared and sprang. There always seemed something not human about her. ...Scorn, triumph, rage, lust and merciless malignity she could represent in symbols of irresistible power; but she had little tenderness, no womanly caressing softness, no gaiety, no heartiness.[1]

Another critic wrote of Charlotte Cushman in her bloodthirsty rendition of Lady Macbeth, enacted repeatedly in London, that "she was inhuman, incredible, and horribly fascinating."[2] Locating these performances on the borderlines of gender and margins of humanity allowed the male observer to enjoy them untroubled, or with an exciting *frisson*. Thus the hero of a theatrical novel by Horace Wyndham (1907) is unwilling and unable to believe that a mere woman could hold him so utterly "spellbound" as the actress Grace Bellingham has done. Adrian Merrick prefers to imagine instead that she is "a visitor from another world" who has somehow transcended the usual categories of gender. "It seemed impossible," he reflects, "that she could be a mere woman like the thousands of others he passed on the streets every day."[3]

This medley of fear and admiration was rooted in a nervous perception that the exceptional actress could and sometimes did work free of the constraints of her gender, trespassing on the territory of men. William Winter, the American critic, writes of Charlotte Cushman's "inate grandeur of authority" on the stage, acknowledging that it may make some observers uneasy. "You might resent her dominance, and shrink from it, calling it 'masculine,'" Winter says, but "you could not doubt her massive reality nor escape the spell of her imperial power."[4] Even arguing from his perspective of sympathy with Cushman's art, Winter must confront, even if he cannot disarm, the social threat represented by a woman performer's "authority" and "power." Overawed by the melodramatic force of Charlotte Cushman, Winter was less impressed by the more subdued style of Eleonora Duse, who would "wander to the back drop and whisper to the scenery" in a manner "supposedly inspired."[5] Yet Max Beerbohm was made uneasy by Duse's relatively quiet power:

My prevailing impression is of a great egoistic force...In a man I should admire this tremendous egoism very much indeed. In a woman it only makes me uncomfortable. I dislike it. I resent it. In the name of art, I protest against it.

The understated "power" and "strength" of Duse unnerves and makes "uncomfortable" the male observer no less than the more rhetorical Cushman and Rachel – for Beerbohm at least, if not for every spectator.[6] Her "egoistic force," admirable in a man, becomes an irritant and source of resentment even as it explains her powerful presence on stage.

Coyly but with unusual self-awareness, Beerbohm exposes the contradictory lines of thought that both freed and limited the Victorian actress – not only in his own thinking, but in the culture at large. These extraordinary women traveled outside the boundaries that confined others, stunning their audiences, men especially, into an admiration that was disturbed and complicated. Reviewers sometimes expressed their approval of an exceptional actress as if they had experienced an electrical shock, undergone hypnosis, been assaulted physically, succumbed to a malady, or been overcome by a beast or monster in the guise of woman. Oscar Wilde, for example, threw lilies at the feet of Sarah Bernhardt when she first arrived in England and held her in awe for the rest of his life, but in his poem "To Sarah Bernhardt," also entitled "Phèdre," she is a vampire from hell, the recipient of kisses from "the loveless lips" of dead men.[7]

This note of anxiety in Wilde's sonnet is evident in many other assessments of Bernhardt's harrowing style as an actress. George Bernard Shaw, less enthusiastic about Bernhardt, preferred the more natural and "human" effects of Eleonora Duse to Sarah Bernhardt's "egoistic" and, as Shaw would have it, monstrous style. Bernhardt sought to overwhelm not only the audience but the play as well, Shaw wrote, usurping the character fashioned by the playwright in order to stage *herself* and, as herself, exercise dominion over her spectators. Bernhardt's art, therefore, could only be seen as "entirely inhuman and incredible"; it was:

the art of making you admire her, pity her, champion her, weep with her, laugh at her jokes, follow her fortunes breathlessly, and applaud her wildly when the curtain falls...And it is always Sarah Bernhardt in her own capacity who does this to you. The dress, the title of the play, the order of the words may vary; but the woman is always the same. She does not enter into the leading character: she substitutes herself for it.

This imperial woman – uninhibited by the playwright's text, bending her audience into mindless subjection to her own moods – produces spectacular but dangerous effects. One glance at Bernhardt's "Monna Lisa smile" discloses a "brilliant row of teeth," a vampire-face which "not only appeals to your susceptibilities, but positively jogs them." How different are the effects of Duse, as Shaw understood her, an actress less "intense" and yet more "human" than Bernhardt. Although Duse's "comparatively quiet" talent still locates her on the borders of humanity for Shaw – she is like a "panther" in her incredible grace and suppleness of movement – she nevertheless expresses in her art "only the multitude of ideas...of that high quality which marks off humanity from the animals." Acting like Bernhardt's, by contrast, is a type of disease – a sequence of tubercular "paroxysms," as Shaw puts it – and the enjoyment it produces is like that of a public execution, "or any other spectacle in which we still take a hideous delight."[8]

Arthur Symons, a devotee of Bernhardt, felt in her presence "almost a kind of obscure sensation of peril." With a breathless morbidity, Symons reports that Bernhardt "tears the words with her teeth, and spits them out of her mouth, like a wild beast ravening upon prey." Watching all this, he declares, the spectator's pulse "beat feverishly," and yet Bernhardt's passionate acting "mesmerised one, awakening the senses and sending the intelligence to sleep."[9] Lesser actresses – and all, for Symons, were inferior to Bernhardt – subdue the male body and mind with varying degrees of success and therefore inspire greater or lesser fear. Réjane, whom Symons much admired, "skins emotions alive," and even in a mediocre play like *Sapho*, adapted from Daudet's novel and performed in London in 1901, she inspired "an actual physical sensation; the woman took me by the throat." But Olga Nethersole, a less brilliant actress in an English adaptation of the same play at the Adelphi in 1902, merely "forced me to admire her, to accept her; I felt that she was very real, and, as I felt it, I said to myself: 'She is acting splendidly.'"[10] Women in the theatre, successful women at all events, "force" men, placing them under compulsion, overwhelming them; but the actress of mere talent, or even a great actress of a certain type, commands them with less ferocity than a Réjane, and Réjane less than Bernhardt. An actress becomes truly great for Arthur Symons when, like the heroine of his story "Esther Kahn," she generates a magnetic current so intense as to be "almost unbearable" to the audience.[11]

In the case of a less dominating, more sentimental actress than Rachel or Bernhardt, a modified rhetoric had to be employed to write her out of womanhood and humanity.[12] For example, Wilde's poetic tribute to Ellen Terry is devoted to her exquisite suffering as the Queen in W. G. Wills's play *Charles I* (1879), her eyes "marred by the mists of pain, / Like some wan lily overdrenched with rain."[13] Terry herself understood very well the prejudices of her audience, to which she appealed by playing one suffering victim after another with thrilling pathos. Of Wilde's sonnet on her, for example, Terry remarked appreciatively that the "phrase 'wan lily' represented perfectly what I had tried to convey."[14] Clement Scott himself venerated Terry as the greatest actress of the day because of the "ideal" and "mystical" qualities in her pathos-laden enactments, whether as the suicidal Ophelia or the betrayed and maddened women of contemporary plays such as *The Amber Heart* (1887) and *Ravenswood* (1890).[15] Nevertheless Terry's performances and their reception, like Bernhardt's but in a different way, situated the actress on the margins of humanity – she became a delicate flower or a "mystical" force, or, in the words of another of her admirers, a "spiritual essence" more than a woman.[16] Reviewing Terry's performance as the victimized Olivia in a revival of W. G. Wills's adaptation of *The Vicar of Wakefield* (1878), Wilde recognizes that Terry's "power," as he calls it, arises from her genius for thrilling an audience with tender emotions.[17] But even this quiet "power," so much milder than Bernhardt's or Cushman's or Rachel's, was difficult to reconcile with the private and passive roles that Victorian women were usually asked to play in life. Audiences could be reassured by the reflection that Ellen Terry was not so much a woman as a nonhuman, vaguely spiritualized essence – a "wan lily," in Wilde's phrase which so appealed to Terry herself.

These receptions of female power – frantic admiration or even love, complicated by panic and disgust – were symptomatic of male attitudes toward actresses at the beginning of the Victorian period as well as the end. When Harriet Smithson made herself famous as Ophelia at the Odéon in Paris shortly before the Victorian period began, her mad shrieks and distracted gestures aroused the audience to frantic cheering. "There was hardly a dry eye in the house," remarks Peter Raby, the biographer of Smithson, "and men reportedly stumbled out of the auditorium unable to watch further."[18] On the first night of *Hamlet* the young musician Hector Berlioz was even more overwhelmed than most of those who witnessed Harriet Smithson's Ophelia steal the show from Charles Kemble. For Berlioz, the acting of Smithson "struck me like a thunderbolt." When *Romeo and Juliet* followed *Hamlet* at the Odéon, Berlioz was there again to see Harriet Smithson play the heroine. "By the third act," he writes, "hardly able to breathe – as though an iron hand gripped me by the heart – I knew that I was lost."[19] Imagining her acting as an inspired assault, violent, life-threatening, irresistible, Berlioz nevertheless became as infatuated with the actress as with her art, and haunted the Odéon even when she was not on the bill.

In his dread as well as love of an actress, Berlioz resembles the hero of William Black's theatrical novel of 1878, *Macleod of Dare*, who shadows Gertrude White from theatre to theatre, under her "spell," hopelessly "bewitched." Just as Berlioz lost his breath when Harriet Smithson performed, so Macleod in Black's novel finds it impossible to "breathe freely" while watching Gertrude White on stage.[20] Five years later, in Joseph Fitzgerald Molloy's novel *Merely Players* (1881), actress Beatrice Barrington exhibits a "subtle power" on stage which leaves her male spectators gasping for breath, as if their lives were imperiled.[21] The metaphor varies – "enslaved," for example, is the term that novelist John Bickerdyke uses in *Daughters of Thespis* (1897) to describe the domination of his threatened hero by an actress. Eric Fairlough falls hopelessly in love with "captivating and seductive" Patta, to whose performances at the Cosmos Theatre he is drawn nightly, like an automaton, "by an influence which was too strong for him."[22] Dorian Gray in Oscar Wilde's novel is robbed of his will and at least the appearance of health whenever he thinks of actress Sybil Vane. "Hectic spots of red," like the marks of a fever, burn on his cheeks, and every night, involuntarily, he visits a dingy theatre in Holborn to see his beloved actress perform – "I can't help going to see Sybil play," he explains, "even if it is only for a single act."[23]

In this early phase of his love for an actress, Dorian belongs in the company of impressionable men like Raoul de Chagny in *The Phantom of the Opera* (1910), who falls into a kind of "fever" listening to the powerful, "irresistibly triumphant" voice of the young opera singer Christine Daaé. Like the voices of actresses in other theatre-fiction and criticism, Daaé's in *The Phantom of the Opera* is physically and mentally disabling to the male spectator. The strains of her voice "went through Raoul's heart" and "seemed to deprive him of all his will and all his energy and of almost all his lucidity at the moment when he needed them most."[24] The only cure for his malady is the domestication by marriage of what is termed in *The Phantom of the Opera* the "superhuman exaltation" of the performing woman. Toward this dénouement the novel by Gaston Leroux moves inexorably, as did Berlioz in his life and Macleod, with unforeseen and disastrous results, in William Black's novel.

MARRIED TO THE STAGE

By invoking marriage to neutralize the power and independence of actresses, theatrical fiction draws attention to the fact that, despite their improving social status and frequent self-conceptions of respectability, women of the stage remained unassimilated by the domestic ideal and could still be seen as incompatible with it. Once married or betrothed, women in these novels are expected to subjugate themselves to a man and give up their professional lives – "an immense sacrifice," as the hero of a novel called *Through the Stage Door* (1884) confesses. Yearning for the stage, where she was "a hundred times happier," the actress suppresses her own wishes in deference to a familiar male anxiety: "Don't return to the stage, Lettie: I could not bear it – promise me..." pleads her husband-to-be, who as usual was first attracted to her in a theatre.[25] She thus confronts a stark choice – on one hand independence and happiness as a performer, a prospect "unbearable" to her mate, and on the other hand obedience to a man within the confines of domestic "law." Her acting, immensely satisfying to herself, can thus be seen as an act of crime and violence against the male, as the hero of William Black's *Macleod* makes clear when he explains the consequences of Gertrude White's refusal to quit the stage and live quietly with him. "This," he says, "is worse than taking my life from me."[26]

This deadlock was broken on occasion in both life and art. *Through the Stage Door*, written by actress Harriett Jay, finally negotiates a compromise in which an actress is allowed a domestic life without altogether sacrificing her work on stage. But even the theatrical trade press and many actors and actresses themselves recognized a deep-seated incompatibility between women performers on one hand and wives and mothers on the other. Elizabeth Robins, as a bride just beginning her acting career in the United States, resisted the urgent pleas of her husband, actor George Parks, to leave the profession and devote herself entirely to him. When she declined, the result was as "unbearable" for Parks as it was for anxious husbands in stage novels – he hurled himself into the Charles River, weighed down by a suit of armor from the Boston Museum acting company.[27] Robins's suicidal husband was merely acting on familiar assumptions that made actresses seem wholly incompatible with wives and mothers, especially if living on their own, exposed to the unique temptations of their chosen career. The eminent critic Clement Scott felt compelled as late as 1897 to speak out on the "temptation" surrounding an actress "in every shape and on every side," dividing her irremediably from domestic femininity:

All I can say is that I marvel at any mother who allows her daughter to take up the theatrical career, and still more am I astonished that any man should calmly endure that his wife should become an actress, unaccompanied by himself. He must be either a fool or a knave.[28]

George Parks proved himself to be neither, according to the reasoning of Clement Scott, when he leapt to his death in the Charles River.

Desperate measures such as these help to explain the force of George Moore's argument in "Mummer-Worship" that a great woman artist cannot be an "ideal mother," virtually paraphrasing the actress Alcharisi in George Eliot's novel *Daniel Deronda*.[29] "The dramatic profession has been, is, and always will be," says Moore, "a profession for those to whom social restraints are irksome, and who would lead the life their instinct dictates."[30] Moore's contrast between the freedom of an acting career with the "prison" of motherhood and domesticity was not an original thought, but one deeply ingrained in Victorian understandings of what an actress was, and was not. Moore's theatrical novel *The Mummer's Wife* (1885) is devoted, in fact, to tracing the impermeable boundaries dividing the woman performer from successful domestic life. The initiation of Moore's heroine Kate D'Arcy into professional acting coincides with her desertion of an ailing husband. Achieving a sudden and effortless success, the usual rationale for a woman's triumph in male-authored novels about actresses, Kate D'Arcy slides into adultery, alcoholism, and madness. Violent quarrels with her lover leave him scratched and torn, and the death of her infant puts an exclamation point to the sentence that Moore levies against the actress – namely, her incompatibility with domestic life, its duties and rewards. Moore's actress is less a woman at the end of the novel than a bloated and raving caricature of femininity as the Victorians understood it. If the self-defining, independent woman of the stage could be seen as somehow inhuman or as a deformation of real femininity, then the anxiety she would otherwise inflict could at least be moderated because the source was in some sense not authentically female.

In this context the success of a woman in theatrical work could easily be attributed either to her being single or to her supposedly undomestic nature. The *Era*, in a profile, attributed the achievements of actress-manager-playwright Janette Steer to long hours, "love of independence," and a single life. "Her stage career has been one of sheer hard work for the love of the thing – the stage is her god and goddess," the anonymous writer says of Steer, for a time manager at Terry's and the Comedy theatres. "She seeks no other ties and is proud of her freedom."[31] Even the *Stage Directory* seemed to confirm, in an article entitled "Actors' Marriages" (1880), an irrevocable disparity between women of the stage and domestic life:

How can the actress whose whole life had hitherto been passed upon the stage be expected to understand domestic arrangements, and all those little tricks and plans about household management, which tend to make a home happy? As a rule it is hopeless to look for it...³²

Against this background it is easy to see why Peter Sherringham in Henry James's *The Tragic Muse* simply assumes that Miriam Rooth will inevitably give up her acting career when she becomes his wife – his "appendage," as the actress remarks bitterly in rejecting his proposal.³³ Once domesticated in marriage, the actress was expected to look back without regret, even with loathing, upon her life on stage. When her husband hesitantly suggests that she might like to go back to acting, her profession before she knew him, the title character of Robert Buchanan's novel *The Martyrdom of Madeline* responds impetuously. "It is impossible," she exclaims. "I hate the stage. Rather than return to it I would die."³⁴ She adds for the benefit of her surprised but relieved spouse that "I am quite, quite happy here with you. Yes, when we are alone together, when we are away from the world and all its feverish tumult, I am more than happy – I am at peace."³⁵ Similarly the actress-heroine of the novel *Merely Players* is described as marrying into a new role in a different kind of "drama" – what author J. F. Molloy calls the "drama" of her new domestic life, with a fixed plot and enforced representations.³⁶ In this theatre of domesticity the Victorians could stabilize and control the multiple selves that made actresses, in Gordon Craig's words, "impossible" as wives and mothers.

In real life this was precisely the choice of Mary Anderson, who writes in her memoirs of the relief she felt upon leaving the stage to be married. "I have never had a single wish," she declares, "to walk its boards again." The quiet, passive life of domestic women was thus made to seem irreconcilable with the independence and power associated, if not always accurately, with actresses. As Mary Anderson expresses it from the vantage point of her own retirement, "I have always thought that no woman can serve two masters: public and domestic life."³⁷ No one expressed this duality with greater force than Gordon Craig, who, as the son of Ellen Terry, felt himself a hapless victim of it. Incapable of recognizing mother and actress in the same person, Craig writes of "Mother" as an autonomous individual, separate and at war with the actress Ellen Terry:

E. T. was always getting in the way of my mother...I continue to speak of them as two, because although one and the same person, they were leagues apart and agreed to differ on almost every subject...E. T. was the "strongest" of the two, but Mother was more cunning, and the dearest – no woman could possibly have been a better mother, a truer wife, a more faithful, unswerving guardian and guide...had it not been for E. T. – that public person who came between us.

Ellen Terry, "two persons in one body," seems to have recognized this doubleness herself and regretted it – "so imperfect," Craig quotes her as having said, "unable to be one thing or another...never entirely one."

Far from being peculiar to Ellen Terry, this incompatability with domestic life was seen as common to actresses, at least the best ones:

> Great actresses and singers as a rule don't marry with success. Great actresses evidently *must* be impossible people. Bernhardt, Duse, Rachel, Siddons, Jordan, Sophie Arnould, la Gabrielli – I could add a hundred to this brief count of those who were not possible persons as wives. There is no other explanation for it, and it had best be faced. One can't be possible *every* way...I don't see how you can rock the cradle, rule the world, *and* play Ophelia perfectly, all in the day's work.

Power and performance, in this equation by Gordon Craig, join to eliminate any capacity to "rock the cradle" as a successful wife and mother. Aside from an occasional exception, such as the happily married Adelaide Ristori, domesticity was almost inconceivable for a great actress, indeed a contradiction as far as Craig was concerned. Actresses, those of the highest order like Ellen Terry, were sadly belated in their attempts to be wives and mothers, for they were already happily married – "married to the stage," as Craig says.[38] "What have we to do with homes, and hearths, and firesides?" asks Peg Woffington on behalf of all actresses in the hit play *Masks and Faces* (1852). "Have we not the theatre, its triumphs, and full-handed thunders of applause? Who looks for hearts beneath the masks we wear?"[39] A "mask" without a "heart," scarcely human, let alone female, Woffington remains to the end a practitioner of her art, divided from other women, the door to a domestic life irrevocably closed to her. Even the heroine of *Teresa Marlowe, Actress and Dancer* (1884) – "pure, spotless, and free from great fault" – feels unworthy to become a wife, although the man she loves has proposed marriage. To be of some use in the world, Teresa Marlowe can only embark on a life of renunciation in "the becoming blue serge...of Wapping's East End London Deaconesses."[40]

MYRIAD LIVES: TRANSFORMATIONS OF SELF AND SEXUALITY

The extremity of her situation – even though it was represented differently, and often moderated, in other texts and other lives – illustrates the difficulty experienced by Victorians in attempting to find a place in their thought and values for the actress. The idea of woman's free and flexible selfhood, as Nina Auerbach has shown, contradicted Victorian thought about the self in general and woman's self in particular. Indeed, performance by its very nature endangered the Victorian belief in a stable identity, the true or "buried" self that lies for Matthew Arnold at the core of being.[41] Actors as well as actresses, with their multiplication of personalities, suggest that character is unreadable, volatile, and subject to transformations. "I hardly knew myself when I sang," confesses Christine Daaé in *The Phantom of the Opera*.[42] Similarly the actress heroine of Anna Cora Mowatt's *Mimic Life* (1856) is startled by her own multiplicity while practicing a part before a mirror:

> She gazed in wonder at the haggard, terrified expression, and then laughed to see the look change to one of surprise. It seemed to her as if she were scanning the face of another. She was indeed "losing her identity."[43]

But as William Black's novel *Macleod of Dare* illustrates, the instability of the actress's character could seem especially threatening from a masculine perspective. The title character of Black's novel, a Scottish laird visiting London, goes to the Piccadilly Theatre to watch the performance of Gertrude White, an actress whom he has met in society, a "grave and gentle" young woman, one appropriately interested in his stories about himself. On stage, however, she is a "gay madcap," not at all the person he knew. "Where was," Macleod wonders, "the silent and serious girl who had listened with such rapt attention to his tales of passion and revenge...Surely that sensitive and vivid imagination could not belong to this audacious girl, with her laughing, and teasings, and demure coquetry?"

As he falls in love with the actress, the laird becomes more and more uneasy in the face of her kaleidoscopic transformations. "Which of them all was she?" wonders Macleod with some urgency, certain that there must be, or should be, a core of true and stable identity in Gertrude White. "Which should he see in the morning? Or would she appear as some still more elusive vision, retreating before him as he advanced?"[44] Nor is his condition improved by the explanation of Gertrude White's actor-father that the performer must transfer his soul into his creation – "his heart beats in another breast; he sees with other eyes." Macleod explains to her the appalling effects of this point of view:

Your father was talking the other day about your giving yourself up altogether to your art – living the lives of other people for the time being, forgetting yourself, sacrificing yourself, having no life of your own but that. What must the end of it be? – that you play with emotions and beliefs until you have no faith in any one – none left for yourself; it is only the material of your art. Would you not rather like to live your own life?

It is not exactly her own life, however, that Macleod wants the actress to lead, but rather a life defined and controlled by himself – a conventional domestic life. Had Gertrude White been more experienced, the novelist reflects, she would have said to herself, "*This man hates the stage because he is jealous of its hold on my life.*"[45]

Actresses in Victorian novels of the theatre often show themselves vulnerable to the accusations of men like Macleod, fearing that their make-believe lives have cut them off from the real, and from themselves. Angela Clifton, the actress in *Sunlight and Limelight* (1898), worries that acting may be too absorbing a career "to be really good for me," that it "interferes with the real life," making it somehow "less real, less intense." On the stage, she feels, one loses oneself in the staging of "imaginary emotions" until in the end the actress's own life "gets to be something of a make-believe." Her lover Herbert Phillimore is made miserable by his inability to possess the actress, who eludes his grasp by slipping out of one self into another with appalling dexterity. Like Macleod, this young man in love with an actress is "jealous of the stage," where she seems to him more passionate and engaged than when "living her own life." So he stands, as novelist Francis Gribble writes, "at the gates of a paradise which he could not enter, tortured by a tantalising vision of its glories; and after the first ecstasy was over he got more pain than pleasure from his love."[46]

Placed in a similar situation, the worldly hero of Oscar Wilde's novel reacts quite differently to the transformations undergone by an actress. Falling in love with Sybil Vane precisely *because* of her flexible identity, Dorian Gray is exhilarated with his discovery that she is "never herself," but instead "Rosalind one night, and Portia the other." This freedom of personality, however, turns out to be an intolerable burden for the actress in *The Picture of Dorian Gray*. Whereas earlier "it was only in the theatre that I lived," Sibyl has since fallen desperately in love with Dorian and can only find "reality" in her love for him. Her turn toward domestic womanhood is at the same time a turn away from the theatre, its antithesis for the Victorians:

Take me away, Dorian – take me away with you, where we can be quite alone. I hate the stage. I might mimic a passion that I do not feel, but I can not mimic one that burns me like fire...it would be profanation for me to play at being in love.[47]

As she chooses a domestic self in preference to her dazzling self-transformations, Sybil Vane reprises the anxieties and misgivings of the actress in *Macleod of Dare*. Similarly, the actress in Francis Gribble's *Sunlight and Limelight* feels compelled to embrace a domestic life. Actresses, she decides, are denied the primary satisfactions of other women – domestic satisfactions. Ordinary women "could love as she could not...could win one man's heart, and cleave to it, and grow old tranquilly, knowing that they had not loved in vain."[48]

Real-life Victorian actresses also experienced a revulsion against the multiplex world of the drama and yearned for the solidity of a one-dimensional life at home – the life of an ordinary woman. "My marriage has not only brought me the happiest and most peaceful years of my life," writes Mary Anderson, "but was incidentally the means whereby I could reasonably leave the stage," which had been proving irksome for many years before. "I was perpetually longing for the *real*, and wishing to abandon the make-believe life," Anderson recalls, "and I have found the real, more rich, more beautiful and more engrossing than its counterfeit."[49] The great danger of the theatre, as Anderson writes elsewhere, is that it encourages a certain carelessness about "the great realities of life," which on stage are principally of concern in the creation of "dramatic effects."[50] Gertrude White in *Macleod of Dare*, like Mary Anderson in life and Sibyl Vane in Wilde's novel, contrasts a core of true feeling with the exhibition of feigned emotion on stage and the ambiguous subjectivity of an actress who must play many parts:

It is a continual degradation – the exhibition of feelings that ought to be a woman's most sacred and secret possession. And what will the end of it be? Already I begin to think I don't know what I am. I have to sympathize with so many characters – I have to be so many different people – that I don't quite know what my own character is, or if I have any at all.

As her actor father recognizes, Gertrude White is contemplating the sacrifice of her unique freedom to a conventional kind of womanhood. "Was she really envying," he asks incredulously, "the poor domestic drudge whom she saw coming to the theatre to enjoy herself with her fool of a husband, having withdrawn for an hour or two from her house-keeping books and her squalling children?"[51]

This downright opposition between performing and domestic women defines as well the character of Alcharisi in *Daniel Deronda*, a singer and actress whose "myriad" lives and "double consciousness" divide her irremediably from what Wilde would later describe as "ordinary women." Her elasticity of life as a star performer goes hand in hand in George Eliot's novel with her contempt for domesticity in all its forms. Desiring neither to marry nor have children – "not to be hampered with other lives," as she says – Alcharisi gives away her son to be reared by a lover. Eliot, like many drama critics of the time, tends to define the actress on the borders of womanhood and even humanity as a way of explaining, or perhaps neutralizing, what she represents – "as if," writes Eliot, "she were not quite a human mother, but a Melusina, who had ties with some world which is independent of ours." The actress herself, however, rejects any such idea:

Every woman is supposed to have the same set of motives, or else to be a monster. I am not a monster, but I have not felt exactly what other women feel – or say they feel, for fear of being thought unlike others.

But such expressions – like Dorian Gray's celebration of Sybil Vane as "more than an individual" – really reinforce from another, unexpected direction the tendency of Victorian culture to isolate the actress in a ghetto of the imagination, unassimilable with other women and what Mary Anderson, having quit the stage herself, calls the "great realities" of their domestic lives. To the son she abandoned as an infant, Alcharisi makes no apologies and offers no pretense of maternal affection, either in the present or past. "I did *not* feel that," she tells her son eventually, defining herself, an actress, through the negation of domesticity. "I was glad to be freed from you."[52]

In *The Picture of Dorian Gray* the discovery by Sybil Vane of love and the prospect of marriage causes Sybil to turn from the stage in disgust and denounce as a "sham" her revolving identities as an actress. In her last performance Sybil plays Juliet without emotion or conviction, her power as an actress having been consumed by her love for Dorian Gray. This failed, "self-contained" portrayal estranges Dorian from the actress whom he had loved only hours ago: "You have killed my love," he explains; "I can't see you again." When the actress learns that her longing for a life with Dorian can never be realized, she swallows poison and dies instantly. Like so many actresses in other Victorian texts, Sybil Vane cannot span the chasm between acting and a domestic life; she is written out of love and marriage, and, again like other actresses in other texts, written out of humanity too – "the girl never really lived," as Lord Henry Wotton explains to Dorian, and even in taking her own life "she has never really died."⁵³

The Victorian stage realized another world – "some world which is independent of ours," as Alcharisi says in *Daniel Deronda* – where the normal categories of gender could be modified. The otherness of this world was marked forcefully by Victorian theatrical conventions such as the darkened auditorium, a lighted performing space, the proscenium framed like a painting, and the stage curtain itself – reminders of less tangible barriers dividing audience from actors. Within this privileged zone actresses might transcend a fixed domestic identity, cultivating "myriad lives" and exercising a power and independence thought incompatible with wives and mothers. Actresses, that is, were permitted some of the prerogatives of men – indeed, they were remarkable in the Victorian period for enacting the roles of men in unprecedented numbers. "It is curious to note," wrote the late-Victorian male impersonator Vesta Tilley, "that there are few leading actresses who have not played or aspired to play masculine roles."⁵⁴ In incorporating male as well as various female identities, the "myriad lives" of actresses could seem only the more disconcerting to thoughtful Victorians who conceived of identity as fixed and indissolubly linked to transcendent categories of gender.

But the phenomenon of actresses portraying men on the Victorian stage was both complex and contradictory. Women performing men's parts were seizing professional opportunities unavailable to actresses in the Victorian theatre, but their tights, cinched waists, and ornately trimmed knickers called attention to their femininity and transcribed their sexuality into the realm of male desire. Moreover, the fact that many actresses undertook male roles was a virtual metonymy of the gender transformations in which women performers were implicated, living the kind of public and professional lives that were thought to be inconsistent with femininity. At the same time, as Tracy Davis has pointed out, the roles of men provided actresses with strong and heroic parts that surpassed their limited opportunities in the usual women's roles – ingenues, shrews, and adventuresses.⁵⁵ Male impersonation by Victorian actresses thus formed an intersection where women's hopes for greater opportunities and men's anxieties over gender relations came together – and sometimes collided.

These crossdressed performances caused some uneasiness on the part of critics who reflected upon the implications of what they saw. Even progressive reviewers such as William Archer, eventually the champion of Ibsen in England, were sometimes troubled by the spectacle of women playing the roles of men. Archer was appalled, for example, by J. Palgrave Simpson and H. C. Merivale's *All for Her* (1875), an adaptation of *A Tale of Two Cities* which, unlike Dickens's novel, introduces the heroine in male disguise. "It is perhaps carrying the romantic too far," Archer writes, "not to mention that, in point of taste, a woman masquerading as a man is always questionable."[56] Two decades later, in 1894, amid the Ibsen movement and the stirrings of British feminism, Archer begins his review of a crossdressed performance of *As You Like It* by acknowledging that in these times men should think twice before laying down laws about what is "womanly" and "seemly." Nevertheless he can find no redeeming feature, nothing pertinent even, in an all-female performance of Shakespeare:

> What does it exemplify? What does it illustrate? A performance by men alone might help to illustrate the conditions of the Shakespearean stage; but this performance has no bearing on either the past or the future, for I do not understand that even the most vindictive champion of her sex proposes to take revenge for the sixteenth century by entirely excluding men from the stage of the twentieth or twenty-first. There was no sociological principle at stake, no artistic lesson to be learnt. The performance had not even the comprehensible attraction of burlesque, that appeal to the average sensual man which lies in the display of "shapely" limbs; for jack-boots were the only wear in the Forest of Arden.

Clearly Archer's position has shifted since he reviewed *All for Her* in 1875. No longer is it the case that "a woman masquerading in male attire is always questionable," but clearly it remains so on some occasions for Archer. What makes this production of *As You Like It* objectionable, from his point of view in 1894, is that the actresses who performed in the matinee at the Prince of Wales's Theatre went too far in their impersonation of men. His reaction, Archer suggests, would have been moderated if the women performers had aimed their crossdressing efforts toward some discernible artistic effect, or even if their rationale had been the familiar and somehow reassuring one of using male disguise as a pretext for displaying "'shapely' limbs" to an audience of prurient men. Instead, the whole point of the performance seemingly was to transgress the boundaries of gender – thus leaving this all-female production of *As You Like It*, in Archer's opinion, with nothing to "exemplify" or "prove," a "purposeless curiosity."

Archer notes that men's roles had been played by women long before his own time – indeed, before the nineteenth century, by Peg Woffington, for instance, and Sarah Siddons. Thus what troubles him in 1894 is less the fact of women playing men's parts in a matinee of *As You Like It* than the extremity of their representation:

Innumerable boys or boyish characters have been performed by women ever since women first appeared on the stage. But...I certainly cannot remember that, until the other day at the Prince of Wales's, I ever saw anything beyond the least indication of a moustache on a female face on the stage. The next time I want to see a bearded lady, I shall seek her in her proper habitat – the caravan.

Actresses who played male parts in the past, Archer points out with emphasis, "have almost always chosen beardless ones." In imitating men to the extent of wearing beards, the actresses in *As You Like It* obliterate their own femininity and with it the possibility of expressing either truth or beauty. Becoming too much like men, as Archer would have it, these women performers abandon the possibility of making any "sociological" or "artistic" point, or even appealing to their audience through "the comprehensible attraction of burlesque." Thus does Archer rule out the possibility of rational discourse being applied to such gender transformations as those at the Prince of Wales's Theatre. This staging of Shakespeare with an all-female cast is described by the champion of Ibsen with the vocabulary of disfigurement and suffering – "ugly," "uncomely," "grotesque," and "painful."[57]

Similar rhetoric is employed by Max Beerbohm in his review of Sarah Bernhardt's portrayal of Hamlet at the Adelphi Theatre in 1899. Like Archer, Beerbohm casts about for an intelligible reason that would account for such an undertaking, and like Archer he comes up empty-handed:

Gentleness and a lack of executive ability are feminine qualities, and they were both strong in Hamlet. This, I take it, would be Sarah's own excuse for having essayed the part. She would not, of course, attempt to play Othello – at least I risk the assumption that she would not, dangerous though it is to assume what she might *not* do...But in point of fact she is just as well qualified to play Othello as she is to play Hamlet. Hamlet is none the less a man because he is not consistently manly...Sarah ought not to have supposed that Hamlet's weakness set him in any possible relation to her own feminine mind and body.

What troubles Beerbohm – as it troubled Archer in watching the bearded actresses of *As You Like It* a few years earlier – is the destruction on stage of barriers dividing masculine from feminine. Hamlet, the "hoop through which every very eminent actor must, sooner or later, jump," becomes for Beerbohm an inadvertent comedy in the hands of an eminent actress. Bernhardt's Hamlet is an "aberration" and "painful," words drawn from the same lexicon that Archer had used to characterize the all-female production of *As You Like It*. Beerbohm, moreover, states what Archer only implied – that actresses impersonating men are really rewriting or usurping the text of the male playwright. As Hamlet, Beerbohm charges, Bernhardt portrayed no one but herself, "and revealed nothing but the unreasoning vanity which had impelled her to so preposterous an undertaking." In a sense Bernhardt had become her own playwright, substituting herself for Shakespeare's hero and making Hamlet "from first to last, *très grande dame.*"[58]

The crossdressed actress, when she departed from the burlesque tradition of male disguise and attempted a serious impersonation, was thus liable to be seen as eliding crucial distinctions of gender and magnifying her own importance to the point of irrationality while denying her own femininity and even humanity. "It is only the unsexed woman," said the *Era* on the occasion of Bernhardt's Hamlet, "the woman who, physically and physiologically, approaches nearly to the masculine – the monstrosity in short – who can deceive us as to her gender on the stage."[59] Women playing Hamlet and wearing beards and authentic male costume suggested a range of feminine identity and potential that was not only unwelcome but alarming to many critics, even comparatively progressive men like Archer and Beerbohm. But the anxieties of male reviewers were raised to an even higher pitch by any suspicion of lesbian sexuality in crossdressed productions. The *Theatrical Inquisitor*, for example, deplored the appearance of Madame Vestris in *Don Giovanni* at Drury Lane in 1820 as the "libertine" title character who seduces women, fights duels, and at the end of the comic afterpiece marries happily. To the critic's dismay, Vestris seems to have followed the precedent of Jo Gould, the aggressively masculine woman who preceded her in the role a few years earlier and defined it in a manner that could only be hinted at:

The disgusting woman who undertook this libertine character at its outset, prepared us very fully for the only result that can ever be drawn, in the nicest hands, from its loathsome repetition; and we, therefore, feel bound to treat it as a part which no female should assume till she has discarded every delicate scruple by which her mind or her person can be distinguished. That any modern manager will bestow a single thought upon the tarnished virtue of his company, is not an event we are entitled to expect; but there is a reluctance, at least, to be evinced by the victim of his power, in discharging her nauseous duties, which should conciliate the judgment that decency has arrayed against her. We could not trace this reluctance in the efforts of Madame Vestris, who seemed to have swathed her slender form in rolls and bandages to fill out the garb of the character, and testified altogether that sort of ease and gaiety against which, for the honour of the sex, we still deem it our duty to protest.[60]

The review draws to an end by counseling Vestris "rather to do any thing than adhere to a task that is fraught with viler consequences than we shall venture to describe."

What disturbed Victorian men, therefore, was not only the actress's dramatization of many selves, but of varied sexualities as well. "It maddens me to see all those hundreds of eyes on you," says the anxious hero of a fragmentary novel by Elizabeth Robins, concerned that audiences have access, for a price, to the body of the woman he loves – "any ruffian may go and look at you for a shilling."[61] In *The Flare of the Footlights* (1907) the emphasis again is laid upon a man's discomfiture over the sale, as he sees it, of the body of the actress. It can never be pleasant, declares a character in this novel, "for a man to see a girl he's fond of having to submit to being slobbered over by a greasy actor for so much a week and half salary for matineés. Well-bred women. . .have a natural objection to earning money in this manner."[62] Beautiful perhaps, but dangerous, irresistible yet deadly, the actress with her uncontained sexuality could seem to the Victorian male a "weird combination of Delilah, Monna Lisa, and Mélisande."[63] As a character in Geraldine Jewsbury's *Half Sisters* puts it:

I have got a real horror of all professional women. A woman who makes her mind public, or exhibits herself in any way, no matter how it may be dignified by the title of art, seems to me little better than a woman of a nameless class. I am more jealous of the mind than of the body; and, to me, there is something revolting in the notion of a woman who professes to love and belong to you alone going and printing the secrets of her inmost heart, the most sacred working of her soul, for the benefit of all who can pay for them.

The speaker is troubled by actresses because they cannot "belong" absolutely to one man – their thoughts and feelings, as well as bodies, seem to be commodities in a free market of men at large. Their lives have become texts for a mass audience, and they themselves writers and printers, "publishing both mind and body too." As a published text the actress is available for anyone to "read," rather than the property of one man, a fact which links her in the mind of Geraldine Jewsbury's young hero to prostitution.[64]

Actresses, as William Charles Macready observes in his *Reminiscences*, were trained to proclaim to the world the passions that proper ladies were made to conceal.[65] This public dimension of the actress's life is what most disturbs the hero of William Black's *Macleod of Dare*, who asks himself, regarding the performer with whom he has fallen in love, "What was she doing here – amidst all this glaring sham – before all these people?"[66] Not only was the actress a public figure on stage, but off as well, as Macleod recognizes only too well:

I dared scarcely open a newspaper, lest I should see her name. I turned away from the posters in the streets: when I happened by some accident to see her publicly paraded in that way, I shuddered all through – with shame, I think.

Macleod recognizes that, like a prostitute, his beloved earns her living by the sale of feigned emotions, "an exposure of her own feelings to make people clap their hands."[67] Merely by being the subject of comment in newspapers the actress entered a textual domain which made her body seem ominously public. "I wish you had never seen the stage," cries the fiancé of an actress in the novel *My Sister the Actress* (1881), driven wild by the way in which the press "presumes to comment on your face, and your dress, and your acting."[68]

Actual rather than implied prostitution has been at least an interlude in the life of the actress in George Moore's novel *The Mummer's Wife*, a woman whose slide into degradation begins with a signature song announcing her public nature: "Look at me here, look at me there." An old actor in *Through the Stage Door*, by Harriett Jay, extends Moore's equation of actress and whore into a globalizing assertion. "I know what the profession, is, and I know the sort of women we've got in it," he remarks, " – women who can't advertise themselves in any other way than by going on the stage." One of the actresses in Jay's novel, in fact, has become a "bad" woman after finding how difficult it was to succeed in the theatre as a "good woman." Even offstage, actresses in *Through the Stage Door* discompose a stuffy colonel with their luxurious costumes, painted faces, heavy drinking, and unrestrained conversation:

How the women drank down the champagne! how boisterously they laughed! and what coarse jokes they made! Some of them had not washed the paint from their faces, and many of them were arrayed in the finery in which a few hours before they had strutted on the stage. [69]

The equation between actress and prostitute which suggests itself to the anxious mind of the military man in Harriett Jay's novel was symptomatic of Victorian attitudes toward women of the theatre even late into the nineteenth century. Moreover, Victorians were afraid that femininity, as they understood it, was peculiarly vulnerable anywhere in the theatre – whether on stage or off.

It remained unusual to the end of the nineteenth century for respectable women to attend the theatre unaccompanied by a man, and at venues where unescorted women were regularly admitted – as at the Alhambra music hall – "you may be sure," as a policeman put it, that most were "women of the town." Because women were admitted alone, one American visitor was moved to characterize the Alhambra as "the greatest place of infamy in all London."[70] The predominance of "harlots" and their customers in the galleries and refreshment rooms of early Victorian theatres had led physician and social reformer Michael Ryan to ask in *Prostitution in London* (1839), "Is not a theatre a brothel?" The two, he reasoned, "are linked together by mutual interests and mutual pursuits," their morals "identically the same."[71] Prostitutes no longer solicited openly in legitimate theatres as they had at the beginning of the Victorian period, thanks in large part to the efforts of Macready in sealing the auditorium from an "improper intrusion" which, writes William Archer years later, "had hitherto been a scandal to public decency."[72] Notwithstanding this exclusion of prostitutes from the performance site, the distinction between playhouse and whorehouse seemed from the perspective of authority to be problematic still. As late as 1896 the *Theatre* was lamenting the popular identification of real-life prostitutes with actresses, including the fact that many women of the street were identified as actresses in newspaper reports, although "the so-called 'actress' has no theatre except the thoroughfare, and no stage but the pavement." The explanation for this state of affairs was that the newspaper writer "has only one word in his vocabulary to describe a Rachel and a woman arrested in Piccadilly for disorderly conduct." The word "actress" was, in other words, a euphemism for "prostitute" in the press, where the meanings of the two words were at times indistinguishable.[73]

The official censor, E. F. S. Pigott, portraying himself as the protector of "order and decency," told a parliamentary committee in 1892 that his duty was to prevent "turning theatres into disorderly houses, if not houses of ill fame."[74] Censorship of the English drama, even late in the Victorian period, was therefore a mechanism for enforcing with state power the wavering, still indistinct boundary between houses of prostitution and theatres. The line dividing them, the censor believed, was insufficient, without interventions by him, to protect playhouses from transformations that would render them indistinguishable from brothels.

The actress, however much applauded and admired, was thus the object of anxiety and dread by men, who discerned at times in her independence and power a challenge not only to the prevailing social order, but to the integrity of self. Under these circumstances going to the play could be an apocalyptic experience, and the theatre itself a kind of hell. Perhaps this is the reason that many Victorian novels of the theatre turn their plot upon the death of an actress or the physical destruction of a playhouse. Thus in *Fairy Phoebe; or, Facing the Footlights* (1887) members of the audience are trampled to death in a panic when the whole stage is enveloped in "a sheet of lurid flame" and the roof falls in with a tremendous crash.[75] In *A Leading Lady* (1891) "a mighty sheet of flame" and an asphyxiating cloud of smoke engulf the theatre. The performing space in Henry Herman's novel has become "a hell of heat and sparks."[76]

In the theatre-inferno of Victorian imagination the actress is often submitted to patriarchal discipline and pays a price, at least a symbolic one, for the life she has led. Thus in *A Leading Lady* the face of young actress Sybil Collier is horribly scarred in theatre hell-fire, leaving her no choice but to retire from the stage. In *Fairy Phoebe* a youthful actress is snatched from the flames by a fireman in the nick of time, her gossamer frock, however, "having been scorched by the far-reaching flames."[77] Phoebe will never act again, nor will the eponymous heroine of *Teresa Marlowe, Actress and Dancer,* who forsakes the stage, with its "thraldom of surroundings so desperate," in order to become a deaconness in the East End.[78] Artistic fame has also marred the life of the persona of a poem by the Polish actress Helena Modjeska, which Oscar Wilde "translated" – so he termed it – for a theatrical gift book edited by drama critic Clement Scott in 1880. The speaker in this poem by an actress has prayed for fame – the "laurel crown" – and won it, but as a result bears the stigmata of "red wounds of thorns upon my brow."[79]

And Generva Romaine, heroine of *The Life and Love of an Actress,* wants only to die, feeling cut off from life by having poured all her energies into make-believe worlds. Although her wish is denied, many of the actress-heroines in Victorian novels of the theatre die extravagantly, often onstage in the flush of professional triumph, or shortly afterward. Others – especially actresses of great power – are felled by vague illnesses which interrupt their careers or cut them short. Narratives such as these contributed to, as well as reflected, the anxiety with which

Victorians regarded the actress, and were part of the disciplinary process by which the supposed excesses of theatre women could be moderated.

Toward the close of the nineteenth century Richard von Krafft-Ebing diagnoses female crossdressing on stage as a manifestation of the "homosexual instinct," itself the result of a physical malady – "functional degeneration."[80] This attempt by Krafft-Ebing to bring actresses under medical observation was one manifestation of a rhetoric of disease through which the subversive potential of actresses was represented and controlled. In being absorbed into medical discourse, furthermore, actresses resembled not only homosexuals but prostitutes – "public" women of another sort who were persistently associated with actresses throughout the Victorian period. In the 1860s the Contagious Diseases Acts compelled women suspected of prostitution to submit to internal examination and, at the option of authorities, be interned in a locked hospital. These women, whether ill or not, were seized by police and made to submit to medical examination on the grounds of protecting military garrisons from the spread of venereal disease.[81] Regarding actresses and prostitutes as in some sense diseased, or potentially sick, was a means of controlling the public bodies and feigned emotions of these women who had exceeded the boundaries containing respectable wives and daughters. They belonged to the tiny minority of Victorian women who lived with any degree of virtuosity, making their own way in the world, exempt from, or at least not strictly bound by, the usual restrictions and taboos.

Moreover the absorption of actresses into medical discourse placed them, in effect, under treatment, negotiating subtle corrections in their personalities while at the same time drawing attention to a social dilemma. Part of that dilemma, as Charles Macready himself pointed out, was that actresses inevitably gave expression to emotions that well-bred women were taught to conceal. And for Victorian psychiatrists the asylum was the proper place for "young women of ungovernable temper...or who want that restraint over the passions without which the female character is lost."[82] Thus actresses were virtually mad by default, and necessarily the objects of medical concern. At the same time, however, their ability to express irrationality and violent emotion on stage provided an escape from the constraints of femininity – a kind of empowerment through the representation of madness. As Florence Nightingale points out in *Cassandra*, an unsettled mind and illness generally could become "feminine forms of protest" against a life of immobility and powerlessness.[83] In positing mental illness as a form of feminine rebellion, Nightingale anticipated feminist theorists of our own time – Phyllis Chesler, Hélène Cixous, Xavière Gauthier, Sandra Gilbert, Susan Gubar, Elaine Showalter, and others for whom madness has appeared a feminine mode of expressing rage and rebellion against a narrowly defined femininity, even if inwardly and without hope of success.[84] Such rebellions could be allowed because they produce no upheaval in society itself, being centered within the individual, monitored and controlled by medical authority. Thus the "freedom" attained through madness is acted out in confinement.

Nevertheless, in adopting an attitude of mental disruption on stage, actresses were realizing in public the same drama of "protest," as Nightingale calls it, which was being performed in Victorian homes. The more authentic this simulated madness appeared to be, furthermore, the greater the tolerance of the public for displays of power and control on the part of the actress. Harriet Smithson's landmark performance as Ophelia in 1828 was sensational in its realistic depiction of madness – "true madness," as one critic put it, adding that "we have never seen it before."[85] The emotional force of Smithson's performance – which brought the audience to its feet and Hector Berlioz to his knees – was fueled by her anguished face, wild outcries, and real tears. Actresses throughout the nineteenth century continued to find in the framework of madness a space for powerful effects that had no place in the usual female roles of ingenue and adventuress. The scope offered by a mad role was striking, even when, like Ophelia, it did not dominate the play and the actress had comparatively few lines. In an adaptation of *The Bride of Lammermoor*, for example, Ellen Terry recalls in her memoirs that in the last act "I had to lose my poor wits. . .and with hardly a word to say I was able to make an effect."[86]

Throughout the period actresses left some of their most spectacular impressions in such roles – Adelaide Ristori as a glassy-eyed Lady Macbeth, Sarah Bernhardt as the bloodthirsty Tosca, and Elizabeth Robins as a cool but seemingly psychotic Hedda Gabler. Indeed it seems likely that *Hedda Gabler* was licensed for performance – instead of being banned, as Robins feared would be the case – partly because the censor elected to interpret the characters and events of the play from a medical perspective, thus containing the force of Hedda's character while providing it space for enactment. As Edward F. S. Pigott, the examiner of plays, expressed it in a letter to Robins after reading the script and approving it for performance:

> The license for representation will be forwarded in due course, and meanwhile may be considered as received. I wish I could honestly believe that all your trouble and talent were well-spent on this eccentric piece, but I must confess that, to my poor perception, all the characters in it appear to have escaped from a lunatic asylum.[87]

This supposed derangement, however, is what makes Hedda Gabler's character imaginable and its enactment possible. Feminine depth of character can be comprehended by locating Hedda Gabler outside the borders of rationality – in an asylum, specifically – and thus the role can be discredited even while allowing it a performance. Reviewers fell readily into step with Pigott's own rationalization of the play. A. B. Walkley, for example, called Hedda a "monstrous specimen" of womanhood, and the play itself a dramatic presentation of "mental pathology" – as if the Vaudeville Theatre had become a kind of sanatorium during the brief period that *Hedda Gabler* was being performed there.[88]

This linkage of theatre and asylum had already been made explicit in Anna Cora Mowatt's *A Mimic Life*, in which the actress-heroine shrieks to her colleagues on stage, "Mad! Mad! Yes – that's it! . . .who isn't mad here? We are all mad!"[89] Lunacy has become a condition of the theatre in Mowatt's novel rather than a manifestation of any particular role or play. Although it manifested itself in various ways, this association of actresses with madness and disease is so pervasive in the Victorian period as to constitute a discernible cultural pattern. For example, the actress and title character in George Moore's *A Mummer's Wife* purchases her career on stage at great cost – a steep decline into unrestrained emotionality, drunkenness, violence, disease, physical deformity, and finally death. Indeed, her potential as an actress is most manifest to her colleagues when she is least rational, as in a jealous rage against her husband:

> The long black hair hung in disordered masses; her brown eyes were shot with golden lights; the green tints in her face became, in her excessive pallor, dirty and abominable in colour, and she seemed more like a demon than a woman as her screams echoed through the empty theatre. "By Jove! we ought to put up *Jane Eyre*," said Mortimer. "If she were to play the mad woman like that, we'd be sure to draw full houses." "I believe you," said Dubois; but at that moment he was interrupted by a violent scream. . .[90]

Medicalized and demonized in this way, the actress, whether in her own person or the part she played, claimed a latitude of speech and behavior that was beyond the experience of most women. More latitude – but at the same time the actress as madwoman was framed in a rhetoric of pathology that both monitored and disarmed her subversive potential. Thus the Victorians constructed their ideas of the theatre, and of the actress specifically, so that – as Foucault remarked of the modern asylum – they validated "the great continuity of social morality."[91]

This political basis for placing the actress in opposition to physical and mental health was usually left unstated, doing its work under various disguises. For example, what was seen as the excessive labor and overstrained emotional life of an actress could lead, it was feared, to a disordered mentality blurring the real and the imaginary. Thus an actress in *A Mimic Life* slips into the insanity of Ophelia when she represents her on stage:

> When Stella appeared upon the stage in the fourth act, – her hair unbound and dishevelled, her eyes dilated until they appeared of the jettiest black, and luminous with the peculiar light of insanity, her white drapery disordered, her movements rapid and uncertain, – her personation of the distraught Ophelia became painfully real.

During the performance the actress collapses on stage, paralyzed and raving, a condition which her doctor pronounces as "brain fever" brought on by "injudicious mental stimulus." Stella's "unstrung mind" can be healed only in absolute quiet, the physician advises, far from the feverish excitements of the theatre. "I foresaw this," announces the concerned brother of the actress; "I dreaded the effect of this turbulent existence upon her; but she would not heed my counsel."[92] The physical and mental strains upon an actress, particularly in demanding roles, seemed inconsistent with her gender, and her ability to bear up under their weight sometimes surprised critics. "The actress exerts herself with an intensity so untiring," wrote a reviewer of Sarah Bernhardt's Hamlet, "that it is marvellous how she can bear the strain of such arduous effects."[93] Much more to be expected is the decline or demise of the overtaxed woman performer, such as Trilby, the title character in the novel by George Du Maurier. She sinks toward death, her lovely voice broken and tuneless, once the supernatural and quasi-medical support of the hypnotist Svengali has been withdrawn as the result of his own death. Under Svengali's mesmeric power Trilby was "the other Trilby…an unconscious Trilby of marble…a singing machine – an organ to play upon – an instrument of music – a Stradivarius." With Svengali's death, however, she was a woman again, weak, sick, and unable to sustain, physically or emotionally, the burden of her success on stage.[94]

In *Violette le Grande, or The Life of an Actress* (1853), a play by William Suter, the heroine sickens at the height of her popularity, brought down by the nervous pace and strenuous effort of her public life. A physician is brought in to announce that Violette le Grande must avoid "great exertion" and "all excitement" – a prescription which she, like women in other theatrical narratives, is inclined to accept. Thus she submits herself to the will of her fiancé, who would have her "bid adieu to the feverish profession that would destroy you" in hopes that "health will revisit your cheeks, and we shall be happy, so happy." For Violette, however, it is too late, and at the final curtain, acknowledging "the wreck I now am," she breathes her last and becomes a fatal casualty of the theatre.[95] Like her, the actress Bianca in the novel *The Half Sisters* (1848) diagnoses her own condition – "I am wretchedly tired; indeed I am always weary now," leaving the inevitable physician to do little more than fill in the blanks. He fears that, in the actress's case, "there is such an alarming debility and general prostration that the worst results may follow." Medicine, as such, can do little for her. What is required, as in the case of Violette le Grande in Suter's play a few years later, is a complete change of scene. "She must be removed [from her life on stage] immediately," the physician declares, "or I will not answer for the consequences."[96]

Victorian novels of the theatre, most of them long forgotten, are replete with exhausted and diseased actresses, beautiful but dessicated. Like Myra Kenneth in *An Actress's Love Story* (1888), their wasted features give their friends cause to worry and express alarm – "you look so white and wan and ill," a confidant tells her.[97] Actresses in these narratives are typically attended by physicians who in a moment of crisis or consultation trace their patients' maladies to the rigors of professional life. In *The Life and Love of an Actress* (1888), for example, Generva Romaine is paralyzed by her labors on stage, unable to move a muscle. "I cannot lift my head from the pillow," she complains; "I should fall if I attempted to walk across the floor." Dr. Tom Winthrop, her physician – "after taking her temperature, and noting her pulse, and inquiring carefully after the most minute symptoms" – declares that the actress is, like many others in this genre of Victorian fiction, "very sick," threatened by "brain-fever." Broken in body and in mind, Generva Romaine can recover health only by removing herself from the stage and its excitements. "She will not be able to play to-night, nor to-morrow night," Dr. Winthrop announces to her manager, "and for all I can promise several weeks to come."[98] Similarly, in the novel *The Moth and the Footlights* (1906), Dr. Peter Blake warns that the theatre – with its "excitement, fatigue, anxieties, worries, draughts" – is no place for the fragile and delicate Gillian Ralph. Pursuing a stage life anyway, despite expert medical advice, she displays symptoms of "brain fever and a feeble heart."[99] A leading lady in Florence Marryat's novel *Facing the Footlights* (1883) finds that she had "worn myself out...body and soul" by twenty years on stage, then follows her doctor's orders to retire to the country for "rest, and a complete change."[100]

The title character of *Only an Actress* (1883) is physically devastated by her work, "deathly pale" and "overstrained to exhaustion."[101] The health of Margherita La Mara has worsened after a particularly splendid performance, and indeed much Victorian writing about actresses indicates that their "illnesses" are more or less grave in proportion to their success on stage – the most brilliant and dominating actresses being also the sickest. The correspondence between a woman's dramatic power and endangered health is made unusually explicit in a novel by Rita (also entitled *Only an Actress*, published nearly three decades after its predecessor of the same name), in a scene in which the heroine rehearses a new part:

While the fire of genius burnt so fiercely within her and all her energies were fanning it to brighter flames, the vital powers of her physical nature were growing weaker and weaker, the long strain was telling on her more and more.

The actress, Irene Vernon, thus makes herself "ill," as Rita puts it, to the same extent that she makes herself a great actress.[102] In the story "The Candle's Flame" (1909) an actress of genius suffers "heart attacks" and dies in the aftermath of an arduous production in which she "never spared herself."[103] And in *My Sister the Actress* (1881) Bertha Selwyn finds herself famous after an electrifying performance as Juliet, but is in no condition to enjoy the rewards of her labor – "too exhausted to care" about her success, she seems "pale, worn-out, and almost ready to fall."[104]

At the end of *The Martyrdom of Madeline*, the theatrical novel by Robert Buchanan, a former actress pronounces herself determined to live in the country, screened from the contamination of the theatre. "The excitements of the stage," as her husband realizes, "were not beneficial to a nature so overwrought as that of his wife," good neither for her peace of mind nor "health." But he worries also about the effects upon the actress of the theatre itself, with its "mercenary specu-lators" and "coarse admiration of the dregs of the public."[105] Such an analysis locates the performing woman within a system of monetary exchange and exposes her to a gross carnality that could be employed as easily in the description of a prostitute as an actress. Later, in a memoir, Elizabeth Robins would draw attention to the Victorian ten-dency to join the actress, the prostitute, and illness into a sinister triad. Acting, she recalls, was generally supposed to lead women to "loitering in the streets," and to propagate "the particular variety of affliction known as Exhibitionism."[106] This triangulation of acting, prostitution, and disease is what brings about the conclusion of *Through the Stage Door*, the novel by Harriett Jay in which an actress turned courtesan dies of a "spasm at the heart" in her expensive rooms in Park Lane amid an elegance purchased by the "shameful" conduct she learned in the theatre.[107]

Thus constructed by the rhetoric of disease and prostitution, actresses could seem hopelessly remote from, and incompatible with, what was often termed the "real" life of domesticity. Life on stage from this perspective was no life at all for a woman, but death. The title character of Buchanan's *The Martyrdom of Madeline* responds impetuously, there-fore, when her husband suggests that she might like to return to acting, her profession before she married him and went to live in the country: "I hate the stage. Rather than return to it I would die."[108] These words – "I hate the stage" – are uttered also in *The Picture of Dorian Gray* by Sybil Vane, whom Oscar Wilde leaves, as Madeline is left in Buchanan's novel, choosing death rather than to continue as an actress. Sybil had lived "only in the theatre" – as Juliet and Rosalind, Cordelia and Beatrice, believing the "painted scenes" and "shadows" of the stage were real – before falling in love with Dorian Gray and learning "what reality really is." In this she resembles the magnetic performer in the novel *My Sister the Actress* (1881), for whom "Juliet's troubles are the only realities she knows" until she falls in love on her own and her stage personae lapse into insignificance.[109] Sybil Vane's discovery of love and the prospect of marriage, what Mary Anderson calls the "great reali-ties," cause her to turn from the stage in disgust and denounce as a "sham" her revolving identities as an actress.

In her last performance Sybil Vane plays Juliet without emotion or conviction, her power as an actress having been consumed by her love for Dorian Gray. Where Wilde departs from the usual script of Victorian thought and fiction, however, is in expressing through Lord Henry Wotton the view that acting "is so much more real than life," and in making Dorian prefer Sybil the actress to the "real" Sybil who loves him. Instead of allowing the actress to marry and retire to a domestic life in the country, Wilde gives her a lover, Dorian Gray, who is more exhilarated than worried by her transformations of self on stage. He learns to think of the actual person Sybil Vane as nothing but a "dream," one who "never really lived," and thus to accept as reasonable that "the moment she touched actual life, she marred it, and it marred her." Despite these ingenious reversals of customary thinking about actresses, however, Sybil Vane is left in a familiar dilemma, the usual dilemma of the Victorian actress as conceived by others and often by herself – helpless, that is, to combine the rewards of a career on stage and those of a domestic life. Written out of love and marriage, she is, like other actresses in other texts, written out of humanity too – "The girl never really lived," as Lord Henry Wotton explains, and even in taking her own life "she never really died."[110]

In her sickness and death Wilde's fictional actress thus performs the doom of actresses generally, as the Victorian imagination tended to conceive it. They suffer from brain fever, like the brilliant actress in "The Tale of a Peacock," written by leading lady Fanny Bernard-Beere, or fall victim to vague maladies like the heroine of "Chances!", written by another actress, Marie Litton.[111] They are physical as well as mental wrecks, like the heroine of William Suter's play *The Life of an Actress* (1853) – casualties, they learn, of the "feverish profession that would destroy you." They kill themselves, off stage like Sybil Vane, or in the middle of a show, like the heroine of *The Life and Love of an Actress*, who stabs herself in a performance under the stunned gaze of the man who just broke off their engagement. Her lithe body swaying to and fro like a reed, Generva Romaine raises a "glittering dagger" and plunges it into her panting breast as the audience cheers wildly, thinking the actress's suicide a brilliant pretense, the crowning glory of her impersonation of Ophelia. In fact, however, Generva Romaine had long been weary of a life that was passed only in the realm of art, like Sybil Vane's in Wilde's novel. "Wrapped in her art, living for it alone," starved for the love of a man, she had felt before this night "utter desolation" and "a longing to die."[112] She is like the actress Irene Vernon in Rita's novel *Only an Actress* (1911), whose most magnificent performance occurs in response to the desolation she feels from the loss of love. In her big scene, to a thunder of applause, Irene Vernon's arms fall nerveless to her side. "My love!" she wails, "my love!" – then, at the moment of her greatest triumph as an actress, and greatest failure as a woman, staggers across the stage and falls dead.[113]

Women like Generva Romaine and Irene Vernon are desperate cases, mentally and physically, although in principle they could be restored to health easily enough. "A quiet home shared with the man of her heart," as the audience of *The Life of an Actress* was informed, would bring color back to the cheeks of Violette le Grande.[114] Similarly, when Sybil Vane has come to "hate the stage," she expresses the remedy with a plaintive cry: "Take me away, Dorian – take me away with you, where we can be quite alone."[115] Like Sybil and the speaker of Wilde's poem "Sen Artysty," the actress gives up everything – her happiness, her hope of love, even her womanhood and humanity – in exchange for the rewards of a public life. As Francis Gribble describes this dilemma in his novel *Sunlight and Limelight*, the actress is perceived to exist in a shadow-land of gender – not like other women at all: "Other women lived by sunlight, lived without the excitement and the music and the applause, and never wanted it, and were happier than she was."[116] This irrevocable gap between the actress and the experience of most women is reluctantly expressed by the heroine of Florence Marryat's novel *Facing the Footlights* (1883), who recognizes that "the quiet pleasures that satisfy other women, who have married the men they love, and have children, and domestic happiness, are not for me."[117]

In their own lives, moreover, actresses sometimes acquiesced in the judgment that their expenditures of hard work and intense emotion exposed them to the risk of both physical and mental maladies. Like the women in theatrical narratives, they confirm dubious judgments of themselves by their own compliance. Mrs. Patrick Campbell, describing her "nervous breakdown" of 1897, offers little resistance to a physician's analysis that her work on stage, with its attendant excitements, was responsible for her condition:

As the doctor held my pulse I laughed, with tears pouring down my cheeks, declaring I was all right. He said gravely, "All the acting has done this."...The doctor – Dr. Emberton, now dead – was an extraordinarily gentle, kind man; he used to hold my hand and tell me I had "worked too hard, and felt too much," and that all I needed was sleep...[118]

Elizabeth Robins underwent a similar rest cure after complaining of "illness and exhaustion," feeling in retrospect that "I drove myself too hard."[119] The American actress Mary Anderson felt compelled to retire from the stage in 1889 after the "great and continuous" exertions that it exacted from her. Her career had become a medical crisis, and "her health required relief from care" in the restorative atmosphere of marriage and a domestic life.[120] Anderson herself came to believe that there was something unhealthy in the "sunless, musty" buildings in which actresses and actors worked – something that caused her, as she calls it in a book of memories, "physical *malaise*."[121] Doctors hovered over actresses in life as in fiction, anxious about the effects of these women's work upon their mental and physical well-being. When the pre-Victorian actress known as Miss O'Neill collapsed in a scene of hysterical despair in *The Gamester*, it seemed obvious to medical men what the problem was: "Doctors shook their heads ominously when they were called in and said such nerve strain could prove fatal."[122]

For actresses, moreover, illness could become the necessary and even desirable outcome of their arduous and therefore "unfeminine" lives, as if they were performing, albeit offstage, society's judgment of them. Elizabeth Robins woos her own sickness, "wishing heartily that I had some important disease" to account for the vague but overwhelming mental and physical malaise she was experiencing.[123] Adelaide Ristori, in her autobiography, reflects on the connections between her work as an actress, her volatile temperament, and illness in general:

Sometimes I fell victim to an inexplicable melancholy, which weighed on my heart like lead, and filled my mind with dark thoughts. I believe that this strange inequality of temperament might be entirely attributed to the excessive emotion I experienced in performing my most impassioned parts. For I so entirely identified myself with the characters I represented that, in the end, my health began to suffer, and one evening, when I had been acting in *Adrienne Lecouvreur*, the curtain had scarcely fallen after the last act, when the great tension of nerves and mind and body I had undergone during that final scene of passion and delirium brought on a kind of nervous attack, and an affection of the brain which deprived me of consciousness for a good quarter of an hour.[124]

Ristori's account of her mad scene in *Adrienne Lecouvreur* recalls uncannily the scene in Anna Cora Mowatt's *A Mimic Life* in which the actress playing Ophelia is infected by the madness of the character she is portraying – the implication in both cases being that the arduous emotionality of acting overwhelms the actress's own reason. Mowatt described herself, moreover, as suffering from the same "brain fever" that afflicted the fictional actress in her novel.

These self-dramatizations of illness could take other forms as well.

Ellen Terry, whose own spirits rose and fell between exhilaration and deep depression, visited madhouses in search of inspiration for the parts she enacted on stage. Adelaide Ristori also felt "impelled," as she said, to visit the asylums of the cities she visited, aware that "mad girls were those who attracted my deepest sympathy; their sad, tranquil lunacy allowed me to penetrate into their cells without danger of any kind, and I was able to stay long with them, to gain their affection and confidence."[125] These forays into asylums and hospitals, and the self-identification with madness and disease expressed by actresses, suggests that the social formulations linking theatrical women with derangement was being incorporated into the consciousness of individual actresses. In their own outbreaks of "brain fever," and in their yearnings and affinities for sickness, women of the theatre internalized to some degree the social mechanism that worked to disarm their disruptive potential.

Max Nordau applies this well-established pathology to a particular dramatic author and group of plays in his attack on Ibsen in *Degeneration* (1895). Whereas most previous discussion had focused on the supposed lunacy of actresses and their susceptibility to disease, Nordau finds symptoms of feminine derangement in the new drama emanating from Norway more than in the performers of it. He can make sense of Ibsen's women only by seeing them as insane – casualties of an epidemic of mental and physical "degeneration" undermining the foundations of the social order. What makes Ibsen's women characters "sick," in Nordau's analysis, are the same qualities which made actresses seem ill or subject to illness in the Victorian period generally – their strong sense of self, or "ego-mania" as Nordau terms it, and their violation of the borders of domesticity.

With Ibsen woman has no duties and all rights. The tie of marriage does not bind her. She runs away when she longs for liberty, or when she believes she has cause of complaint against her husband, or when he pleases her a little less than another man... Woman is always the clever, strong, courageous being; man always the simpleton and coward. In every encounter the wife is victorious, and the man flattened out like a pancake. Woman need live for herself alone. With Ibsen she has even overcome her most primitive instinct – that of motherhood – and abandons her brood without twitching an eyelid when the caprice seizes her to seek satisfactions elsewhere.

These violations of the established domestic order are what certify Ibsen's women characters as diseased, or, in Nordau's fevered rhetoric, "raving so wildly as to require strait-jackets." For the enactment of such characters, Nordau can imagine only a fantastic, feminized theatre with an audience dominated by women exactly like those in Ibsen's plays. Although masquerading as advocates of women's independence, this female audience would in fact consist of hysterics, nymphomaniacs, and prostitutes who recognized their own lawless selves glorified in a Nora Helmer or Mrs. Alving. The theatre of Nordau's nightmare thus becomes a madhouse in which an audience of lunatic women applauds "their own portrait," their own suffering degeneracy, in representations of women mad like themselves.[126]

The grave defect of "women of this species," as Nordau calls them, is that they find "all discipline intolerable." His overheated comments are an attempt to impose discipline, to stigmatize a degenerate femininity associated with the theatre, and to confine "women of this species" within a framework of rhetoric which subjects them to the guardianship and correction of "rational men." Nordau's analysis belongs to a Victorian discourse of madness and disease which was aimed at the enactments of female aspiration and power that took place in the theatre. By construing these performances as deranged or diseased, by associating them with death and the negation of "real" life, the Victorians were able to neutralize to some extent the threat that they posed to the hierarchy of gender and the social order as a whole.

TIGERS IN THE DAIRY: THE ACTRESS DOMESTICATED

From beginning to end, therefore, the Victorian period was able to tolerate the actress, with her unique powers of speech and action, by confining her within rhetorical structures of madness, disease, prostitution, deformation, and inhumanity. Seen as sick, depraved, and exotic, these independent women could not easily present a serious threat to the social order which in normal circumstances would have rendered them, as women, idle and silent. At the same time, however, a related and contradictory discourse – one emanating largely from the theatre itself – functioned to neutralize the actress by bringing her under the auspices of domesticity instead of banishing her from it. A collectivity of audience and players, organized round the icon of the chaperoned young woman, yet troubled by nightmares of feminine power and aggression, looked for ways to check the disruptive tendencies of the theatres. This work could not be accomplished, however, without the collaboration of actresses, whose assumption of seemingly masculine attributes on stage could seem inimical to health, sanity, and humanity itself. Interpreting the actress as being refined and respectable, harmonious with Victorian domesticity, might seem to have worked against the rhetoric of disease and death which also framed performing women throughout the period. But these two modes of representing actresses served one purpose, that of monitoring and limiting the imagined excesses of women on stage and reinforcing the battlements of male privilege.

The cup-and-saucer comedies of Tom Robertson at the Prince of Wales's Theatre beginning in the 1860s intensified a campaign already begun to make theatres respectable. Charles Kean, for example, had brought back to the theatre – for his historicized reconstructions of Shakespeare at the Princess's in the 1850s – a middle-class audience that for a generation had been mostly absent. Macready and Madame Vestris banned prostitutes from the promenades and refreshment areas of their theatres, and the Theatre Licensing Act of 1843 reduced the annoyance of drunken playgoers by forbidding legitimate theatres from selling alcohol. As theatres came to seem more like homes and less like houses of prostitution, the carriages of respectable families could once again be seen stopping outside.[127] Queen Victoria herself witnessed William Charles Macready's farewell performance in 1851 at the Haymarket, and was a patron of the Lyceum Theatre when Madame Vestris and her husband Charles Mathews were managing it. Samuel Phelps began in 1844 the formidable task of transforming the unruly Sadler's Wells Theatre into a center of Shakespearean performance that attracted middle-class audiences for almost twenty years under his management.

In plays like *Society* and *School* – cited in their own time for "unquestionable taste, elegance, and refinement" – Tom Robertson's drama of middle-class life was performed before middle-class spectators at the Prince of Wales's.[128] Under the husband-and-wife management of Squire and Marie Bancroft the theatre was being reinterpreted as an English home rather than the brothel or madhouse imagined by critics alarmed by the staging of unconventional femininity. Although Victorians would continue to confuse playhouses with whorehouses, the Bancrofts' theatre lent momentum to a counterforce that would complicate the distinction between theatre and home. They recall with satisfaction in their joint autobiography how characters on the stage of the Prince of Wales's Theatre "move and talk and demean themselves just as English people of the class represented would do in English homes."[129]

The homelike quality with which the Bancrofts tried to infuse their productions was often remarked upon by contemporaries who had grown up with an idea of the theatre which suggested little or nothing of the kind. Playwright and critic Justin McCarthy would write in *Portraits of the Sixties* that Marie Bancroft, in particular, "could express human emotion exactly as it might express itself in the life of an English home."[130] Bancroft productions, as Henry James observed, presupposed "a great many chairs and tables, carpets, curtains, and knick-knacks, and an audience placed close to the stage. They might, for the most part, have been written by a cleverish visitor at a country-house, and acted in the drawing-room by his fellow-inmates."[131] At the Prince of Wales's, as William Archer puts it, "society flocked to see itself reproduced."[132] Thus the subject of the drama on stage was the audience itself, which left the theatre charmed by the "refined gaiety" and "delicate emotion" of Mrs. Bancroft and the manly good nature of her husband's impersonations. The Bancrofts liked to think that their spectator returned to his actual home in "good-humour, smiling to himself," satisfied and reassured by the "truth" of the domesticated theatricals that he had witnessed.[133]

Dispensing with the exaggerated gestures and highly rhetorical utterance that were customary with actresses before her, Marie Bancroft made herself into the young woman of the Victorian home as well as an actress. As Naomi Tighe in *School* and Polly Eccles in *Caste* she helped to define and sustain femininity as most Victorians would understand it. Performances like hers at the Prince of Wales's thus became part of what Michel Foucault has described as a "discourse" of power, an activity of regulation through public discussion. While involved in redefining gender through public enactments on one hand, however, on the other the stage itself was being regulated. By the 1860s and 1870s the audiences at London theatres – not only the Prince of Wales's – seemed to some observers an ominous middle-class presence, one that could exert a sinister influence over the performance on the other side of the footlights. Henry James, for example, found that the London audience of the 1870s "suggests domestic virtue and comfortable homes," consisting of dull-eyed girls, mothers in knitted shawls, and honorable-looking fathers in evening dress.[134] This "genteel" audience limited the possibilities of the theatre, James believed – a view seconded by William Archer, who complains that Victorian gentlemen who brought their young daughters of 15 to the dress circle "resented the slightest shock to their innocent ignorance."[135] Even late in the century, as Virginia Woolf recollects, respectable young women could not go to the theatre "unaccompanied."[136] Consequently playwrights found themselves writing for chaperoned young women and their watchful guardians – for families as such – thus closing all the more the gap between the theatre and domestic life.[137]

The line dividing respectable audiences from professional actors was further blurred in late Victorian times when amateurs from good society began to appear in professional roles on the West End stage while at the same time actors were received more often than before among the elite. "They appear in society," writes an exasperated Henry James about actors, "and the people of society appear on the stage; it is as if the great gate which formerly divided the theatre from the world had been lifted off its hinges."[138] The Lyceum under Henry Irving was the first theatre to open its doors to amateurs, and its wings "stank of debs and Debrett," complained Kate Phillips, a long-time actress at the Lyceum, speaking from the point of view of a woman for whom acting was a livelihood.[139]

Fiction also provides some indication that the infiltration of the stage by well-to-do amateurs, while contributing to the prestige of the drama generally, was an unwelcome development from the perspective of at least some professional actresses. "What right has she upon the stage at all?" asks a leading lady in Florence Marryat's novel *Facing the Footlights* (1883) when she has been displaced in her part by a titled amateur. "She has plenty of money of her own, and it's a mean thing to try and take the bread out of the mouths of those who have worked hard for it."[140] The actress-heroine in a novel of 1868 by Mary Elizabeth Braddon loses her part in *The Hunchback* to an amateur of independent means, but loses no time in expressing her outrage:

And are you aware that it is you, and ladies of your class, who bring discredit upon the profession which you condescend to take up for the amusement of your idle evenings?" It is this – amateur – element which contaminates the atmosphere of our theatres, and the manager who fosters it is an enemy to the interests he is bound to protect.[141]

Managers like the one in Braddon's novel, however, welcomed well-to-do amateurs, knowing that their friends would fill the private boxes and bring with them an aura of respectability and fashion. To a degree, therefore, actresses themselves were the victims rather than beneficiaries of the growing social acceptance of women on stage.

This domestication of the theatre was not without its critics. A. B. Walkley regretted the falling of barriers that separated actors from people on the other side of the footlights. At a dinner of the Actors' Benevolent Fund he reacted cooly to speeches by Henry Irving and John Hare, who were "congratulating themselves on their rise in 'social position'" while ostensibly attacking prejudice against the stage. "They are becoming emburgessed, as the French say," Walkley complains of actors, "– desirous of merging themselves in the ruck of mere commonplace citizens, of being enrolled in the mandarinate."[142] In an acerbic essay George Moore takes actors to task for going to church and writing self-important memoirs in order to enroll themselves among the respectable. Overvalued, "lifted out of their place," they were becoming, according to Moore, increasingly bound together with their audiences – a trend that he believed was irreversible. "The flame of mummer-worship shall be blown higher," he laments; "society shall embrace the mummer, the mummer shall return the embrace more ardently."[143]

It was just such an embrace that concluded *Masks and Faces* in 1852 when the actress Peg Woffington entwined herself round Mabel Vane, "an angel of truth and goodness" and virtuous young wife. "Sister! oh, yes!" cries the actress Woffington at the end of the play; "call me sister!"[144] Hearing "that sacred name" of sister from the lips of the angel-wife initiates the actress into the Victorian family and extends the rule of domesticity into the theatre itself. Audiences and players, less and less distinct from one another, were therefore moving toward the mutual embrace that George Moore imagined, organizing themselves into a community of shared values. Together they aspired toward the "cohesive public" that Herbert Blau argues has disappeared in our own time – a like-minded community whose "threshhold of approval" determines what can be attempted in the theatre.[145] But to make the theatre congruent with home, the actress would have to become unequivocally a woman. She would have to reject the masculine dress and freedom of crossdressed roles and aspire to what was considered "real" femininity – like Marie Bancroft, whose fame came at first from her "astonishingly impudent" performances as a boy. "Oh, dear me!" Bancroft exclaimed, "why can't I be allowed to be a girl?"[146]

Being a "girl," a "sister" – embracing rather than overpowering the audience – was one way in which the actress could demonstrate her solidarity with it. She could enact flattering representations of the public, charming it into laughter or tears by dramatizing its most cherished ideals. Such acting, however, would never inspire the praise that William Hazlitt heaped upon Sarah Siddons before the dawn of the Victorian period, raising her to the ranks of gods and prophets in announcing that "Power was seated on her brow."[147] Siddons had dominated the stage with her flashing eyes and clarion voice, spellbinding her audience and sometimes rendering other actors mute when they were supposed to speak. The absence of this power is what Gordon Craig laments in the irreverent biography of his mother Ellen Terry, the most eminent of late Victorian actresses. "Faced with the public," he complains, "rather than carry the public along, or fight it, she would side with the cow-like animal and begin to imitate its face and to drop tears all over the place." Siddons, unlike Ellen Terry, "refused to be dominated" by her audience, refused to be "made tearful by it when she was about to scorch and brand it."[148] In dramatizing the weepy sentimentality with which the Victorian public invested its women, whether playing Ophelia or Lady Macbeth, Terry was overcome by the prejudices of an audience which her son believed she had the genius to master.

But others reserved their highest praise for Terry's performances in dramas of besotted sentimentality such as Alfred Calmour's *The Amber Heart*, in which the critic for the *Referee* declared that the actress showed "greater delicacy" and "deeper pathos" than ever in playing a distracted woman rejected by her poet-lover.[149] In such roles Ellen Terry seemed "a living embodiment" of pictures by Sir Laurence Alma-Tadema and Albert Moore, whose art resembles the publicity photographs of Victorian actresses with eyes downcast, vacant, or tear-stained, their bodies in postures of submission – kneeling or shrinking backward, hands uplifted in mute appeal or covering their eyes in self-effacement. "The bow of grief seemed to pass over her soul," exclaims an ardent reviewer for the *Theatre*, "wringing from it a chord of deep pathos that vibrated through every heart, while tears, real tears, flowed from her eyes."[150]

Earning £200 a week as perhaps the best-paid woman in England, Ellen Terry was a preeminent star in her own right and yet, as Nina Auerbach points out, as dependent on Henry Irving as Victorian wives were upon their husbands.[151] "We must have no more of these Ophelias and Desdemonas!" her father once exclaimed, dismayed by Irving's assigning "second-fiddle parts" to his daughter. "I might have had 'bigger' parts, but it doesn't follow that they would have been better ones," responds Ellen Terry somewhat defensively in her memoirs.[152] At the Lyceum Theatre she played a mild Ophelia to Irving's Hamlet, a passive and pure Margaret to his titanic Faust. While Sarah Bernhardt, Eleonora Duse, and Mrs. Patrick Campbell were impersonating powerful women – murderous queens, suicidal and deranged society ladies – Ellen Terry was melting audiences at the Lyceum as the suffering wife in *Cymbeline* and the victimized but pure Olivia in W. G. Wills's adaptation of *The Vicar of Wakefield*.

Shaw complained that Ellen Terry, despite her genius, played down to the usually inferior roles she was given, and her actress-sister Marion Terry was beloved of playwrights who permitted no tampering with the plays they wrote. "Their method suited her," reflects Kate Terry Gielgud in her memoirs, "– she could fit the embroidery of her individuality into any design."[153] Not all women could be so self-effacing, however. "If I were a man," exclaims the actress Bianca in Geraldine Jewsbury's novel *The Half Sisters*, "I should enjoy playing 'Hamlet.' You do not know, you cannot imagine, the bitterness of heart, the intense envy I have felt...when a grand play has been put on, and I have no hope, no prospect, of getting beyond my own little part of two dozen lines! Oh, the maddening mortification I have had to devour!"[154] As Nina Auerbach writes, Ellen Terry herself annotated the part of Hamlet more extensively in the Lyceum script than that of her own Ophelia – her way, perhaps, of expressing the same longing as the fictional actress Bianca to play men's parts and act on a "grand" scale.[155]

What Ellen Terry and her fictional counterpart could only wish for, however, many other Victorian actresses put into practice. Charlotte Cushman, for example, won critical acclaim for her portrayal of Romeo in 1855, the *Illustrated London News* commenting that "for force and passion it exceeds that of any male performer, and yet avoids exaggeration."[156] Sarah Bernhardt's controversial Hamlet was the most notorious, but by no means the first and by some accounts not even the best female representation of the part. "I have seen several far better female Hamlets," the Victorian playwright Chance Newton writes, although acknowledging Bernhardt to have been "supremely beautiful" in the death scene. Newton recalls in particular Mrs. Bandmann-Palmer, who was said to have played the role a thousand times and whose Hamlets were "among the most striking performances I have seen of the character." Sophie Miles played Hamlet at the Britannia Theatre and Clare Howard at the Pavilion, while Julia Seaman, Florrie Groves, and Sybil Ward each took on the part at one time or another. Miss Marriott, who made her reputation as a tragic actress at Sadler's Wells Theatre, portrayed a Hamlet that, Newton recalls, was "one of the very best I have ever seen."[157] Even Clement Scott, the conservative theatre critic

1. Helen Faucit as Pauline in *The Lady of Lyons*, 1838.

for the *Daily Telegraph*, was impressed by Bernhardt's Hamlet, judging her to have risen to challenges that her other roles – as women – never offered her. "As Hamlet," Scott writes in a little book on late-Victorian actors of the part, "I see her as a greater artist than ever, because her task was heroic in its significance and importance." It was a performance, he says, that one was "bound to admire," and even in later years "not forget."[158]

Ellen Terry never played Hamlet, and even her enactment of Lady Macbeth was trimmed to the proportions of a Victorian dame – "she was *not* a fiend, and *did* love her husband," she once wrote."[159] But her capacity to act on a larger scale seemed obvious: "She could play any part and hold any audience," Shaw Desmond recollects in *London Nights of Long Ago*; "no female creature that has lived on this earth ever had more primal vitality."[160] Gordon Craig agreed with this estimate of his mother's abilities, but added a crucial qualification. "If there was ever anybody born in nineteenth century England to give a real and painful interpretation of *Lady Macbeth* it was Ellen Terry, if only she had not been frightened of that British public."[161] The foremost Shakespearean actress of her time, Terry nevertheless seemed more a spirit on stage than a woman of depth and force – "ideal, mystical, and medieval," as her most influential critic, Clement Scott, once characterized her, in what was meant as a compliment.[162] What Shaw Desmond called her "primal vitality" was mediated and subdued by "a sort of spiritual essence that seemed to come from some interior fount."[163]

Ellen Terry was by no means alone in being trapped within roles that stunted her potential as a commanding presence on stage. Janet Achurch, the first Nora in an English production of *A Doll's House*, turned from Ibsen to play Mercy Merrick in Wilkie Collins's *The New Magdalen* in 1895, causing George Bernard Shaw to doubt the evidence of his eyes. "I can as easily conceive," Shaw exclaims, "a tigress settling down in a dairy as Miss Achurch...domesticating herself...and receiving an offer of marriage from such a sample of good form as Mr Horace Holmcroft" – the eligible young man in Collins's drama.[164] Janet Achurch might well have preferred to play another Ibsen heroine instead of Mercy Merrick, just as Elizabeth Robins a few years earlier declared her preference to act in something more challenging than an Adelphi melodrama by Robert Buchanan, and Ellen Terry confessed her longing for the chance to act Rosalind in *As You Like It* instead of another suffering victim of a Henry Irving character.[165] Women

2. Charlotte Cushman as Romeo and Ada Swanborough as Juliet – a sketch
from *The Illustrated London News*, 1855.

characters in male-authored Victorian plays were typically what Micheline Wandor has called "ciphers" or "objects of displacement" for the male protagonists.[166] Even in plays in which actresses portrayed the title role – for example, Bulwer's *The Lady of Lyons* and Wilde's *Lady Windermere's Fan* – the woman character remains trapped in male-centered territory and, in the case of Wilde's play, not only adjunct to the main action but ignorant to the end of what is going on round her.

But among the luckiest actresses, in fact, were those "tigers in the dairy" trapped in male-determined roles that limited their potential as actresses and women, for at least they had employment of some kind in the theatre. A more extreme means of constricting actresses' professional and personal development was to maintain a state of affairs in which most of them could not find work at all. As recent studies by Tracy C. Davis and Mary Jean Corbett have emphasized, the theatrical marketplace for women was overcrowded with job-seekers and fiercely competitive – so much so that, as actress Irene Vanbrugh relates, the actress's life was "one long fight...There are others, many others, in the field and if she stops fighting for a single moment she will be trampled underfoot."[167] For every actress life is a "lone battle," Vanbrugh continues; "for every individual who succeeds in the theatre there are scores who fail." One who failed abysmally was the nameless author of *Diary of an Actress: or Realities of Stage Life* (1885), who reflects the despair with which an ordinary actress, one without prospects and just beginning her career in provincial theatres, could view the desperate competition before her:

If I could only earn enough to live, I would do my best and work hard at anything. But it is dreadful to think of being here alone in lodgings, with no money, and no means of earning any...Is my life all a mistake?...after all my anxiety and waiting, what prospect is there before me? Why should I expect to be more fortunate than hundreds of other women, cleverer, better-looking, nicer in every way than I?[168]

The life of an actress, as another, earlier, Victorian wrote, is "a state of war without bloodshed," a contest in which only a few could prevail.[169] Even the most successful actress was not exempt from the competition, as Irene Vanbrugh points out: "She can never rest on her laurels unless she wishes to be passed in the race by others who are quicker and cleverer than herself." Florence Farr was still lamenting by 1910 that in contrast to a few wealthy stars, the average successful actress could earn only £10 a week or £500 a year, part of a widespread discrimination for which the remedy, she argues, is "reorganizing the market value of women's labour."[170] Even when starring in *Mrs. Dane's Defence* (1900), Lena Ashwell recalls that she made only £20 for eight performances a week.[171] The wage of only £1 or £2 a week earned by Mrs. Patrick Campbell when she began her professional career was roughly typical for a woman at the time – low pay, but as much or more than she could earn in many other vocations opening up to women by the 1880s.[172]

One way for an actress to survive and prosper in such an atmosphere was to provide her public and the actor-managers with the type of performance they expected from her. Caught in a web of masculine power, her primary role would be as the object of that power, enacting womanliness as defined by a patriarchal culture. Victorian actresses – many of them – were extreme examples of what Sue-Ellen Case has described as the alienation of women performers from the theatre.

Within the patriarchal system of signs, women do not have the cultural mechanisms of meaning to construct themselves as the subject rather than the object of performance. A wedge is created between the sign "woman" and real women that insinuates alienation into the very participation of women in the theatrical representation or within the system of communication in the dominant culture.[173]

Ellen Terry, in becoming what W. Macqueen-Pope calls "womanliness personified," was supplying a masculinist public with what it demanded – a representation of itself, its prejudices and ideals.[174] This type of self-censorship was extremely common among Victorian actresses, many of whom embraced Victorian social morality, especially as it touched on the representation of gender, as the governing purpose of their work on stage.

Helen Faucit, for example, who acted for six years with William Charles Macready at Covent Garden theatre, declared that the stage should be a moral influence by dramatizing for audiences "the types of noble womanly nature as they have been revealed by our best dramatic poets, and especially by Shakespeare."[175] She was lauded by Mrs. C. Baron Wilson in *Our Actresses* (1844) for living up to her own ideal, representing "a feminine grace and delicacy that deserved the highest applause."[176] Faucit's husband, Sir Theodore Martin, writes that "people saw in her not only a great actress, they felt themselves in the presence of one who was herself the ideal woman of whom poets had written."[177] Inseparable from Helen Faucit's womanliness, as Mrs.

Wilson perceived it in *Our Actresses*, was "her great excellence...in characters of tenderness" who were "deeply pathetic."[178] Acting of this kind, emphasizing sympathy, gentleness, and tears, could be construed as the epitome of womanhood. Indeed it was this capacity to be "pathetic," even as Lady Macbeth – "to drop tears all over the place" – that later would define the "womanliness" of Ellen Terry on stage and elicit the disgust of her son Gordon Craig, who knew the virility of which his mother was capable, and could exercise if allowed.[179]

But Ellen Terry, by her own account, "made them cry as much as I would, and as much as I could," achieving with this philosophy of tears an unparalleled success on the Victorian stage. Madge Kendal worried that "I cry so much that I perhaps do not do my author justice," and reassured herself with the reflection that the distinctive contribution of an actress was to bring "sympathy" into a play to complement the "intelligence" supplied by male performers. Like Faucit, Terry, and other actresses, therefore, Kendal construed her acting as an exemplification of authentic womanliness.[180] Whereas Florence Nightingale and others had seen the stage as providing women with the hope of liberation from Victorian femininity, some of the most successful actresses underwrote the very conventions of passivity and private feeling that made other women yearn for the "freedom" of theatrical life.

Although she was praised for a kind of power – for example, "a power of saturating herself with the vital essence of what she read" – Helen Faucit's perceived womanliness was the distinguishing feature of her acting, both in her own mind and in the opinion of others.[181] Famous for acting Shakespeare's heroines opposite Macready beginning in 1837 at Covent Garden, she later wrote of these roles in terms of gender ideals – "providing all that gives to woman her rightest charm, her most beneficent influence." Faucit was thinking of "thoughtful, reticent, gentle Ophelia" and Portia, "the perfect wife," but she even played Lady Macbeth, she recalls, without ferocity, seeing her as above all a woman promoting her husband's welfare, "urging her husband forward through her love for him." When playing Beatrice she sought to emphasize the character's "heart of gold" and "a soul, brave and generous as well as good," despite her raillery and high spirits.[182] One of Faucit's admirers, the American actress Mary Anderson, was praised by critic William Winter for performing, as he calls it, "the strongest and highest feelings of a true woman's heart." Winter lauds Anderson for renouncing the "delirium and convulsion" sometimes taken for power in actresses, commending her reticence and approving her mode of acting

3. Ellen Terry in *The Amber Heart*, 1887, illustrating the actress in relation to "mystical womanhood."

that kept the world at arm's length. What made Mary Anderson a great actress, Winter urges, is her grace, refinement, and restraint – the abiding presence in her art of "the woman herself," a monitor of what femininity should be.[183] Similarly it was the "melting power of pathetic tenderness" that, in Mrs. Wilson's book of 1844 on actresses, characterized the pre-Victorian performer Miss O'Neill – the quality that distinguished her from a Sarah Siddons and accounted for the "glowing admiration" of her audiences.[184] And Marie Bancroft, looking back over a long career, remembers as one of her high accomplishments the "pathetic ending" that she tacked on to Tom Taylor and Charles Reade's *Masks and Faces*. By transforming the heroine Peg Woffington from a flippant but dominating actress to a self-sacrificing domestic female, she surprised the co-author of the play, Charles Reade, and reduced him to tears at the same time.[185] "If Charles Reade had not allowed me to alter the end of the play I could not have acted the part," she writes in her memoirs.[186]

Thus actresses, however threatening to Victorian men, could with the proper oversight or self-policing be counted among the mainstays of domesticity and feminine virtue. In her autobiography Lillah McCarthy describes, for example, how a performance of Wilson Barrett's religious drama *The Sign of the Cross* influenced a young girl in the audience to understand what would be required of her as a woman. "Your personal representation of what was most beautiful, the noblest and the sweetest of what one looks for in womanhood," the girl wrote to Lillah McCarthy in later years, "was so inspiring that I can assure you that perhaps you created something which actually proved to be a real influence for the future in at least one obscure life."[187] In her *Autobiography of an Actress*, written many years earlier, Anna Cora Mowatt concedes the satisfaction she derives from "the power of swaying the emotions of a crowd," but emphasizes that the actress must seek the true justification of her art elsewhere – in communicating "purifying influences" and exciting "*reverence* as well as admiration."[188] Madge Kendal, who managed the St. James's Theatre with her husband W. H. Kendal and John Hare, was noted for her unimpassioned stage presence, yet ruled the company with an iron fist, enforcing the strictest decorum upon young performers and superintending their work down to the smallest detail. It was due in part to her own vigilance that Mrs. Kendal could announce with some degree of accuracy in 1884 that "there is at last a recognized social position for the player." This dignity, as she calls it in her memoirs, could be maintained only if actors and actresses lived with the same respectability demanded of others, leading "such lives that those who have regarded the Stage with a suspicious eye will at last give it its proper place in the world of Art."[189]

The mother of Jessie Millward, eventually to become William Terriss's leading lady at the Adelphi, reluctantly agreed to her daughter going on the stage instead of becoming a governess – "provided you start with Mrs. Kendal." While other Victorians worried about whether the theatre and the family ideal could be reconciled, the Matron of the Drama, as Mrs. Kendal was known – "not for nothing," as Jessie Millward recalls – was busy applying domestic standards of conduct to actors and actresses and making the theatre itself into a home. Once, for example, Millward became flustered in a performance of *Still Waters Run Deep* and kissed John Hare, the leading man, "instead of letting him kiss me" – an error which caused Mrs. Kendal to summon her after the show. "After some severe remarks on decorum," Jessie Millward remembers, "she concluded her reproof by describing my lapse as 'the most unmaidenly performance I have ever seen in my life.'"[190] Mrs. Kendal, for her own part, always acted opposite her husband, declaring that "the greatest amount of domestic happiness was possible to exist on the stage provided husband and wife were never separated."[191] Although the atmosphere at the Lyceum was described as less crushing than at the St. James's where Mrs. Kendal held sway, Henry Irving also displayed an anxiety to reproduce the domestic milieu inside the theatre; indeed, his "obsession – or passion" on this point was remarked upon by a friend. Spouses always traveled with Irving's company on the road, for, as he explained, "I have never – to my knowledge – parted any such husband and wife – and please God I never *will!*"[192] In this environment Ellen Terry's son imagined the Lyceum Theatre as a family, and Irving as "the head of the house."[193]

Attempts to harmonize the actress with domesticity took other forms as well. From one point of view, as W.H. Davenport Adams writes in *Woman's Work and Worth* (1880), women are naturally "at home" on the stage because their reputedly feminine traits can find expression there as nowhere else. "That faculty of expressing the passions which is the peculiar gift of women," Adams writes, "their natural grace of movement, their power of sympathy...their charm of voice, their eloquence of gesture – all of these are attributes which tend to ensure their success in dramatic representations."[194] The theatre, as Victorian social theorist Havelock Ellis saw it, also called upon the "emotional explosiveness" of women – "much more marked than men possess, and more easily within call." While others expressed alarm at hearing women on stage give voice to emotions that they were not really feeling, Ellis perceived that all women were actresses, whether performing on stage or in a drawing-room. "They are, again," writes Ellis, "more trained in the vocal expression both of those emotions which they feel and those which it is considered their duty to feel. Women are, therefore, both by nature and social compulsion, more often than men in the position of actors." Women's supposed susceptibility to "admiration and applause" further explained and justified their success on stage, Ellis believed.[195]

It was possible, or becoming possible, therefore, to construe acting as appropriately and particularly feminine rather than a subversive deviation from gender norms. Sarah Bernhardt, for example, insisted that "the dramatic art would appear to be rather a feminine art; it contains in itself all the artifices which belong to the province of woman: the desire to please, facility to express emotions and hide defects, and the faculty of assimilation which is the real essence of woman."[196] Such pronouncements worked toward the reconciliation of normative femininity and the theatre, making the presence of women on stage seem appropriately in the nature of things. When Polly Eccles, played by Marie Bancroft, announces in *Caste* (1867) that she and her sisters are performers at the Theatre Royal, Lambeth, she adds significantly: "We're not ashamed of what we are."[197] By the turn of the century this attitude had become so widely accepted that an attack in print on the character of actresses elicited outrage from many readers, including playwright and actor David Christie Murray, who solemnly declared that "actresses are among the most honest women in the world."[198]

Thus the malevolent, death-dealing, even inhuman actress of the male imagination was also construed as a proper lady from the beginning of the Victorian period, long before Mrs. Kendal became Dame Madge and her former colleague at the Prince of Wales's was elevated to Lady Bancroft. Indeed, the incessant self-monitoring of prominent women performers such as Kendal and Bancroft made them, in effect, collaborators with the power that in various ways constrained their independence of action and the strong speaking voice that men feared in actresses. These competing constructions of the actress – diseased monstrosities on one hand, refined and respectable ladies on the other – were of course polarized and incompatible in one sense. But they were both part of the combustible mixture which formed the Victorian idea of the actress, and they contributed, each in its own way, to the same result – tempering and marginalizing the power of women who had to be restrained in the interest of relieving male anxiety and preserving the status quo.

CHAPTER 3

Actresses, managers, and feminized theatre

No woman has ever won reputation in this profession.

(From a memoir on Sara Lane, long-time manager of the Britannia Theatre, arguing for women's unfitness to be theatre managers.)

For the majority of actresses, survival rather than respectability was the main concern, and their precarious careers were at the mercy of the actor-managers who selected plays for production and cast them according to their own prejudices and interests. "Twice in the course of my life on tour," recalls Cicely Hamilton, "I was thrown out of work to make room for a manager's mistress; no fault was found with the playing of my part, but it was wanted for other than professional reasons, and therefore I had to go."[1] In a letter to the *Era*, actress Charlotte Morland lamented that too often for a woman in her profession "success or failure are consequent on her powers of fascinating the one man who has her career in his iron grasp, and who can make or mar her according as she yields or resists to his will and pleasure."[2] Despite a growing emphasis on the respectability of Victorian actresses, couch politics could still make or break their careers, and sexual attractiveness to men was almost essential to success.

Although heroes in late Victorian drama might be any age, recalls the actress-manager Lena Ashwell, all the heroines had to be young and lovely. Ashwell herself was discouraged from going on the stage by George Alexander, actor-manager at the St. James's Theatre, "as it was necessary for such a career to be beautiful, or at any rate good-looking, and...I was very plain."[3] Women who were not "reasonably good-looking," Ashwell says elsewhere, "had little chance of achieving great success. They always had to play subordinate parts."[4] An experienced performer confided to the young Violet Vanbrugh – who would become a star with Irving and Tree – that "I know I can act, but I am very plain, and I don't look the parts; that is why I shall never be a leading London actress." Vanbrugh could not deny it, saying only that "it was a pity."[5] Many a Victorian actress would have recognized familiar truth in the case of Flora Sandford, the actress-heroine of the novel *A Lost Eden*, who gets her chance on stage only because her appearance beguiles the actor-manager who hires her: "D—d pretty figure," says the actor-manager Burley, running his eye over her slender form "as deliberately as if he had been looking at a horse in Tattersall's yard."[6]

Shaw was probably right in declaring that "indispensable" actresses of commanding talent "can be, and *are*, what *they* like," their prospects not depending on their compliance with the sexual desires of their managers – "though," Shaw added, "those of their humbler colleagues do."[7] In their autobiographical reflections, however, even major Victorian actresses are keenly sensitive to the control that actor-managers exerted over them. Ellen Terry writes of Henry Irving's "despotism" as the "sole superintendent of his rehearsals" at the Lyceum Theatre, and Ellaline Terriss reflects with awe on the almost Foucauldian supervison by Charles Wyndham of his players at the Criterion Theatre:

He might not be on the stage, or even in sight. But he heard all right – and he saw. He had a room in the wings, with a porthole that looked on to the stage, and we used to say, trembling, "Is it open tonight?" There was a mirror, too, which reflected all that was going on. He missed nothing.[8]

Genevieve Ward recalls an assistant "bearing a huge pasteboard trumpet" through which he bawled criticisms and curses when the manager became too hoarse to utter them himself.[9] W. S. Gilbert was a despot of respectability at the Savoy Theatre, prohibiting most backstage visitors and assigning actresses to dressing-rooms that were on the opposite side of the stage from men's. Augustus Harris of the Drury Lane Theatre was said to be "ubiquitous" in his auditorium, "directing everything and everybody":

Now he interrupts a leading lady with 'No, my dear, that's not it', and proceeds to illustrate how the words are to be uttered and the action performed that is to accompany them. Now he takes another by the hand, and leads her along, and postures her and poses her till she acquits herself to his satisfaction.[10]

John Douglass of the Standard Theatre, like many other managers, had a system of fines for his players; and when exasperated, flung off his hat and stamped on it. Seymour Harris, according to his wife, "would rave and he would drive, he would break his umbrella on the orchestra rail to emphasize his points."[11] Men like these were the prototypes of fictional characters such as Arnold Sidney of the Sheridan Theatre in a novel by Horace Wyndham. "In his own theatre he was supreme," Wyndham writes of his fictional actor-manager, "and he ruled the establishment with a rod of iron."[12]

These authoritarian actor-managers cast a jealous eye at any woman who might threaten their own place in the limelight. William Charles Macready, for example, worried that in *Money* "Miss Faucit had quite the advantage over me."[13] Such anxiety was the rule, not the exception among managers. "There was one thing my old friend Herbert loved devotedly," writes Chance Newton of H. Beerbohm Tree, "– that was to have plenty of limelight thrown upon him! Not, however, that he was by any means singular in that!"[14] Similarly Henry Irving was un-enthusiastic about a suggestion that he showcase Ellen Terry in *As You Like It* at the Lyceum: "Good – very good –," he commented blandly, "but where do I come in?"[15] Actor-managers were fierce competitors by nature, as Genevieve Ward points out in her memoir *Both Sides of the Curtain* (1918), citing Irving as her example. "This composite being necessarily tends to fight for his own hand," she writes, "and to choose the pieces that suit him. It precludes a company 'of all the talents,' such as the Comédie Française tries to get, and often does."[16] "After all," as the actor-manager De Mortemar says in a forgotten novel by Mary Elizabeth Braddon, "what does it matter how the women's parts are played?" As for his leading lady, De Mortemar takes care to keep her back to the audience while he rants at her from the center of the boards.[17]

Only by entering management could actresses free themselves to shape their own careers. Thus Marie Wilton, later Bancroft, was "in despair and did not know what to do" with her hopes of playing more than Cupids in Strand Theatre burlesques until her brother-in-law asked "How would it be if you had a theatre of your own?" and lent her £1,000 to open the Prince of Wales's.[18] The late-Victorian Janette Steer, in reply to the question why she became her own manager at the Comedy Theatre and elsewhere, replied "Simply because I hate having to play parts I don't like, and because now I can choose what I please."[19] And Eleanor Calhoun, one of many American actresses transplanted to the London stage, imagined a theatre which would rise above the "vulgar and common plays" that were ordinarily staged in the West End by self-interested managers. In due time, she believed, the theatre could eliminate the exploitative manager, and with progressive leadership – the kind that Eleanor Calhoun aspired to provide herself – rise to "a standard of perfection and form" of classical dimensions. Her ideas of a noncommercial theatre inspired by "truth" and aesthetic value rather than by profit may have influenced the even grander and more organized ideas of theatrical reform that would emanate from another American emigré, Calhoun's friend Elizabeth Robins, in the 1890s.[20] Such projects flew in the face of the opinion, expressed by the biographer of Britannia Theatre manager Sara Lane, that "no woman has ever won reputation in this profession." The appearance that Sara Lane had accomplished just that, writes Alfred Crauford, was illusory. She was amiable and a good actress, but "wanting in judgment as a manageress," he declares, and particularly inept in selecting plays to be produced at the Britannia, including some written by herself.[21]

In general women who thought of management on their own were interested in enlarging the opportunities available to actresses, including themselves, as well as altering the theatre as an institution. For example, Mary Anderson, bored and disgusted with the theatre by the time she came to write her memoirs, recalls with genuine excitement her foray into management in 1887 to produce *The Winter's Tale* at the Lyceum, a bold experiment in which she played both Hermione and Perdita her daughter.[22] Elizabeth Robins, Florence Farr, Janet Achurch, and other women organized their own productions in the 1890s, and in the process afforded themselves more challenging parts than would have come their way from managers like Alexander and Irving, who believed the success of actresses depended more on looks than professional skill. In 1891, for example, Florence Farr produced *Rosmersholm* and played the leading role of Rebecca at the Vaudeville Theatre, only weeks before Elizabeth Robins, despairing of playing a woman's role of depth and power in a regular West End production, produced and starred in *Hedda Gabler* at the same theatre. Lena Ashwell, manager of the Kingsway Theatre, followed the lead of Eleanor Calhoun and Elizabeth Robins in advocating a "people's theatre" or "national theatre" which would corrrect the excesses of commercial drama and attempt to "broaden men's minds."[23] For this project she hoped to recruit unknown authors – "the young writers, the poets, the thinkers" – as being the likeliest to create a new and more purposeful drama outside the orbit of commercial theatre. At the same time Ashwell sought to stabilize the working conditions of actors and actresses by engaging a company for an entire year. The project began to bear fruit in 1905 with her first production, *Leah Kleschna*, in which Ashwell played a woman thief, and continued with her launching of Cicely Hamilton as a playwright. *Diana of Dobson's* (1908), with its reversal of the Cinderella myth and critique of familiar gender roles, realized Ashwell's objective of "broadening men's minds" through the theatre. But her long-range goal of creating a "national theatre" remained unrealized, and her own part in envisioning it un-recognized.[24]

Just as women producers could imagine a theatre very different from the West End establishments dominated by male actor-managers, they also proved themselves capable at times of running a theatre effectively without tyrannizing over the performers who worked for them. Madge Kendal, a forceful woman whose authority was rarely called into ques-tion, directed her actors and actresses by a method of collaboration rather than the intimidation for which Irving, Alexander, Tree, Hicks, and many others were noted. Always demanding, she nevertheless helped both male and female performers realize the characters they enacted by constantly encouraging them and building their self-confidence. "Very definitely," recalls the actress Violet Vanbrugh after touring America with the Kendals, "her method was to make one think for oneself and use one's own brains, and to work with one's own method and personality." For example, Vanbrugh recalls having once unconsciously imitated her famous manager in the rehearsal of a difficult scene. Madge Kendal stopped her abruptly:

"Can't you see, can't you understand?" she cried; "we are different types, you and I. Circumstances wouldn't affect you as they affect me. Don't imitate me; look to your own feelings, your own emotions, and imagine for youself what you would do in such a situation." And she dismissed rehearsal and sent me home to think.

Kendal, as Vanbrugh recalls her, was a "genius" as a producer, the cleverest and above all the "most sensitive" of any for whom she worked – "in fact quite the finest stage manager of them all." She differed from other managers in recognizing that, as Vanbrugh puts it, "the method for getting the best work out of a sensitive, vibrating personality is to awake, not to destroy or crush intelligence or individ-uality."

Certainly Kendal's style was not shared by all women managers of the period. Ellen Terry remembered working as a girl under the direc-tion of Madame de Rhona at the Royalty Theatre and crying when the manager "flew at me like a wild-cat and shook me."[25] Madge Kendal, by contrast, was quick to acknowledge improvement and to encourage "thoughtful effort," Vanbrugh says, but even more remarkably she displayed none of the notorious tendency of actor-managers to hog the limelight. Once Vanbrugh unintentionally positioned herself above Kendal when the Matron of the Drama had a great outburst of emotion to portray. Vanbrugh apologized, but Kendal had taken no notice of what another manager would have resented as scene-stealing. "My dear," Kendal exclaimed, "I don't care two pins where you are! I should be ashamed of myself if I couldn't convey my feelings through my shoulder or my back, as well as through my face! Every bit of you has to act, if you can act at all."[26]

Sara Lane was said to have ruled the Britannia Theatre in the East End as a kindly autocrat – the Queen of Hoxton whose control of her huge working-class theatre was unchallenged over several decades, but who was able to maintain a "close personal friendship" with her players and indeed with her large audiences.[27] It had been different at the Britannia when Sara's husband Sam Lane had been alive, exacting from his wife, with her "delightfully amiable disposition," a meek submission to his own rule and guidance.[28] Even as managers, therefore, women were sometimes constrained by the men with whom they were in partnership, whether their own husbands or other men – and paid a price when they were not. Madge Kendal, although a demanding personality who overawed even the most wilfull actors, always deferred to the authority of W. H. Kendal, her husband and partner at the St. James's Theatre and elsewhere. "When I write *I*," she says in her memoirs, "I mean *we*, and when I write *we*, I mean *he*."[29] She never played opposite anyone but W. H. Kendal despite pleas from some of her fans that "it would be more interesting to see another man embracing me."[30] Her subordination of her own career as an actress to the interests of her husband and the Kendal organization "confined her genius," as Violet Vanbrugh says in a memoir. The public confirmed her popularity in a certain genre of domestic comedy, but as Vanbrugh says, "great as her triumphs were, there were other high triumphs within her reach which circumstances denied her the chance of winning." These limitations of time and place were like those which restrained Ellen Terry from enacting parts such as Rosalind and Lady Teazle in which, as Vanbrugh says, "Terry would have excelled."[31]

Likewise Marie Bancroft ceded final authority at the Prince of Wales's Theatre to her husband. "Mrs. Bancroft from the beginning placed perfect confidence in my judgment," writes Squire Bancroft, "not only with regard to the business side of our work, but in the choice of plays, and accepted my opinion in nearly all important matters, even when, unfortunately, it chanced to be at variance with her own."[32] Running a theatre, Squire Bancroft believed, required a masculine hand at the controls, and that required a subordinate role for his wife – "by my side," "modest" and "faithful" during their long joint management of the Prince of Wales's Theatre. "At the age of twenty-six," explains Squire Bancroft, "I found myself face to face with the responsibility of sparing my wife the more laborious side of managing a London theatre."[33]

Like actresses, women theatre managers had difficulty in being perceived as proper ladies unless they abdicated their power or disguised what one critic referred to as their "strongly-marked individuality." One woman manager who made few concessions of the kind was Mrs. John Wood, who raised the St. James's Theatre to a high position in the 1860s and 1870s. "Many ladies can hardly understand Mrs. Wood," writes an anonymous critic in *The Stage of 1871*, "and are inclined to think she is vulgar." On the contrary, argues the critic, Mrs. Wood's confidence and boldness merely represent a "style of her own" and help to explain her success as a manager. Such comments demonstrate that women of strong individuality could succeed in Victorian theatre management, and at least earn the admiration of some observers – but at the risk of seeming incomprehensible from the perspective of "ladies," and of doubtful gender by implication.[34] Although women managers sometimes went to great lengths to demonstrate their own respectability, they acknowledged on occasion the obvious and vast difference that set them apart from most women of the period. Madame Vestris, for instance, shortly before Victoria's reign began, took over the Olympic Theatre and in a prologue spoken on the first night of her management referred to herself as "a warrior woman, that in strife embarks, / The first of all dramatic Joan of Arcs." She had become, as she said, the first woman "that ever led a company" – a distinction that she recognized as dividing her from ordinary women and associating her instead with the combative and androgynous Joan, whose crossdressing as a man was reprised again and again in Vestris's career at the Olympic and later at Covent Garden and the Lyceum theatres.[35]

Toward the close of the Victorian period an increasing number of women produced plays written by women, or, like Ibsen's dramas, seriously concerned with women, before audiences largely constituted of women. Madge Kendal, for example, produced *Little Lord Fauntleroy* by Frances Hodgson Burnett at Terry's Theatre before an audience that was said to be predominantly female. Ibsen's dramas were frequently produced by women in matinee performances attended largely by women, who were free to come in the afternoon and appeared to be less shocked than men by the unconventional themes of plays such as *Ghosts* – staged in the out-of-the-way Royalty Theatre managed by Kate Santley. This prospect of a feminized drama – staged and patronized by women – elicited amusement as well as contempt and even anxiety from some men. One critic described the audience for Madge Kendal's production of Ibsen's *The Pillars of Society* (1889) in comic terms – as consisting of people of dubious gender, out of place in the playhouse and in life. The audience, he writes, was composed of "masculine women and effeminate men," a foolish band of "women worshippers" who misconstrue the play, applaud at the wrong times, and have no more idea of how to get into a theatre than what to do once inside:

Outside the circle doors of the Opera Comique...there were assembled some twenty to thirty of these manly women, eager to listen to Ibsen. The whole crowd, walking in one after the other, could have found seats in the middle of the first row; and yet they fought and struggled round the pay-box as if there were only room in the whole theatre for the first ten...The fearful business made by these two dozen members of the superior sex in getting into a theatre was the most appalling thing of its kind we have ever witnessed. They knocked each other down, and trampled on each other. They dragged each other away from the pay-box, and pushed each other downstairs. They crushed each other up against doors, and kicked each other.[36]

Similarly, on the occasion of Mrs. Patrick Campbell's production of Edith Lyttleton's *Warp and Woof* (1904), critic A. B. Walkley offered a grotesque vision of what happens when women appropriate the theatre, offstage and on. This play, written by one woman and produced by another, was attended by "other mundane ladies," Walkley opines, "who have written original modern comedies themselves, or might have done so if they had chosen, or are intending to do so the very next wet afternoon." Even on stage there are no men in Walkley's whimsical nightmare of a theatre in which, as he says, the "exaggerated brims and monstrous crowns" of ladies' hats on both sides of the curtain blot out every other consideration. The drama, now degraded into a fashion show, has become a "feminine" spectacle that has little to do with either life or the theatre.[37] Such, for Walkley, is the stupefying irrelevance of women producing plays written by other women for the amusement of an audience consisting, for the most part, of still more women.

Walkley's comments on Mrs. Campbell's production of *Warp and*

Woof suggest that a theatre loses its identity and proper function when women assume control of it – as producers, writers, and audience – in addition to their traditional function as actresses. This interpretation of the theatre as a masculine institution, one incompatible with female authority, appears also in Walter Besant's speculative novel *The Revolt of Man* (1888), concerned with the consequences of women seizing control of the state and its various institutions. In Besant's matriarchy that used to be England, sovereign woman has destroyed industry and commerce, placed the writings of Shakespeare and other men under lock and key, usurped the property of their husbands, and taken over the theatres. Although "the perfection of the drama" is the thing on which the matriarchy most prides itself, the drama in fact has been reduced to performances of the irrelevant before small and inattentive audiences. On a typical night at the play, for example:

The whole audience with one consent fell to talking among themselves; the actors went on with the piece unregarded, and the curtain fell unnoticed...The old tragedies, in which women played the secondary part, were long since consigned to oblivion...It was resolved...that to make merriment for others was quite beneath the notice of an educated woman; and that the drama must be severe, and even austere – a school for women and for men. Such it was sought to make it, with as yet unsatisfactory results, because the common people, finding nothing to laugh at, came no more to the theatre; and even the better class, who wanted to be amused, and were only instructed, ceased to attend.[38]

Besant's analysis in *The Revolt of Man* represents a classic Victorian reaction to manifestations of feminine control in the theatre, particularly when women assume the executive roles of manager or playwright. Instead of real plays, Besant suggests, women prefer to write and stage dramatized tracts or sermons, and their clumsy attempts to reconcile the drama with their ideas of "the dignity of woman" result in dull, ideological performances and diminished audiences.

Besant was scarcely alone in his desire to keep the theatre under masculine control, and in particular to define good plays and playwriting so as to exclude women authors, whether implicitly or overtly. Victorian playwrights associated with one another in men's clubs such as the Garrick and the Savage where they would meet for a drink and dinner and enjoy the company of men in other predominantly masculine professions, such as law and journalism – fields to which many playwrights could trace their own origins. "We really did try to help one another," recalls Clement Scott in his memoir *The Wheel of Life* (1897), "if not by lending our spare cash, at least by giving one another a hoist up the literary ladder."[39] These men's clubs resemble the Owls' Roost in Tom Robertson's play *Society* (1865), an association of journalists, playwrights, novelists, and other would-be "great men" who provide one another with encouragement, social, and professional connections, and in time of need an occasional 5 shillings.[40]

Their exclusion from these coteries helps explain why women were never prominent among Victorian managers and playwrights. But just as a few women became managers in spite of the odds against them, others wrote plays, especially in the last two decades of the nineteenth century when the number of theatres increased and the earning potential of dramatists rose significantly. Playwrights, who at the beginning of the Victorian period often earned only a few pounds for each of their plays and had to write them in copious numbers to make a living, had begun sharing in the profits of their dramas in West End theatres and in a few instances amassing large fortunes.[41] Few if any women benefitted from these windfalls, because none of the Victorian women who wrote plays in the last three decades of the century experienced the long runs that brought large sums to some of their male colleagues – Dion Boucicault, R. C. Carton, Sydney Grundy, Henry Arthur Jones, Arthur Wing Pinero, Oscar Wilde, and others. By the end of the Victorian perod Walter Besant's vision of a woman's theatre was only a nightmare, not a reality, thanks in some measure to the efficiency with which women were denied meaningful access to the profession of playwriting.

PART TWO

Gender and Victorian playwriting

CHAPTER 4

The impossibility of women playwrights

I don't think any woman can succeed in writing a good play – at least they never do.

(The Life and Love of an Actress, 1888)

In *A Room of One's Own* Virginia Woolf searches a bookshelf "where there are no plays by women," looking for works that were "not there." But Woolf was by no means the first to detect that there were no plays by women on bookshelves, or to hear, as she puts it, that "women cannot write the plays of Shakespeare."[1] These were observations that many Victorians had made already, both directly and indirectly, whether rationalizing an absence of plays by women – usually the purpose behind such statements – or asking, and sometimes theorizing, why women were underrepresented among dramatic authors.

The growing number of women writing plays by the end of the Victorian period was ignored in most of these discussions, and in some the exclusion of women from the ranks of acknowledged playwrights could only be inferred from what was left unsaid. Even William Archer, in *The Old Drama and the New* (1923), omits any notice of women playwrights – although he knew several personally – in his attempt to draw up a canon of recent English drama.[2] The assumption noted by Virginia Woolf that women could not write good plays was so deeply rooted, therefore, that it could go unspoken and still carry force. And that assumption was probably reinforced, as Micheline Wandor suggests, by the incongruity of a woman playwright's claiming the authority to make other people speak and act when the theatre, as an institution, most often made women seem invisible, or merely glamorous.[3] Sue-Ellen Case has suggested that the prejudice against women playwrights may have been less strong at an earlier period, in the late seventeenth and early eighteenth centuries, when with the example of Aphra Behn's success before them, women were responsible for scores of plays staged in London. In any event, as Case points out, the absence of these women in traditional theatre and literary history has effectively meant the suppression of a tradition of women's playwriting.[4]

Women who aspired to become playwrights did not always realize the extent of the bias against them until it was pointed out. At the close of the Victorian period Cicely Hamilton, for example, "most of all. . .desired to write a good play," but learned from a manager, when her first one-act piece was about to be produced, that "it was advisable to conceal the sex of its author until after the notices were out, as plays which were known to be written by women were apt to get a bad press."[5] This point is not lost on the heroine of *Our Flat* (1889), an aspiring woman playwright who signs her first play with her husband's name, withholding her own identity as author "till the agreement is signed."[6] A few years after *Our Flat* was staged Florence Bell and Elizabeth Robins disguised their authorship of *Alan's Wife* from Beerbohm Tree, who they hoped would produce it, being well aware of his view that "women can't write."[7] By the 1890s – when plays by Pearl Craigie, Mrs. Musgrave, Mrs. Pacheco, and Madeline Ryley earned the distinction of one hundred performances or more[8]– there was some evidence of a growing awareness of women playwrights, although little appreciation of their work. In a piece called "Women as Dramatists," for example, the popular magazine *All the Year Round* drew attention to the surprising fact that two plays by women had been staged at notable theatres during the theatrical season of 1894. "Though we can count women novelists by the score," the anonymous critic observed, "the number of women dramatists is extremely limited, and can easily be told off on the fingers."

This "unusual experience" of seeing two plays by women – Constance Fletcher's *Mrs. Lessingham* and Lady Violet Greville's *An Aristocratic Alliance* – staged at major London theatres at the same time was moderated, however, by the opinion of the reviewer that "neither made a conspicuous success."[9] In the same year the *Era* wondered in a gossip column why "our lady dramatists" did not write plays of their own in reply to caricatures of progressive women in Henry Arthur Jones's *The Case of Rebellious Susan* (1894), Sydney Grundy's *The New Woman* (1894), and other dramas by men:

There are Mrs. Burnett, Mrs. Oscar Beringer, the Misses "Michael Field," Mrs. Craigie, Mrs. Hugh Bell, Miss Nora Vynne – half a score of lady dramatists, earnest, alert, advanced. Why do they not commission a *corps d'élite* to issue a counterblast?[10]

The *Era* was inviting women to write plays in response to men instead of considering the merits of works they actually produced, many of which dealt with women in a sustained, reflective, and original fashion. Indeed, women playwrights had already characterized the New Woman in dramas of their own, plays which, upon reflection, would have made ridiculous the *Era*'s easy assumption that women playwrights were outdone by men even on the ground of female characterization and needed the prompting of male journalists in order to find their way.

But there was never any shortage of men to advise women playwrights what to write, or how to write it, while at the same time tending to theorize playwriting in a way that emphasized certain qualities of mind – scientific, technical, intellectual – that Victorians rarely associated with women. In our own time Hélène Cixous, among others, has argued that women are suited to write drama of a type distinctly different from male-authored plays, a drama in which linear plot, even language as such, would be of diminished importance, while gesture and the body itself take on increased significance.[11] The insight of Cixous that women dramatists might produce work of a different kind from men's writing for the stage, and no less worthy in its own way, was not a possibility which occurred to most Victorians. Only a few – often women – seem to have recognized the possibility that plays could be written in some way other than what the male-dominated theatres of the time required.

An example of the Victorian tendency to define playwriting so as to exclude women, implicitly at least, appears in Frank Archer's *How To Write a Good Play* (1892). "Play-making may not be one of the exact sciences," the author concedes, "but it is more nearly allied to them than appears at first sight. It can fairly be described as a sort of *sympathy in mathematics.*" The playwright, by this analysis, is a sort of architect whose "constructive ability" arises out of an analytical mind that the Victorians rarely associated with women.[12] This prejudice also finds expression in a theatrical story by Henry James, "Nona Vincent," in which a male playwright discovers with satisfaction that his craft relies upon qualities of "line and law" that Victorians reflexively considered to be masculine. The "dramatic form," observes dramatist Allan Wayworth in the story by James, "had the high dignity of the exact sciences, it was mathematical and architectural. It was full of the refreshment of calculation and construction." Women, with their abundant reserves of emotion, must be called on for the "vulgar" necessity of acting Wayworth's first play, but only he – a man – could actually write it.[13] If a woman wrote a good play, as critic William Archer believed was the case with Constance Fletcher's *Mrs. Lessingham* in 1894, the fact could be explained by the woman playwright's masculine style. "I fancy," Archer comments in his review of the play, "it would be a very keen critic who should detect a feminine hand in the workmanship," even though in a modest way *Mrs. Lessingham* displays a bent "rather towards emotion than analysis." Because this woman's play is "strong" and "actable," Archer asserts, it found a reception in the West End theatre. No woman who can write like a man, he seems to say, "need despair of finding a hearing."[14] Similarly, in the play *Our Flat*, the success of a woman playwright's drama is explained on the grounds that, as one character says, it is "impossible to tell it's a woman's work."[15] And the author of "Women as Dramatists" explains the success of Joanna Baillie's writing for the pre-Victorian stage on the basis of the supposed "masculine strength and vigour" of her prose.[16]

More and more women were attracted to playwriting as it became remunerative during the Victorian period. By 1892, in an article entitled "The Finance of the Drama," the *Era* noted that the relatively new arrangement of a playwright's receiving 10 percent of the gross – on the average, £20 for a sold-out performance in a West End theatre – meant that "even a moderately successful run must bring in a little fortune to the author of the piece."[17] Before the Victorian period it had not been unusual for an author, even a woman playwright, to be offered £200 or more, as Mary Mitford was for *Julian* in 1823, and Fanny Kemble for *Francis the First* in 1827. Elizabeth Inchbald received £300 for her first comedy, then £900 three years later for *Such Things Are* (1787).[18] As early as the 1820s, however, theatres were becoming financially beleaguered, and the earnings of playwrights began to drop precipitously – Douglas Jerrold, for instance, being paid only £50 for the smash hit *Black-Eyed Susan* (1829) at the Surrey Theatre. On the usual system of fixed payment the typical fees of established playwrights like Charles Reade and Tom Taylor could be £50 an act, or less, and even Tom Robertson was paid £3 a night for each performance of *Caste* at a time when star performers could receive £50 nightly. The situation for playwrights was worse, however, at theatres outside the West End, where the going rate was no more than £2 to £10 for a pantomime and house dramatists like George Dibdin Pitt of the Britannia Theatre would write fifteen or twenty plays a year for only a few pounds each. The situation began to alter in favor of the playwright when in 1860 Dion Boucicault negotiated an arrangement which gave him a share of profits rather than a fixed payment for *The Colleen Bawn*, and made a fortune in the result. Profit-sharing and the risk associated with it became increasingly common, so that by 1895 the scale of remuneration for authors typically ranged from a low of 5 percent to 15 percent of the gross in prestigious West End theatres. Oscar Wilde, for example, negotiated a sliding scale of royal-ties up to 15 percent for full houses for the production of *The Importance of Being Earnest* at the St. James's Theatre.[19]

The increased prosperity of playwrights in the later Victorian period helps explain why the cupboards and work-tables of actor-managers were overflowing with manuscripts from hopeful playwrights, many of them, as Madge Kendal observed, young women writers. "The drama is now the only line which pays largely," novelist Mary Elizabeth Braddon observed, " – & anyone who can write a play does wrong to write anything else."[20] Although Braddon thought she could write a play, and several times did so, none of her dramas was successful and some remain unproduced, including an ambitious work entitled *A Life Interest*, written in the early 1890s, which she hoped would be staged in one of the prestigious London theatres.[21] It was a common misconcep-tion, as an actress said in a letter to the editor of the *Era* in 1895, to think that "the untried dramatist has his play at once accepted by a West End manager" and earns a large sum of money from it.[22]

Most playwrights came to their work from some other male-dominated area of employment – for example, stage-management (like Ben Webster and George Conquest), or journalism and dramatic criti-cism (J. M. Barrie, John Oxenford, G. B. Shaw, George R. Sims, Tom Taylor, Edmund Yates). Men's clubs like the Arundel brought together members of the varied professions from whose ranks writers for the stage typically emerged. Thus the usual routes into playwriting were difficult for a woman to enter, a fact which helps explain why most women playwrights were primarily writers in other genres, almost invariably fiction, and that even their novels were usually dramatized by men.[23] Actresses, however, had connections with powerful men in the theatre who facilitated the making of playwrights, and so it is not surprising that actresses were prominent among the numerous women who became dramatists. Among them were Elizabeth Robins, Cicely Hamilton, Harriett Jay, and perhaps the two most commercially suc-cessful women playwrights of the age – Madeline Lucette Ryley and

Clotilde Graves. Indeed, when asked by an interviewer how she came
to write plays, Clo Graves accounted for her seemingly anomalous
position as a woman playwright by virtue of having been an actress
first.[24] Yet actresses rarely established themselves as professional playwrights – the double career as actress and author being, in the words of
Anna Cora Mowatt, one of the few women who experienced it, "*to say
the least*, a bold experiment."[25] The plight of the heroine in Constance
Woolson's story "Miss Grief" could stand as representative of women
playwrights generally. The title character has written an inspired
drama, thrilling in its "earnestness, passion, and power," but never
performed because Miss Grief lacks any entrée to the theatre managers
and playwrights who could assist her with getting it prepared and
accepted for production.[26]

The likely outcome for women playwrights was to have their would-
be dramas interred with other doomed playscripts in the Kendals'
cupboards, or discarded after a peremptory glance. Even if a woman's
play were produced, the author might ot benefit from the generous
profit-sharing arrangements that became increasingly common after
1860. Although established dramatists insisted on and received such
terms, the woman playwright was on uncertain ground and thus unable
to deal from a position of strength and experience. As Elizabeth Robins
reports in a letter, Herbert Beerbohm Tree was prepared to spend
£6,000 on mounting the production of her play on Benvenuto Cellini at
a time when £1,000 was a typical sum to lay out for a fairly lavish
production such as "an ordinary comic opera."[27] But Tree, complained
Robins, was willing to spend very little on compensation for the author –
was trying to "do" her, as Robins confided to a friend, and in the end
her play was never produced.[28]

Women, even well-connected actresses like Robins, fell outside the
usual boundaries of acknowledged playwrights – a coterie defined in
part by gender, and access to which was controlled through the masculine domains of theatre management, law, journalism, and men's clubs.
Unsurprisingly, therefore, Robins's previous plays had been summarily
rejected by a variety of actor-managers, and in Tree she was dealing
with one who had long held the prevailing opinion that women were
incapable of writing good plays.[29] Women writers were handicapped, as
Robins's case shows, by the common opinion that their gender disqualified them from writing drama, a prejudice which influenced a situation
in which their plays would in fact be rejected, thus making it impossible
for women to assemble the kind of credentials as playwrights that would

count with actor-managers. This trap may explain the fact that plays by women were more often than not mounted at theatres outside the West End – where the rewards were greatest and the access for untried playwrights most difficult.[30] The increasing tendency to engage plays for long runs of a hundred performances or more reduced the opportunities for trying out new playwrights in the West End even at a time when the number of theatres in the fashionable district was increasing from the 1860s through the 1890s.[31] Yet it was only the West End that mattered, as William Archer points out. "I cannot recall a single play of the slightest importance that has been produced outside of the West End of London," he writes. "To all intents and purposes...the seed-plot of the English drama may be said to fall within, and well within, the two-mile radius from Charing Cross."[32] This widely held view consigned most of the dramas by women in the Victorian period to a level of absolute insignificance.

Women were thus excluded from playwriting, especially from the branch of it that mattered most and paid best, purely on the grounds of gender. It was obvious to anyone who thought about the matter that women had won recognition as playwrights before the Victorian period, if not during it – women like Hannah More, for example, and Joanna Baillie. When these women were recollected by the Victorians, as sometimes they were in theoretical discussions of playwriting, their success could be explained by the "power of influence" and "good offices" exerted on their behalf by male friends – David Garrick in the case of Hannah More, or Sir Walter Scott for Joanna Baillie.[33] Masculinity, by contrast, was counted as a qualification for writing plays, and as an attribute of the theatre as an institution. The author of *The Stage of 1871*, for example, identifies playwrights as *men*, specifically those with wide experience of the world – "men who, in addition to literary ability, have mixed much with all classes, and experienced the ups and downs of life."[34] Another reviewer expressed the view that a good dramatist "must be everything else" – a man, naturally, but with the kind of wide experience no Victorian woman could know. "He must be a politician, a historian...and an orator...a man of action and of thought...above all, he must directly and publicly impress a crowd of other men."[35] The best plays would therefore be written for, as well as by, men – the ideal audience being, in the words of no less advanced a critic than William Archer, "principally masculine of course."[36]

There was reason for surprise, therefore, when Clo Graves's *A Mother of Three* scored a box-office success at the Comedy Theatre in 1896, at the same time as another play co-authored by her was being performed in London. The *Sketch* observed that "probably it has never before occurred in the theatrical annals of London that two plays by the same woman have been running at the same time" – the other being *A Matchmaker*, which Graves co-authored with Gertrude Kingston for the Shaftesbury Theatre. In the same year appeared Madeline Ryley's *Jedbury Junior*, and several plays in which women authors collaborated with male playwrights, as in *The Strange Adventures of Miss Brown* by Harriett Jay and Robert Buchanan. In this atmosphere the *Era* launched "an inquiry into the subject of female playwrights, not many of whom have achieved any lasting success or fame up to the present period." Despite good reviews and large audiences, *A Mother of Three* by Clo Graves is portrayed by the reviewer as a curiosity – "an example of what can be achieved by industry" rather than a cause to re-examine the assumption that women were constitutionally unfit for play-writing.

As was customary, the anonymous writer for the *Era* finds in the supposed nature of women an explanation for their underrepresentation as dramatists. Their use of language is undisciplined, he argues, lacking the architectural rigor believed necessary for good playwriting; and their personalities generally lack the comic sense that most plays require:

Chiefly, perhaps, because most women are devoid of deep and mirthful humour, and on account of their prolixity of diction and their tendency to introduce an abundance of small irresponsible details into their writings, as witness the lady novelist and her methods, female dramatists have been few and far between, though quite a large number of authoresses have essayed to write for the stage.[37]

Thus the success of women as novelists is offered by the *Era* as a reason for their failure as playwrights, even though, as the writer acknowledges, "a large number" had made the attempt. The novel seemed to complement women's experience in obvious ways by virtue of its concern with private, domestic experience and its production and consumption in a home setting.[38] Plays which were conspicuously domestic risked not being received as plays at all; *A Doll's House*, for example, was dismissed by one critic because "it is as though someone has dramatised the cooking of a Sunday dinner."[39] Such narratives were thought better suited to fiction than to the stage. Moreover, as one critic pointed out, the leisurely pace of fiction allowed the imagination to supply "what is so often wanting in the novelist" – namely, knowledge of the world and experience of life.[40]

The *Era* reviewer was not alone, moreover, in holding that the quality of language required of a play was different from that of a novel. William Archer, for example, explains in *Play-Making*, his manual for aspiring playwrights, that the drama requires an "art of condensation" while the novel permits a "license of prolixity" in language. Archer has in mind the subtle gradations of change in persons and their circumstances in some fiction, which by comparison with drama lacks the startling crises and sharp outlines that characterize what he believes to be good writing for the theatre. These prejudices were sometimes aired when women novelists wrote for the stage, as happened in 1853 when *The Cruel Kindness*, by fiction writer Catherine Crowe, was produced at the Haymarket. The reviewer for *The Times*, like others who had thought through the matter, defined playwriting in a way that necessarily excluded virtually the only women who could be considered professional writers – namely, women novelists. "That an author who has gained favour as a novelist should fail in delineating those sharply marked characters which are most effective in drama need be no matter of surprise," writes the critic for *The Times*, "since the principle of art in the one department of literature is precisely the reverse of that which is valid in the other."[41]

This supposed requirement in drama for broad strokes of character and action means, as William Archer believed, that each act should contain at least one and perhaps a group of crises. Unlike the novel with its almost imperceptible developments and "long, slow processes," a play must unite strong, even violent incidents into a well-crafted whole, thus achieving a "carefully calculated proportion, order, interrelation of parts – the unity of a fine piece of architecture." Archer, acknowledging that this conception is "dramatic" in a traditional sense, offers two exceptions to the rule – both of them early twentieth-century plays by women. In Elizabeth Baker's *Chains*, Archer concedes, the absence of a marked crisis allows a different kind of drama, the story of a woman who thinks of marrying but decides not to, and a man who considers emigrating but stays where he is. In a sense nothing "happens," just as in Florence Bell's *The Way the Money Goes* no "story" can be detected in the drama of a woman who feels bowed down by her secret of having run into a debt of £30. Although drama ordinarily requires "moments of crises" and even "shocks to the nerves," Archer allows for the possibility that the concept of the dramatic need not always be so conventional. In a certain type of drama, one attempting a broad portrayal of a "social phenomenon," the style of writing may depart from the conflict model adopted by most male playwrights and place a higher value upon observation, nuances of feeling, and the domestic. Archer, however, relegates his two examples of such plays, both by women, to a reduced-type footnote in his manual on play-making.[42]

Like James and other Victorian men, furthermore, Archer finds an analogy for playwriting in the "law" which governs the work of the architect, whose profession, like that of the playwright, seemed inherently scientific and technical and thereby, of course, masculine. Archer construes the first act of a play, ideally, as "the porch or vestibule," or at least a "threshold," upon which the body of the "structure" is to be raised. The good play, like a successful building, is "informed by an inner law of harmony and proportion," built up by "a principle of selection, proportion, composition, which, if not absolutely organic, is at any rate the reverse of haphazard."[43] By this analysis women who wished to write good plays would have to approach language from a "masculine" perspective, stripping their plays of "social theories and political opinions" and focusing on a sequence of action "stripped of all undue elaboration."[44] This formalist understanding of good drama – as stated in the handbook *How To Write a Good Play* – blocked women from pursuing the kind of elaborative prose which had brought them success in fiction, and branded as undramatic any expression of political views arising out of their position as women. Whether written by men or women, plays which were structured by discussion of political or social issues more than by interconnected crises of action and character were likely to face interrogation as to their status in genre. That is why reviewers could think *A Doll's House* less a play than a dinner conversation, or *Mrs. Warren's Profession* a fragment of a well-written pamphlet, "not a drama." As Max Beerbohm put it in dismissing Shaw's play, "no development: no drama."[45]

Although women were necessary to the stage as actresses, as even the characters of Henry James realize, there was no compelling reason for Victorian men to encourage female incursions into the other theatrical professions. "The chief lesson to be learnt," wrote a critic for *The Times* in reviewing a play by Ella Stockton, "is that ambitious actresses should not write their own plays." Just as the woman novelist was believed constitutionally unsuited to write plays, so the actress was held to be better off "only as an actress," as a character of Henry James phrases it. "I mean the stage in general, dramatic or lyric," as Peter Sherringham says in *The Tragic Muse* (1890); "it's as the actress that the woman produces the most complete and satisfactory results."[46] It was almost predictable, therefore, that actress Ella Stockton's adaptation of William Black's novel *Madcap Violet*, staged at Sadler's Wells Theatre in 1882, was held to suffer from the architectural or "constructive" defects that seemed inevitable whenever women tried to write plays. *Madcap Violet*, complained *The Times*, was merely "a series of pretty scenes" rather than a well-designed work for the stage. "Of what may be called the logic of the drama, the telling response of prompt action to strong motive, the masterful leading up from well-grouped incidents to impressive results, there is nothing whatever."[47]

Women themselves were sometimes persuaded by such arguments of their incapacity to write drama. Pearl Marie Craigie, who wrote plays as well as novels under the name John Oliver Hobbes, believed that dramatic authorship required what she termed a "constructive capacity" and "vast co-ordinative power" which, regrettably, women rarely if ever possessed. "How few women-dramatists there are," she exclaimed in an interview, "or ever have been, in comparison with men."[48] Craigie was one herself, although lacking in confidence, and when she died Ellen Terry noted with regret that "the great play of which I know she was capable had not been written."[49] Actress Fanny Kemble, like Craigie a dramatist in her own right, states in a memoir her own pessimistic views about the potential of women as playwrights. What makes it impossible for women to write successfully for the stage is their essential "feminine nature," Kemble says, and their lack of a wide experience of life:

I think it so impossible that I actually believe their physical organization is against it; and, after all, it is great nonsense saying that intellect is of no sex. The brain is, of course, of the same sex as the rest of the creature; besides, the original feminine nature, the whole of our life and training and education, our inevitable ignorance of common life and general human nature, and the various experience of existence, from which we are debarred with the most sedulous care, is insuperably against it.[50]

Kemble imagines that women on the borders of gender – "manly, wicked" women such as Cleopatra or Semiramis – might have been capable of writing plays because of their estrangement from normative femininity. "But they lived their tragedies instead of writing them," she observes.

This self-doubt of women dramatists was reflective of a larger cul-

tural doubt about whether women could work successfully as dramatists. Thus William Archer expressed surprise when John Hare, actor-
manager at the Garrick Theatre, produced a play in 1894 by Constance Fletcher (or George Fleming, as she called herself), a short-lived
production under the name of *Mrs. Lessingham*. Archer was less surprised that a woman could write a good play than that a West End
manager would "produce a first play, by an untried author, and that
author of the sex which has commonly, of late years at any rate, been
considered destitute of dramatic faculty."[51] That general opinion "of
late years" explains why Generva Romaine, the title character of *The
Life and Love of an Actress* (1888), draws a skeptical reaction when she tells
a male confidant that she is writing a play. "I don't think any woman
can succeed in writing a good play," her friend responds, – "at least
they never do." Generva Romaine perseveres, however, in writing the
play that she entitles *Her Drama*, but before the play can be produced
it must be revised by a man named Carlysle, "the most brilliant
and withal most unassuming of dramatists." Pleased to find "good
material" in the rough version of this play written by an actress,
Carlysle sets to work on *Her Drama* and produces in the end "a powerful
play."[52] Clearly the result would have been different without the modi-
fications that his "brilliant" masculine intelligence introduced into this
dramatic text by a woman. Likewise, a male author in Constance
Woolson's story "Miss Grief" offers to correct the "barbarous shor-
tcomings" of a powerful but ineptly plotted drama written by an
aspiring woman playwright.[53] It was not unusual for women who
actually wrote plays in the Victorian period to submit them to men for
revision. Anna Cora Mowatt, for example, gave up the script of her
play *Armand* to an unnamed London dramatist and critic, who marked
it up "abundantly" before it was staged at the Marylebone Theatre in
1849.[54] Mary Elizabeth Braddon, as part of her doomed effort to have
A Life Interest staged in the 1890s, turned it over to dramatist Jerome K.
Jerome for his suggestions and good offices.[55]

In *The Picture of Dorian Gray* Oscar Wilde introduces the supposed
ineptitude of women as playwrights as shorthand for differences between masculine and feminine mentality, differences which tell, of
course, in favor of the male. "Women never know when the curtain has
fallen," Wilde writes in the voice of Lord Henry Wotton. "They always
want a sixth act, and as soon as the interest of the play is entirely over,
they propose to continue it." If women had their way, moreover, every

comedy would end tragically, "and every tragedy would culminate in a farce." It is this incapacity for dramatic stucture which demonstrates for the character in Wilde's novel the inferiority of women's intelligence and their lack of any "sense of art."[56] In practice, however, men who wrote plays did not always proceed in a fashion as rigorously "intellectual," "scientific," or "architectural" as some Victorian analyses of dramatic authorship imply. The drama, supposed by James and others to be uniquely masculine in its "high dignity" and "mathematical" construction, was in fact at times off-handed and even chaotic when written by Victorian men. Wilde, for example, wrote *The Importance of Being Earnest* in a few hurried weeks, and always consented whenever Beerbohm Tree or George Alexander asked that he restructure a piece, add bits to it, or even, once, lop off an entire act.

But Wilde's casual approach to playwriting seems austere beside that of W. G. Wills – "a brilliant writer," as Madge Kendal once exclaimed of him, who supplied Henry Irving with many of the hit plays which raised the Lyceum to the front rank of late Victorian playhouses.[57] Wills's haphazard method owed nothing to the "constructive capacity" or "vast co-ordinative power" that were supposed to be typically masculine and indispensable for success in dramatic authorship:

> He would lie in bed for days together, scribbling his thoughts and scenes on separate pieces of paper and hurling them one after another on the floor all round the bed! When he had passed a day or two in script scattering thus, Poet Wills would summon an attendant to pick up those pages and try and piece them together.[58]

Irving then would struggle over the piecemeal results of Wills's writing, striking away whole acts and rearranging the disconnected scribbles into something that could be staged. Yet it was W. G. Wills of whom Clement Scott once said that "he has written more real poetry for the stage than any other author of his time," discovering in his tangled compositions the basis of a new "literary drama."[59]

Alfred Calmour, whose *The Amber Heart* (1887) provided Ellen Terry with one of her most pathos-laden roles, was likewise known for composing plays on stray sheets of paper that he scattered round his lodgings in no particular order. Colin H. Hazelwood was more systematic in his work as playwright for the Britannia and other playhouses outside the West End, employing a cut-and-paste method on the work of other writers, as his one-time collaborator discloses:

Hazelwood, or one of us working with him, would run through...periodicals, jotting down the main incidents in the stories thereof, and scissoring out here and there sundry aphorisms, axioms, and moral sentiments and so forth. These were docketed alphabetically, and when Colin was engaged in writing, or in sticking down, a new play for the Brit, etc., he or his assistants would take down from the shelf sundry envelopes...[60]

Thus Hazelwood's plays were more an effort of systematic filing than actual writing. Similarly the licensing manuscript of Bram Stoker's *Dracula* consists of lines cut from the published novel and pasted between brief handwritten transitions. In general the quality of writing in plays was abysmal, as Max Beerbohm laments in a review from 1902 – the dramatic equivalent, he says, of penny-novel hackwork.[61]

Under cover of producing an austere and uniquely masculine art, male playwrights were often composing hasty and even chaotic works that, among their other uses, provided actresses with roles that enforced Victorian conceptions of gender – roles like the passive and pure heroine of Wills's *Olivia*, made famous by Ellen Terry, who at the Lyceum "*drops down, face in hand sobbing*" when she discovers her marriage to Squire Thornhill was a sham, then says dutifully to her father "I would sooner die in a ditch than disgrace you with my presence."[62] Women throughout the period – a few of them, at least – saw through this charade of dramatic authorship as being somehow inherently masculine and conceived the possibility of women themelves writing lines for actors and actresses to speak, rather than leaving that task, along with its prerogatives and rewards, solely to men. Madge Kendal recollects that of the "hundreds of plays" submitted each year to her and her husband by hopeful playwrights, many were written with talent by ambitious young women.[63] In fiction about the theatre the woman playwright is a familiar figure; and if in fact the works of most women playwrights came to nothing, gathering dust on the shelves and worktables of theatre managers, in novels their luck was considerably better. The staging of their plays within the framework of fictional narratives, moreover, raised some of the issues that made the Victorians uncomfortable with the presence of women in theatre generally, and their role as writers of plays in particular. Anna Maria Hall, a playwright herself as well as a writer of fiction, describes in her novel *A Woman's Story* (1857) a young heroine whose first play will "bring another proof to lordly man...that the mind is of no sex." The woman playwright in Hall's novel exults in the power of her new occupation – "the power to quicken the beatings of every heart within [the] arena – to draw tears from every eye – to nerve each hand for applause, to rouse each voice, as the voice of one, in a long shout of approbation." But Helen Lyndsey, the playwright, conceals her gender behind the initials "H. L." – choosing anonymity, just as Virginia Woolf imagined that the unheralded "sisters" of Shakespeare would do in order to avoid supposedly unfeminine publicity. As a result the critics discount rumors that "H. L." is a woman – for "no woman," in the words of one newspaper, "could have written the more philosophic portions of the drama, the report that a *young* lady is the author, being too absurd to need contradiction, as the least practised critic must know that the framework of the play is constructed by a master hand."[64] In common with many other Victorians, the reviewer makes an assumption that only a "constructive" and technical male intelligence could produce good drama.

Dorothy Leighton, a woman playwright connected with the Independent Theatre, introduces a fictional woman dramatist in her novel *Disillusion* (1894). Like "H. L." in Anna Maria Hall's earlier novel, Linda Grey is loathe to make known her authorship of a hit play, for although an ardent feminist, "her shy, reserved nature shrank from any approach to notoriety."[65] The credit goes to her male collaborator, just as in the play *Our Flat* a woman playwright allows all acclaim for her hit play to fall to her husband, who wrote no part of it himself but will "work together" with his playwright-wife in the future on "social dramas."[66] These representations by, and of, women writers suggest that Virginia Woolf was correct in her assessment that women were socially conditioned not to write plays; or if they wrote them, to deny authorship.

But Olive Logan, in her mid-Victorian book on stagecraft, argues that women could contribute to dramatic literature something missing from the plays of men. "It is not too much to believe that if women wrote more frequently for the theatre," Logan says, "they would impart to its exhibitions something of their own grace, purity, and elegance." Her objection to the "licentious" women among the characters in many plays by male playwrights is in its own way typically Victorian. But Olive Logan acutely realizes that male-authored plays provide a means of control over actresses. The woman as playwright would, or could, she believes, raise the horizon of actresses and liberate them from the dictation of men. She would help bring into existence something like a women's theatre, and with it a different kind of drama and an improved outlook for actresses. "By dignifying the drama," writes Logan, "she would dignify that vocation which so many of her sisters follow, and would rescue from the indignation of the censor and the sneer of the scandalous those who are sometimes causelessly blamed."[67]

Representations of women playwrights, however, even those drawn by women writers, are typically etched with illness and death. "H. L.," the playwright in Anna Maria Hall's *A Woman's Story*, is capable of becoming "the great dramatist of modern times" but instead sinks into the life of an invalid, a casualty of "spasmodic attacks, brought on by excitement," and never writes for the stage again. Her attendant describes one such episode:

she put her arms round my neck, as a child would, and I more than half carried her into her bedroom, and laid her upon her sofa; by that time she was white and powerless; and, as her head lay back upon the pillow, tears trickled from between her eye-lids.[68]

The disciplinary function of illness, even in this story by a woman who herself wrote plays, is to reduce the woman dramatist to being calm, dependent, and "powerless." Nor was Anna Maria Hall the only woman to submit her own work as playwright to a process of surveillance and judgment. Women of the nineteenth-century theatre, playwrights as well as actresses, often resemble the inmates of Foucault's asylum – less constrained from outside than by a moral consciousness which regulates their own aberrant lives. They are part of a system, as Foucault says of the madhouse of the same period, "whose essential element was the constitution of a 'self-restraint' in which...freedom, engaged by work and the observation of others, was ceaselessly threatened by the recognition of guilt."[69]

Self-surveillance of this kind is evident, for example, in *George Mandeville's Husband* (1894), a novel by actress and playwright Elizabeth Robins, when the young daughter of a woman dramatist attends the rehearsal of her mother's play in a musty theatre and contracts a fatal "brain fever" as a result.[70] Similarly, in *Mary Iverson's Career* (1914), a novel by Elizabeth Jordan, the drawn-out rehearsals of a woman's play coincide mysteriously with her fiancé's worsening health, which improves when she gives up her work. Mary Iverson, the woman playwright of the story, blames herself for being preoccupied with the details of producing her play while nurses and doctors hover over her betrothed, "watching, listening for the change that meant life or death." In the end she renounces her playwriting career to be a wife: "My professional life...lay behind me," she explains; "little in it seemed to count in the new world I was entering."[71] Constance Woolson in the story "Miss Grief" portrays a would-be playwright who dies in her forties of no identifiable illness, laid to rest in a grave with her manuscripts as a pillow and her masterpiece for the stage unproduced and unread.

Alongside these comparatively sympathetic portraits some others seem almost hysterical in the anxieties that they manifest where women dramatists are concerned. In George Moore's *A Mummer's Wife* playwright Laura Forest – cold, sexless, and intellectual – becomes so engrossed in writing the second act of her new play that she scarcely notices on the other side of the room the death-delirium of the woman she has come to sit with. In a play called *The Female Dramatist* (1782), written by George Colman the Younger at a time when women playwrights were more visible than would be the case a hundred years later, the woman dramatist Melpomene Metaphor is portrayed as deranged and erratic. "If you was but to see her you'd be frightened out of your wits," a servant reports; "– First she takes her Pen, then she takes a Dip of Ink – then she takes a pinch of Snuff, then she dips her Pen in the Snuffbox, and puts her Finger into the Inkstand then –"[72] Symptomatic of her mental disorder is this female dramatist's neglect of ordinary household cares – washing clothes and cooking, for example – in order to spend all her time writing and reading. Similarly, in the late-Victorian play *Our Flat*, the heroine turns to playwriting because, as she says, she has "no genius for the domestic arts."[73]

Disqualified from writing plays in literature as well as in life, women who persevered as dramatists were unlikely to produce the new kind of theatre – a woman's theatre – that Walter Besant and others dreaded and mocked. Nor were Victorian women playwrights in any position to accomplish what Olive Logan hoped they might – an improvement in the condition of actresses, who for the most part moved at the dictation of male managers and spoke the lines provided by male playwrights. In making the woman playwright a curiosity, even a theoretical impossibility, the Victorians confirmed and reinforced their view of the theatre as a masculine institution, and as such a bulwark of patriarchal society. This indeed is the formula of *A Husband of No Importance* by Rita, in whose closing pages an unsexed New Woman is astonished to learn that her own husband is the author of a hit play in a West End theatre, even though, unlike herself, he had never written a line before. It is his having become a dramatist that confirms the husband's masculinity in Rita's novel and reduces his misled wife to tearful contrition as the curtain falls on opening night:

He is right! – he is right! The woman's sphere begins with love, and by love alone she reigns. . .He the Head and she the Heart. . .So may Life's best work be done!

With this epiphany the story can safely conclude, for the male dramatist and the masculinist theatre which his writing sustains have accomplished their disciplinary mission. Husband and wife are reconciled, "understanding one another as but for this lesson they would never have done," and so domestic order is restored through the masculine work of dramatic writing.[74] In Rita's novel the theatre has re-established the hierarchies of gender which, on many other occasions, in life as in art, it disrupted and threatened to destroy.

CHAPTER 5

Textual assaults: women's novels on stage

To myself no payment, not the greatest, could in any way really
compensate for the annoyance and the injury...

(Ouida, 1882, protesting in a letter to *The Times* against a male
playwright's unauthorized adaptation of a novel of hers for
production on stage)

No middle-class Victorian woman, as the previous chapter has shown,
could realistically hope to support herself by writing plays. Of the
hundreds of nineteenth-century plays written by women, none survives
today as part of the literary or dramatic canon, and only a few were
critically acclaimed or commercially successful in their own time. Fiction, of course, was another matter. Written and consumed in a domestic setting, remote from the public spectacle of theatre, fiction provided
an opportunity for women writers to conform to Victorian conceptions
of femininity while pursuing a career of their own.

As Gaye Tuchman reveals in *Edging Women Out*, perhaps as many as
half of all early Victorian novelists were women; and although their
rewards as novelists diminished in the later Victorian period as men
wrote more fiction themselves, women remained numerous in the
growing list of novelists throughout the nineteenthth century and beyond. As Tuchman points out, writing fiction was one of the "few
acceptable ways" in which women could earn a living. As in the
teaching profession, if not to the same extent, women dominated the
early Victorian novel – so much so that men more often wrote under
female names than women adopted male pen names. But by the 1880s
more women were assuming a male persona, indicating, as Tuchman
says, that "later cultural expectations emphasized that novelists were
mainly men."[1]Among the late Victorians far more men than women
were achieving fame as novelists, while at the same time men continued
to enjoy greater access than women to other literary genres. But

whether early or late in the Victorian period, it was fiction alone that women wrote with much popular success – even in the 1880s and 1890s when an increasing number of women tried their fortunes as playwrights – while men achieved fame not only in fiction but nonfiction prose, poetry, and of course playwriting as well. Women who wrote plays for this male-dominated theatre were usually novelists who ventured only rarely into drama, and the plays they wrote were little regarded in comparison with their fiction, if they were staged at all. When novels by women were adapted for the theatre, furthermore, the writers were most often male playwrights rather than themselves.

The masculinist bias of Victorian theatre emerges clearly, therefore, when placed in contrast with Victorian fiction – itself increasingly "masculine" as the nineteenth century drew to a close, yet always a field in which women could win distinction while expressing, if only indirectly at times, their resistance to the subjection of women. An outpouring of feminist literary scholarship has effectively and often brilliantly documented this note of resistance in Victorian fiction – a note struck not only by women novelists, but by some men as well. In *Sisters in Time*, while refuting the idea of a distinctive woman's voice in fiction, Susan Morgan finds in nineteenth-century novels as a whole an emphasis upon the roles played by women, whose struggles, choices, and actions are at the center of narratives for a culture in which women were generally regarded as less important than men. "The great age of the British novel," Morgan writes, "is also the age of the great heroines" – from Elizabeth Bennett and Becky Sharp to Tess of the D'Urbervilles and Clara Middleton.[2] Novels, whether written by women or men, were one area in which women, far from being powerless, had a strong voice in shaping Victorian society. At the same time, Morgan argues, heroines of novels were providing models of social "progress," setting aside the aggressive, erotic, and competitive models of male heroism – as displayed, for example, in fiction of the previous century – to achieve a different kind of empowerment through compassion and love.

Nancy Armstrong, like Morgan, places less emphasis on women writers in *Desire and Domestic Fiction* than upon the novel's focus in the nineteenth century on domestic life and the personal experience of women. This feminization of the novel, Armstrong argues, provided a "complement and antidote" to the values of the marketplace and politics, making the household "into what might be called the 'counterimage' of the modern marketplace."[3] Not birth or wealth, but nuances of behavior in networks of personal relationships regulated by women became the indicators of one's worth. In Armstrong's reading of nineteenth-century fiction women are neither powerless nor the agents of a subversive power; they do not so much challenge gendered categories or offer "alternative modes of culture" as they sustain the middle-class order by restraining its excesses.[4] Mary Barton may know nothing of economics or politics, as she confesses in the novel by Elizabeth Gaskell, but her reserves of love and mercy give her the authority to regulate violent conflicts between workers and capitalists. Thus the novel becomes a means of enforcing household values, setting limits on male aggression, and pointing the way to a modified rather than revolutionary social order in which the domestic authority of women is a civilizing force. The brutal Hareton Earnshaw is tamed at the end of *Wuthering Heights* by young Catherine, and a chastened Rochester is re-educated by Jane Eyre at the end of the novel which bears her name. In *Oliver Twist* the return of Nancy to haunt the murderous Sikes is seen by Armstrong as another instance of the powers of surveillance with which women are bestowed in nineteenth-century fiction.

While Armstrong and Morgan emphasize women's centrality and power in fictional texts – indeed Armstrong argues that novels reinvented womanhood for Victorian culture – other feminist critics have insisted on crucial distinctions between men and women as *writers* of fiction in the nineteenth century. At a time when all self-assertion was "unladylike," as Mary Poovey says in *The Proper Lady and the Woman Writer*, the very act of writing fiction – however inhibited, and despite any concessions in the text to propriety – was in fact a proclamation of a woman's "momentary, possibly unconscious, but effective, defiance."[5] This female "defiance" expressed itself not just in the act of writing, but in the content of fictional texts as well, although it was often disguised rather than explicit. Sandra Gilbert and Susan Gubar have argued that in a period in which women by definition had no story of their own to tell, women writers experienced an anxiety of authorship that sometimes functioned to soften or conceal a socially disruptive level of meaning. In *Jane Eyre*, for instance, the "cover story" of Jane's weakness for the Byronic hero and his charismatic sexuality can be set against Jane's less obvious encounter with her own rebellion and rage in the shape of Rochester's hidden wife. Elaine Showalter makes a similar point in *A Literature of Their Own* – Jane Eyre is, or is partly, the madwoman Bertha Mason. By allowing her a portion of the assertiveness that society figured as madness in women, Charlotte Brontë fashions Jane into a character more passionate and self-defining than the typically sweet, submissive heroines of Dickens and Thackeray.[6] This kind of subtextual rebellion against authorized ideas of gender in the nineteenth century has been documented throughout women's fiction of the period in impressive detail by Gilbert and Gubar, along with Showalter in particular. Even Jane Austen's heroines, for example, can be read as talkative, intelligent, and satirical women who submit to the necessity of male "protection and cover" in order to accomplish anything at all.

The feminized narratives that to a large extent define Victorian fiction are much less influential in the drama of the period, when the woman playwright seemed practically a contradiction in terms. On the one hand Victorians believed that some mysterious lack rendered women unfit to write for the theatre; on the other, they sought to exploit the obvious talents of women writers on other terms. Many successful novels by women proved irresistible to the men who wrote plays for a living and knew how to adapt a woman's fictional text for their own use and profit on stage. No law prevented a playwright from appropriating, without compensation or acknowledgment, the plot and characters, even the title, of a successful work of fiction. In 1861, however, Charles Reade sued to recover damages for an unauthorized stage version of his novel *It's Never Too Late To Mend*, which he had first written in dramatic form under the title of *Gold*, staged at the Drury Lane in 1853. The court of Common Pleas held that G. A. Conquest's dramatization for the Grecian Theatre did not infringe on Reade's rights as author of the novel, but later accepted the plea that Reade's own dramatic version under the title of *Gold* was in fact copyright. Reade was awarded £160 in damages, not because his novel had been adapted for the stage without permission, but because his dramatic version of the novel gave him theatrical rights to his own work of fiction. In the tangled web of dramatic copyright this ruling meant that novelists could protect their work from unscrupulous playwrights only by dramatizing it themselves.[7] "The novel in this country," as one theatre manager pointed out, "seems to be fair game for anybody."[8]

Mary Elizabeth Braddon, whose novels were repeatedly adapted for the stage without her consent, complained bitterly of this violation of her work. Her publisher sought damages for William Suter's unauthorized adaptations of *Aurora Floyd* and *Lady Audley's Secret*, and won, but only because Suter's dramatizations were published. The pirated novels were legal in the form of dramatic representations, the Court of Chancery held, but when Suter brought out his adaptations in print, he was trespassing on the copyright of the novelist. In 1874, however, more than a decade after the victory in *Tinsley* v. *Lacy*, Braddon was still complaining about the unauthorized rewriting of her fiction for the stage: "I have never received the slightest pecuniary advantage from any of these adaptations, nor does the law of copyright in any way assist me to protect what appears to be a valuable portion of my copyright, the exclusive right to dramatize my own creations."[9]

For practical purposes, therefore, novelists' texts remained open to the incursions of pirate playwrights late into the Victorian period. Ouida (Mary Louise de la Ramée) was dismayed to find in 1882 that her novel *Moths* was about to be dramatized and that, as she said in a letter to *The Times*, "I have not been consulted in the matter by even so much as a courteous formality of request for permission or acquiescence." Asserting that the law gave her no protection, and that "book after book of mine is seized by these pirates of the green-room," Ouida protested against "such robbery" and directed her rage as much at the hopeless state of dramatic copyright as at the "purloiners of my ideas and creations." Men and women of genius, she writes in her letter to *The Times*, can be expected to abandon literature "unless the copyright law is purged of the present condonation which it gives to this, the very worst form of literary theft." Her grievance was not only monetary – for money, she said, would not atone for the damage done to her fiction. "To myself no payment, not the greatest," Ouida writes, "could in any way really compensate for the annoyance and the injury which are entailed on any romance...by being dragged on the stage, cut and clipped, travestied, and dressed up in vulgar and ill-fitting clothes."[10] For his part, Henry Hamilton, who adapted Ouida's *Moths* for the Globe Theatre, protested that "I have in no way overstepped the bounds of literary probity, but have merely availed myself of a right which the law gives me in common with all others." He even asserted that he was doing Ouida a favor in dramatizing her novel, for "the fact of a good book being dramatized is not only a tribute to its merits, but an advertisement of them."[11] Hamilton wrote that his play would be an "adaptation" entitled *Star and Flame*, but when it actually opened at the Globe Theatre it bore the same name as Ouida's novel – *Moths*. The actress-manager of the Globe, Marie Litton, wrote her own letter to *The Times* as the controversy thickened, referring to the Charles Reade lawsuits of twenty years before as having established the principle that novelists "may easily protect themselves" against unauthorized stage versions by producing their own dramatizations first, before anyone else did so.[12]

To the audience none of this seemed to matter. "It welcomed Mr. Hamilton as if he were really the author," wrote a reviewer in *The Times*, adding that the large crowd at the first night's performance "seemed to have no views of its own about literary copyright." Nor did it take much notice, apparently, of the ways in which Hamilton's playscript abused the novel on which it was founded, notably its de-emphasizing of the novel's lead female character – a strategy that was predictably employed by male playwrights when they adapted novels by women. "We may say," the *Times* reviewer wrote, "that the adaptation is far inferior to the novel" – particularly, he notes, in its representation of the heroine, whose vitality and force of character in the novel were not translated onto the stage. "Vera Herbert...is in the novel a being who possesses all our sympathy from the first; in the play, even acted with all Miss Litton's ability," according to *The Times*, "she is a shadow, only at one or two moments of crisis seeming to possess the attributes of flesh and blood." Hamilton's play not only shrank the novel's central female character, as the critic noted, but built up the leading man into a monster of brutality who perishes in a sequence of violent deaths that Hamilton introduced at the end of his version of *Moths*. "A more inartistic finale has seldom been put upon the stage," the *Times* reviewer said.[13]

The fictional texts of some men – Charles Dickens, for example – were also abused by playwrights, although not exactly in the same way as the work of women writers. In fact Dickens and a few other male novelists – Sir Walter Scott, in particular – have invariably been cited in theatre history as having suffered at the hands of pirate playwrights. But women novelists were also numerous and prominent among their victims, and in the end it was women writers whose loud complaints made these invasions of novelistic texts both riskier and less common. In *A History of English Drama 1660–1900*[14] Allardyce Nicoll lists six pirated versions on stage of Ouida's *Moths*, four of *Jane Eyre*, three of Elizabeth Gaskell's *Mary Barton*, three of Mary Elizabeth Braddon's *Lady Audley's Secret*, ten of Harriet Beecher Stowe's *Uncle Tom's Cabin*, and fifteen of Ellen Wood's *East Lynne*. By comparison eight versions of Scott's *Ivanhoe* are listed, and twelve of *Oliver Twist*. The tendency to regard male novelists as the main or only victims of adaptation began with the Victorians, and indeed was fostered by protégés of Dickens, not to mention Dickens himself, ever alert to thefts and distortions of his fiction on stage. George Augustus Sala writes in the 1880s of an adaptation of a novel by Edmund Yates, like himself a disciple of Dickens:

You have a series of segregated 'flashes' of the novelist's scenes and characters, and of his real purpose and intent, but a well-linked chain of narrative or action is generally past hoping for. Mr. Edmund Yates has not suffered more in this respect than has his illustrious Master in Letters. There is scarcely one novel of Charles Dickens that a real Dickensian scholar can listen to, as a play, with common patience.[15]

Comments in this vein – accurate in themselves, but citing male novelists as the sole victims of unauthorized adaptation – continue to be a theme in most histories of Victorian theatre. Scott and Dickens, for example, are cited by George Rowell for having their work refitted for the stage time after time.[16] Robertson Davies writes that the fiction of Dickens and Edward Bulwer were "coarsely adapted" as plays, sometimes even before the original had been completed in monthly parts. Where melodrama was present in their fictional texts it was exaggerated on stage, Davies points out, and eccentric characters were made into occasions for shows of professional skill in costume and makeup.[17]

Nevertheless more than one hundred productions in the theatre of Victorian London can be identified as men's rescripting of women's stories, obscure as well as famous – not only *Jane Eyre* and *Mary Barton*, but *Phyllida* by Florence Marryat and *Faustine's Love* by Rita.[18] It is certain that many others will never be identified because they were produced under the adaptor's own title and without credit to the original, like Dion Boucicault's *The Long Strike*, a rewriting of Elizabeth Gaskell's *Mary Barton*. But these dramatizations of women's fiction have attracted little or no attention. Like most adaptations for the stage, and most nineteenth-century plays in general, their texts survive only in rare acting editions or manuscripts. Cumulatively, however, these adaptations of women novelists represent a massive assault against women writers that is both textual and sexual in nature. Women novelists shared with men such as Dickens and Scott the misfortune of having their novels exploited on stage for their melodramatic potential. In addition, however, the texts of women novelists were refitted for a masculinist theatre, with the result that the original texts' representations of gender and sexuality were inevitably disfigured. This was not just an "anxiety of influence" at work, not the "swerving" of a belated author from the example of a father-precursor, attempting only to speak in his own voice. It was an organized plunder of literary "mothers," who could be rewritten against their will with the full sanction of law and custom. The point of this textual violence – quite in contrast with the Bloomian model of literary history – was to make the later work recognizably the *same* as its precursor.[19] But while clinging fast to the original titles, characters, and plot situations created by their literary mothers, male playwrights typically ignored or starkly reversed the central purposes of the women-written novels upon which they imposed themselves. Whereas fiction written by women gave primacy to the experience and values of women, the theatre exhibited a "masculine" perspective even in plays whose title characters were women, or in which women were central to the action. Unlike the leading women of many novels – especially those written by women – Victorian stage heroines, as Robertson Davies writes, "do not so much act as permit themselves to be acted upon; they rarely initiate anything vital to the plays in which they appear."[20] Playwrights who rewrote women's fiction would sometimes exaggerate the melodramatic incidents and eccentric characters of the original texts, as they did with Dickens's, but they also neutralized any tendency in women-authored novels to critique or reconfigure Victorian standards of gender.

An 1867 production of *Jane Eyre* at the Surrey Theatre is a good example of a playwright's seizing the title and other appurtenances of a woman's novel in order to construct a stage play which violates the spirit of its precursor. Jane Eyre, enacted as a "very pretty" ingenue, has the good looks and self-abnegation required of stage heroines, but bears no physical or mental resemble to the plain, proud, and assertive heroine of Charlotte Brontë's novel. At the same time Rochester on stage is given additional lustre by a title he does not possess in the book – at the Surrey Theatre he was "Sir Rowland Rochester." Furthermore, as in most revisions of the novel, the melodramatic potential of the madwoman hidden in Rochester's house is shamelessly exploited. She yells fearfully, appears äd disappears suddenly – but these manifestations have little significance beyond providing the audience with a gothic chill. In the novel the madwoman functions as a realization of Rochester's guilt, in particular of his dehumanizing relations with women – the wife and mistresses who for him have been objects of purchase. His marriage to Bertha Mason had been the result of self-serving financial considerations. At the same time, the novel connects Rochester's mad wife through the imagery of madness and fire to Jane Eyre herself, whose passionate revolt against her own subjection finds expression, if only indirectly, in the madwoman's rage. In the play of 1867, by contrast, there is no bond at all between Bertha and Jane, who regards the mad wife distantly as "that terrible woman" and in fact the beneficiary of Rochester's gruff but kindly nature.

Indeed Bertha Mason is not Rochester's wife at all in the *Jane Eyre* staged at the Surrey Theatre, an alteration which exonerates the central male character in his treatment of her. "Listen," says Rochester after Jane Eyre has saved him from being burned alive in his own bed, "the fiend who in woman's shape would have destroyed me is a raving maniac...Lady Harriet Rochester, my brother's wife. She was my betrothed. My father sent me to London, and I returned to find her married to my brother – the heir of all our wealth." Rochester, the real victim in the stage version, is absolved of having married for money, and can be praised for taking care of Bertha Mason – or Lady Harriet, as she is known in the play – who "lost her reason for ever" after being unfaithful to her husband, Rochester's brother. The madness of this "guilty wife" – as Rochester calls her – is the outward expression of her deviation from authorized femininity, but it has nothing to do with Jane Eyre, who regards her distantly as the object of Rochester's charity. "Nobly have you become the protector of the woman who deceived you," she tells him in the last act of the licensing manuscript of this unpublished play. Jane Eyre also praises Rochester for his conduct with respect to Adèle – in the novel the little girl who may be his illegitimate child, but at any rate is the result of his affair with a Parisian dancer. In the play, by contrast, Adèle is the abandoned daughter of Rochester's late brother and the "maniac." Assured by Rochester, whose profligacy is a major theme of the novel, that he has never before spoken of love to a woman, Jane in the play agrees to be his wife – "yes," says Rochester, "my wife, protected by this strong arm and heart from all persecuting and envious foes."[21] Rochester, blind, maimed, and beast-like at the end of the novel, lacks the ability to help himself, let alone "protect" Jane Eyre.

The heroine in Brontë's original version of the story observes Rochester's immobility and blindness, his unkempt hair and nails like bird's claws, and declares "It is time some one undertook to rehumanise you." Moreover, it is precisely Rochester's "powerlessness," Jane says in the novel, that "touched my heart to the quick." Now he had become "dependent on another" – indeed "he saw Nature – he saw books through me," Jane reflects with satisfaction in Brontë's story. Rochester himself is no less aware of his dependence on Jane at the end of the novel, and his avowal of that dependence is for the heroine both an exaltation and a reason to love him all the more. With tears in her eyes, Jane Eyre as created by Charlotte Brontë confides in Rochester that "I love you better now, when I can really be useful to you, than I did in your stage of proud independence, when you disdained every part but that of the giver and protector."[22] By contrast the Jane Eyre at the Surrey Theatre – lacking what Terry Eagleton has called the "complex blend of independence, submissiveness, and control" with which she domesticates Rochester at the end of Brontë's novel[23] – ends up by gladly submitting herself to Rochester's care and authority, pleased to enter a marriage-prison from which her precursor in fiction had recoiled.

Another rewriting of *Jane Eyre*, produced at the Globe Theatre in 1882 and authored by W. G. Wills, defaces the text of Brontë's novel with a more sophisticated touch than the earlier version at the working-class Surrey Theatre. In Wills's adaptation, just as in its predecessor at the Surrey, little Adèle is no disparagement to the character of Rochester – she is simply "a ward" rather than his or anybody else's illegitimate child. Indeed Rochester is so appealing to Jane Eyre from the first that she turns down an offer of marriage from a persistent man named Prior, a character invented by the playwright Wills, and before the end of Act I declares herself to be "jealous" of Rochester's affections – "Yes I love him," she says to Rochester in his disguise as a gypsy. But in this play, too, the madwoman presents herself to Jane as merely a gothic apparition whose offstage shrieks cause the heroine to exclaim, "Oh, what's that! God protect me, it was like a devil's laugh." This faint-hearted Jane swoons upon sighting the "maniac," falls to the floor, and is revived only by supporting her head on Rochester's knee. The madwoman is indeed Rochester's wife, but it is *her* numerous infidelities which the play emphasizes, while Rochester seems in this play never to have committed an indiscretion. As a reviewer for the *Daily News* of London remarked, the playwright was "mitigating somewhat – and in truth, on the stage they require mitigation – the unscrupulous proceedings of Mr. Rochester."[24]

Jane Eyre sympathizes with Rochester's plight in Wills's play, but because he is a married man leaves him with little or no hesitation, rather than with the agonizing which precedes her withdrawal in Brontë's novel. Nearly blind at the end of Wills's play, Rochester looks to Jane for support – but only to bear patiently with "a crippled man twenty years older than you whom you'll have to wait on,"[25] leaving unmentioned the novel's insistence on the need to "rehumanise" him. Consequently Jane Eyre is more the nurse than the "humanizer" of Rochester when the curtain falls. One review praised the male playwright for offering only "slight departures" from the original narrative and preserving its spirit, but at the same time found Mrs. Bernard-Beere's portrayal of Jane Eyre to be marked by "charm and refinement" – by ingratiation and decorum, in other words, rather than the fiery independence that characterizes Brontë's Jane.[26] *Jane Eyre* as acted by Fanny Bernard-Beere at the Globe was, as one review put it, "very pretty" and "very tender," and the play itself "deeply touching in its pleasant wholesome simplicity." But, he added, "this is not the Jane Eyre over whose trials so many readers have wept during the last five-to-thirty years."[27] The fate of *Jane Eyre* on stage was typical of dramatizations of Victorian novels by women. Male playwrights brought the perspective of their own gender to these hijacked narratives and invariably diminished the importance and power of women in comparison with the roles given them in novels.

In a third dramatic version of the novel – evidently the only one to be published in the nineteenth century – John Brougham, an Irish actor and playwright who also adapted Dickens for the stage, gives Jane the good looks that the theatre demanded of its heroines, making her a "devilish pretty" young woman who at times reflects dimly the fortitude of Brontë's heroine. At other times, however, the Jane Eyre in Brougham's play can seem helpless and abject, as when she moans, "Oh, pity me, for I need pity much. Homeless, friendless, and an orphan; what is to become of me?" A fire breaks out at Thornfield Hall while the marriage ceremony uniting Jane and Rochester is in progress, ignited by the "maniac" wife who discloses herself, torch in hand, at an open window to end Act IV. "My wife!" cries out a candid Rochester just before the curtain falls, and thereupon Jane Eyre "*faints*" against a backdrop of the "*house beyond...in flames.*" Act V opens with the title character living alone a year later, omitting any account of the "ordeal" in which Jane Eyre, in Brontë's novel, is seriously tempted to become Rochester's mistress. A second fire is lit by the "raving lunatic," destroying Thornfield Hall, leaving Rochester maimed and blind. Brougham dilutes the ending of the novel by writing a final scene in which Jane Eyre does not demand but only offers to take charge of the disabled Rochester – "if you wish it, not otherwise."

Instead of humanizing the male and establishing the groundwork for a marriage of equality, Jane Eyre in Brougham's play has only to provide Rochester with slight physical assistance. The day of their reunion is also Rochester's birthday, and the day of their renewed betrothal. The heroine receives at the final curtain the floral tributes and hurrahs of his happy "peasants," who cry out, "A cheer for our kind master and his intended bride."²⁸ Under a canopy of flowers and to the sound of music Jane Eyre is transfigured at the end of the drama by an aristocratic marriage – instead of Rochester being transformed, as in Brontë's novel, by feminine surveillance. Indeed, one of the most noticeable differences between dramatic versions of *Jane Eyre* and the novelistic original is the comparatively vigorous health which Rochester enjoys on stage, leaving him less in need of the heroine's supervision and care.

The most egregious example of a hale and hearty Rochester appears in an adaptation by James Willing and Leonard Rae, *Jane Eyre, or Poor Relations* (1879), in which the master of Thornfield Hall has suffered only a slight and temporary injury to the eye. "But it was given out I was stone blind," explains this hearty Rochester to Jane Eyre; "and anxious to test the sincerity of your love – I feigned blindness." Instead of the rehabilitation of a brutalized male, this drama concerns itself with testing the worth of a well-intentioned but inexperienced young woman whose survival at every turn is the result of some man's largesse. For example, Brocklehurst, in contrast to the abusive proprietor of Lowood School in Brontë's novel, is in this play Rochester's boon companion and Jane's kindly benefactor, determined to have her well fed and clothed "if I have to go without myself."²⁹

Although not dramatized as often as *Jane Eyre*, Elizabeth Gaskell's novel of labor strife in Manchester – *Mary Barton* (1848) – was disfigured by male playwrights along the same lines as Charlotte Brontë's novel. Gaskell's story hinges on the class divisions that fuel a bitter strike, replacing the "ties of respect and affection" between workers and masters with "mere money bargains alone." In this atmosphere of hostility and self-seeking the title character's father – John Barton, a Chartist – murders the son of a mill-owner, and Jem Wilson, who is in love with Mary Barton, is wrongfully charged with the crime. The title character takes upon herself the task of proving her lover's innocence while suspecting that her father is the real murderer, and in the process works toward a general reconciliation in the strife-torn city. "All this I can and will do, though perhaps I don't clearly know how, just at present," Mary Barton declares in Gaskell's novel before setting out by rail and sea to bring back a key witness who will exonerate Jem Wilson in the murder case. Her heroism is reported in the *Guardian* and rewritten for London newspapers. Eventually she negotiates a meeting between her father, the real murderer, and the mill-owner whose son was slain. Antagonism between classes – between oppressor and oppressed – begins to evaporate under Mary Barton's sympathetic influence as John Barton asks and receives forgiveness from the father of the man he killed. The master, for his part, walks away from Mary Barton and her repentant father with a determination to alleviate suffering and treat his workers as human beings rather than the "mere machines of ignorant men" which under his employment they had become.[30]

By contrast, Dion Boucicault's adaptation of *Mary Barton*, entitled *The Long Strike* (1866) and performed at the Lyceum Theatre, introduces Gaskell's characters not only under a different title, but with new names and a spectacular dénouement that has no counterpart in the novel. Posters advertised the play with no acknowledgment of Gaskell or the novel *Mary Barton*, describing *The Long Strike* as a "new drama in four acts...written by Dion Boucicault."[31] The heroic efforts of Mary Barton – called Jane Learoyd in this play – are skipped over in Boucicault's dramatization. The heroine, played by Boucicault's wife, stands by passively while two men, a lawyer and telegrapher, work out the return of the missing witness to testify in Jem Wilson's trial for murder. This scene, with the heroine kneeling in supplication, is represented on the poster advertisement for *The Long Strike*. Unlike Gaskell's novel, moreover, Boucicault's play ends in the courtroom. Absent in the Lyceum Theatre version is any hint of the last hundred or so pages of the book in which the sympathy and forgiveness realized throughout the novel by women in general, and Mary Barton in particular, begin to influence men as well, bringing about a reconciliation between Mary's father and the grieving mill-owner and opening the prospect for more humane relations between Manchester workers and capitalists.

Another adaptation of *Mary Barton*, written by Thompson Townsend and staged at the Grecian Theatre in 1861, also ignores the reconciliation of capitalists and workers negotiated by Mary Barton in "the Spirit of Christ" in Gaskell's novel. Like Boucicault's play, Townsend's version of a few years earlier emphasizes crime and courtroom melodrama at the expense of what Ellen Moers has identified as the concerns of Gaskell's novel – social injustice made possible by forgetfulness of the "essential humanity" of the oppressed group.[32] Mary Barton's powers of love and sympathy that bring the novel to a close are replaced in Townsend's play by a sudden revelation that John Barton, the heroine's Chartist father, was after all *not* the murderer of Harry Carson, the mill-owner's son. The grieving father learns that the killer was actually "Abel Thornley, and he is – Dead!"[33] As he pronounces the word "dead" in triumph, his innocence proven, Mary Barton's father – himself the killer in the novel – falls down and dies at the final curtain. The improbable but spectacular events which bring Townsend's play to an end have little or nothing to do with the social crisis which began the action, or with the heroine after whom the play is somewhat gratuitously named. Mary Barton is a mere onlooker in the final act, not the catalyst for social change that Gaskell makes her in the closing chapters of the novel.

J. E. Carpenter's rescripting of *Adam Bede* for the Surrey Theatre in 1862 retains the character of Dinah Morris, but only as a shadow of the key part she plays in George Eliot's novel of 1859. Eliot's heroine is a Methodist preacher whose message of God's mercy and love, along with her own compassion and sense of purpose, negotiates the conclusion to the book. It is Dinah who visits in jail with Hetty Sorrel, about to go on trial for the murder of her own child, and breaks through Hetty's hardness of heart with this appeal:

God's love and mercy can overcome all things – our ignorance, and weakness, and all the burthen of our past wickedness – all things but our wilful sin; sin that we cling to, and will not give up. You believe in my love and pity for you, Hetty; but if you had not let me come near you, if you wouldn't have looked at me or spoken to me, you'd have shut me out from helping you: I couldn't have made you feel my love; I couldn't have told you what I felt for you. Don't shut God's love out in that way, by clinging to sin...It is sin that brings dread, and darkness, and despair: there is light and blessedness for us as soon as we cast it off: God enters our souls then, and teaches us, and brings us strength and peace.[34]

With that, Hetty Sorrel can tell the truth about her illegitimate child by the young squire Arthur Donnithorne, and come to peace with herself in asking the forgiveness of God as well as of Adam Bede, the honorable working-man who loved her before this trouble. Dinah Morris provides Hetty with "strength and hope" to go through an ordeal that seems certain to end in hanging, and moreover functions as a mediator between the guilty young woman and a forgiving God – for "the pitying love that shone out from Dinah's face looked like a visible pledge of the Invisible Mercy."[35]

A spellbinding preacher and agent of divine love and redemption in the novel, Dinah Morris sinks in the male-authored play to become nothing more than the confidant of Hetty Sorrel. Dinah Morris on stage is a conventional woman whose overriding concern, when she learns of the accusation of child-murder, is with the nature of Hetty Sorrel's relationship with the young squire: "Tell me, were you married to him?" she asks urgently, whereupon Hetty falls swooning to the floor.[36] Adam Bede, the young carpenter who had hoped to make Hetty Sorrel his wife, is preoccupied in the play with his own dignity – "for the honour of his family and the integrity of his name," explains Adam's brother Seth, "is as dear to the working man as to the proudest noble in the land." Even in Eliot's novel, as Susan Morgan points out, the agony of Hetty Sorrel is to some extent rationalized as the means to a bright future for Adam with Dinah as his wife. "What better harvest from that painful seed-time could there be than this?" asks Eliot in the narrative voice. "The love that had brought hope and comfort in the hour of despair, the love that had found its way to the dark prison cell and to poor Hetty's darker soul – this strong, gentle love was to be Adam's companion and helper till death."[37] Nevertheless, Eliot's novel is focused on issues of guilt and redemption arising out of a woman's aspiration – Hetty allowed herself to be seduced by the squire largely because of her dreams of becoming something more in life than a dairymaid.

In J. E. Carpenter's play, however, these concerns are not raised at all. Indeed, Hetty Sorrel as enacted at the Surrey Theatre turns out, by a sensational turn of the plot, to be guilty of nothing – the dead child was not hers at all, but belonged to gypsies, and Arthur Donnithorne, as the audience learns just before the final curtain, was married to her all along! In Act III he rushes into the courtroom where Hetty is being tried for her life – crying "I come to save, to own you" and explaining that for the sake of keeping his inheritance the marriage had to be concealed awhile. Adam shakes the squire's hand warmly as the jury acquits Hetty just before the curtain falls. From the novel's concern with women's dreams, guilt, and redemption through suffering and love, the male playwright fashioned a drama about a magnanimous aristocrat who raises a virtuous girl of the people to wealth and high estate. J. E. Carpenter's defacement of the main women characters in the novel – Dinah Morris and Hetty Sorrel – is what gives shape and structure to his travesty of George Eliot's novel.

As in the dramatized version of *Adam Bede*, the centrality of women was denied over and over, and in ingenious ways, when men rewrote women novelists for production on stage. Jane Tompkins has shown how Harriet Beecher Stowe's *Uncle Tom's Cabin* is "the most dazzling exemplar" of sentimental novels that work through a story of salvation by motherly love to a myth granting women ultimate power and authority.[38] In such incidents as the death of little Eva St. Clare the novelist suggests that social change hinges on a change of heart, and that the Christlike act of giving up one's life for others can have profound political consequences – in Stowe's novel, for example, consequences that would lead to the abolition of slavery. In this revolution of the meek in *Uncle Tom's Cabin*, women and mothers, acting out of compassion and love, point the way to a new world in which slavery and all exploitation will cease. The coda to the novel, indeed, addresses the "mothers of America," arguing that with them lies the power of influence and strength of feeling that could bring an end to slavery.[39] For Stowe, the death of Eva St. Clare is not only a medical and emotional phenomenon but a political act – Eva's protest against inhumanity. Near the end of her short life Eva implores her slaveholding father to adopt her own point of view, hoping to make her death the means – or at least one of the means – by which the slaves will be liberated:

Papa, isn't there any way to have all slaves made free?...couldn't you go all round and try to persuade people to do right about this? When I am dead, papa, then you will think of me, and do it for my sake.[40]

How significant, then, that little Eva is not even among the *dramatis personae* in some of the stage adaptations of *Uncle Tom's Cabin*. In those in which she appears, moreover, the novel's concern with the political implications of her death is typically lost amid the lights and music of a spectacular transformation scene – that "tear-drawing episode," recalls Chance Newton, in which little Eva, "in most of the versions that I have seen, is shown to be received at Heaven's portals by a couple of glittering angels," including once when the part was enacted by a youthful Madge Robertson, later to become the Matron of the Drama as Madge Kendal.[41]

The slave Eliza, driven by love of her child to escape the Shelby plantation, carrying him in her arms as she slips and stumbles across the icy Ohio River to freedom, appears as a character in most of the plays – but invariably a shrunken version of Stowe's heroic woman. In an unpublished 1852 production of *Uncle Tom's Cabin* at the Royal Olympic Theatre, for example, Eliza is able to escape from Kentucky only with the assistance of her husband George, whereas in the novel she acts entirely on her own. "*George drags away Eliza and the child on a mass of ice,*" the stage directions say, "*which he pushes from the bank, with his staff, across the river.*"[42] In Edward Fitzball's version produced at the Standard Theatre in 1852, Eliza doesn't cross the river at all – but her husband George does, hanging precariously on to a log.[43] George F. Rowe's rewriting of the novel, staged at the Princess's Theatre in 1878, preserves much of the anti-slavery sentiment of Stowe's novel and allows Eliza, pursued by the slave traffickers Marks and Haley, to negotiate the ice on her own, without assistance from a man. But a note in the acting edition suggests that some players might be tempted to turn this scene of a woman's heroism into low comedy: "*The person who plays Marks will not indulge in any gags here,*" the author orders just as Eliza eludes her would-be captors. The issue of slavery as an institution is lost sight of in Rowe's last act, which ends spectacularly with a dying Uncle Tom reaching out to a vision of little Eva in heaven, "*surrounded by angels,*" while a "*song of triumph*" is being sung by the chorus.[44] It is not even made clear in the licensing manuscript, nor does it seem to matter much to the author, whether Eliza and George Harris will remain slaves. Unlike their counterparts in Stowe's novel, slaves in the Uncle Tom plays usually have little or no objection to slavery under a kind owner, and in carefree moments enjoy themselves in minstrel-style song and dance. Mark Lemon and Tom Taylor's adaptation for the Adelphi Theatre in 1852 opens in this fashion, with the slaves on the Shelby plantation laughing, singing, dancing, and chanting in unison "good mass'r, good mass'r." Their master Shelby doesn't use the whip "'cept now and den," as one of the slaves says – and all in all, as Eliza herself remarks in the Lemon and Taylor collaboration, "we have great cause to be thankful."[45]

The novel's vehement opposition to slavery is also diluted in the adaptation staged at the Royal Olympic Theatre in 1852. Oblivious to Stowe's program for a matriarchal reformation of society and its institutions, it ends with the return of the "good" slave-owner Shelby, who rescues Uncle Tom, Eliza, and her husband from the clutches of Simon Legree in order to return them to his own slave plantation. The stage directions call for "*movements of joy*" by Shelby's slaves as they resume their lives under this congenial owner by crying out gratefully, "Master! Master!"[46] The novel, by contrast, ends with George and Eliza going as free people, indeed as black nationalists, to "glorious Africa," there to found, as George says, "a country, a nation, of my own" – a civilization perhaps "of even a higher type" than the Christian Anglo-Saxon one they leave behind.[47]

Thus the subversive content that has been detected generally in women's novels of sensation and sentiment is notably missing in men's adaptations of these works for the stage. Mary Elizabeth Braddon's *Lady Audley's Secret* presents its title character ambiguously, suggesting "madness" as the reason for her crimes while offering other explanations, including economic ones derived from her position as a dependent female. She had found out as a child, she says after being exposed as an arsonist, murderer, and bigamist, "what it was to be poor" and that "my ultimate fate in life depended upon my marriage." Lady Audley's criminal behavior arises out of that knowledge, but seems incompatible with femininity in general and the kind of woman she appears to be in particular. As her antagonist and kinsman Robert Audley expresses it:

> If I have wondered sometimes, as it was only natural I should, whether I was not the victim of some horrible hallucination, whether such an alternative was not more probable than that a young and lovely woman should be capable of so foul and treacherous a murder, all wonder is past. . .Henceforth you must seem to me no longer a woman. . .I look upon you henceforth as the demoniac incarnation of some evil principle.

Madness as another explanation for Lady Audley's crimes is also attractive to Robert Audley. Like his reinvention of her as "the demoniac incarnation of some evil principle," the supposed madness of Lady Audley would expose her deviation from normative ideas of femininity as being not only wrong, but irrational and even insane. Even Lady Audley sometimes conceives of herself as mad, but the psychiatrist whom Robert Audley summons for a diagnosis takes a different view:

> I do not believe that she is mad. . .She employed intelligent means, and she carried out a conspiracy which required coolness and deliberation in its execution. There is no madness in that. . .She has the cunning of madness, with the prudence of intelligence. I will tell you what she is, Mr. Audley. She is dangerous.

Nevertheless, believing her innocent of murder, the physician agrees to have Lady Audley confined to an insane asylum as a "service to society."[48] The novel's recognition of Lady Audley's sanity, her authentic womanhood, and the rational bases for her crimes is missing in all of the stage adaptations of Braddon's novel.

In Colin H. Hazlewood's script for the Royal Victoria Theatre, where *Lady Audley's Secret* was staged in 1863, the diagnosis of Lady Audley's insanity is irrevocable – the *dramatis personae* encircle her in the final scene, crying "Mad!" as the title character sinks to the boards, holding her head and emitting a death groan.[49] In William Suter's version, staged at the Queen's Theatre the same year, Lady Audley herself declares "I am mad!", then, according to the stage directions, "*laughs wildly, tossing up her arms – and then dashes herself to the ground*" as the hero Robert Audley looks on, *"petrified."*⁵⁰ In George Roberts's version for the St. James's Theatre (also 1863), West End theatregoers saw a more genteel Lady Audley, continually tottering, swooning, and clinging to sturdy objects for support, declare herself at the final curtain to be "a – MAD WOMAN!"⁵¹

In the 1880s actor-manager Wilson Barrett demanded that two young playwrights, Henry Arthur Jones and Henry Herman, write a play to order for him – "a kind of *East Lynne* turned round." Like many other Victorian managers who were attracted to Ellen Wood's spectacularly successful novel, Barrett insisted on certain revisions in adapting it for the stage. "That is to say," as he explained to the two playwrights, "instead of a fugitive wife and mother coming back disguised and being prevented from seeing or succouring her own children, I want a man (falsely accused of course) put in the same position in the most poignant and most pathetic manner that I can get it. . .write me that *East Lynne* turned round. If you can't, I'll damned well do it myself!"⁵² Jones and Herman responded, not with a play entitled *East Lynne*, but with a drama that would be one of the greatest hits of the age, *The Silver King* (1882). Like most dramatists who rewrote Ellen Wood's novel, whether under the name *East Lynne* or some other title, Jones and Herman imposed a masculine perspective upon a story that, despite its surface conventionality, was marked by a strong undercurrent of woman's dissent.

These adaptations of *East Lynne* gut Ellen Wood's novel of the complex rationale for the heroine's abandoning her husband and children and ignore altogether its dream of a new society in which Victorian notions of the family would be superseded. They pass over or diminish the novelist's insistence upon the unhappiness of Isabel Carlyle's marriage – one formed out of financial and family considerations to a man who is cold and distant, unaware of her obvious unhappiness, and ignorant of the daily abuse she suffers from his own sister. After she leaves her family in Wood's novel, Isabel Carlyle is visited by a series of disasters – abandoned by her lover, she is disfigured in a railroad accident, and suffers through the death of her young son. "My sin was great," she says, asking forgiveness of the husband she left years ago, "but my punishment was greater." This suggestion that Isabel has been dealt with more harshly than she deserves is accompanied by the heroine's deathbed vision of a life beyond the grave in which she and her husband and children will be reunited. In the novel, unlike the many plays based on it, the implications of this reunion in heaven are drawn out to their logical conclusion.

It is no sin to anticipate it, Archibald. For there will be no marrying or giving in marriage in heaven: Christ has said so. Though we do not know how it will be. My sin will be remembered no more there, and we shall be together with our children for ever and for ever.

On earth Isabel Carlyle's conduct has made her inconceivable as a wife or even a rational woman – indeed "madness," as she herself says, is in her own time and place the only explanation of such conduct.[53] In the heaven she imagines, however, the standards governing women's behavior and the family itself will be thoroughly reorganized. And to this vision Isabel's tearful husband whispers his own assent as she dies.

In 1866 an adaptation of *East Lynne* by the playwright John Oxenford was produced at the Surrey Theatre which, like most of the numerous dramas based on Wood's novel, assigns all guilt unambiguously to Isabel Carlyle. Her punishment, moreover, has not been excessive, although Isabel Carlyle in Ellen Wood's novel considered it "greater" than she deserved. "Give me strength," she implores heaven in John Oxenford's play, "to bear the punishment I have righteously deserved." Her out-of-touch husband and vicious sister-in-law are pronounced guiltless by Isabel Carlyle herself, who insists unequivocally that "my crime is to be attributed to my own bad suspicious temper."[54] The licensing manuscript of yet another version of *East Lynne* submitted to the Lord Chamberlain in 1875 is typical in its drawn-out death scene, with cries of "Forgive!" and kisses of peace, erasing all mention of the revaluation of Victorian ideas of gender and family toward which Isabel Carlyle points in her dying words in the novel.[55] Even in the novel she can only imagine this refiguring of the family taking place in heaven, but in Edmund Gurney's dramatization, entitled *The New East Lynne* (1898), heaven itself reproduces the Victorian home – for "Paradise," as the playwright calls it, is nothing more than the house of Archibald Carlyle from which Isabel is forever excluded by virtue of her own culpability.[56]

Women novelists like Ellen Wood were even more disadvantaged than their male counterparts by a legal state of affairs which made their work fair game to any playwright who cared to adapt it for the stage unless they first did so themselves, thus securing dramatic copyright. Many male writers – including Dickens as well as Bulwer-Lytton and Reade – enjoyed access to the theatrical world and were experienced dramatists as well as fiction-writers. Women, however – even the most prominent women novelists – could not readily obtain a hearing as playwrights and remained uniquely vulnerable to textual invasions from dramatists until at least 1888.[57] In that year Frances Hodgson Burnett, fresh from her success with *Little Lord Fauntleroy*, was informed by a young London author named E. V. Seebohm that he had rewritten her novel for the stage. He sent a letter to Burnett, then in Italy, letting her know of his play and stating that "I have naturally had to invent a large amount of fresh plot and action in order to develop the dramatic intensity of the theme." But Burnett was unimpressed by this suggestion that adaptation required mysterious powers that the playwright could explain in only a general way to a woman novelist. She replied to Seebohm that "it would be out of the question to expect my consent to the production of a play founded upon my work without the slightest reference to my rights or consultation with me." When the playwright offered Burnett half the profits for her consent, she was tempted but held back, knowing, as she told a friend, that she could accept no money from Seebohm, "if my dear little boy is spoiled." Seebohm tracked down Burnett in Italy to try to persuade her, but in their only meeting she refused point-blank his offer of profit-sharing. The dramatist decided under the circumstances to produce a dramatic version of Burnett's novel without her permission, explaining to her the law on such matters as it was then generally understood:

By the English law any one may adapt for stage representation any novel, story, or tale published either by itself or in a magazine or journal. The author of the story can prevent the play from being printed and sold as a book, but he or she cannot prevent it being acted. The only way in which the author of a story can reserve for himself the stage rights is by dramatizing it and publicly representing it before its publication as a book. As there is no record of your story having been produced as a play previous to its publication as a book, I am afraid, my dear Madam, you cannot reserve for yourself the sole right of dramatizing it.[58]

Subsequent correspondence to *The Times* on this controversy shows that Seebohm's interpretation of the law was not universally accepted in all respects – least of all by Burnett herself. Nevertheless Seebohm's play took the stage at the Prince of Wales's Theatre on 23 February 1888, in defiance of Burnett's wishes, at about the time Burnett herself boarded a train for England with a generous supply of manuscript paper, pencils, and ink and began to write her own play, pointedly entitled *The Real Little Lord Fauntleroy*, while still riding the rails.

Burnett had been victimized in this way before, with unauthorized stage versions of *That Lass o' Lowrie's* and *Editha's Burglar*. This time she consulted lawyers and filed suit in the court of Chancery with Warne, her publishers, named as plaintiffs. While her lawyers complained that Seebohm had stolen the plot, title, and characters, as well as large chunks of dialogue from her novel, dramatic critics noted that Seebohm had damaged the spirit of the original with a third act of mere "commonplace jesting," ending with "the effort of the low comedian to gain laughter at all hazards." Seebohm, too, had neglected the novel's account of the effect young Cedric Errol has on his grandfather, the proud old earl, who learns from the child how to express love and sympathy – he is, as Burnett says, "made into a human being," like Rochester in *Jane Eyre*. In *Little Lord Fauntleroy* the agent of that change is the mother, Mrs. Errol, and Fauntleroy himself, costumed androgynously in lace, bows, and long curling locks, and played by a girl – Annie Hughes in Seebohm's version, Vera Beringer in Burnett's own dramatization. Little Lord Fauntleroy maintains a unique, virtually undifferentiated relation with his mother Mrs. Errol. "Do you *never* forget about your mother?" asks the earl in Burnett's novel. "No," answers young Cedric Fauntleroy – "never; and she never forgets about me."[59] This unbroken communion with his mother, not merely his girlish costume, is what makes Fauntleroy unique – a point that Burnett was careful to make in her own play derived from the novel. "He is not like other children – I am not like other mothers," explains Mrs. Errol in *The Real Little Lord Fauntleroy*. "We could not live apart."[60] The transfiguration of the old earl into this matriarchal family concludes Burnett's novel and her play based on it, while Seebohm's own adaptation ends instead, as one critic put it, with "a climax of clowning."[61]

Produced under the direction of Madge Kendal, *The Real Little Lord Fauntleroy* appeared to some observers to be a distinctively feminine drama, almost beyond the ken of a male audience. Indeed, one of the remarkable features of the play was that it attracted mostly women to Terry's Theatre, as the reviewer for the *Illustrated Sporting and Dramatic News* pointed out:

It was impossible, if you had the misfortune to be of the sex to which my colleague and I belong, not to feel out of place in a gathering so largely and so impressively female. The few individual male visitors, scattered here and there among the mass of womankind, seemed to be no better than intruders, and looked as though they knew it.

At a time when it was still customary for women to attend the theatre in the company of men, rather than alone or with other women, this feminized audience could only seem a striking, even threatening,

4. Annie Hughes as Little Lord Fauntleroy in the "lost" dramatized version of Frances Hodgson Burnett's novel, the Prince of Wales's Theatre, 1888.

5. A drawing of the all-female audience of Terry's Theatre for *Little Lord Fauntleroy*
1888.

anomaly. Clearly many in the house were not regular theatregoers; indeed, the reviewer was certain that he saw "aged gentlewomen at Terry's who had never been to any theatre before." Not only was there a new kind of audience on hand for Burnett's play, but the play itself seemed of a new type – a theatrical enterprise founded upon "strictly regenerative principles." Nor could the reviewer, as a man, react to the play with the "sobs" and "weeping" that women in the audience accorded it. "I did not shed a tear of my own, nor did my colleague," he remarks coolly.[62] When the curtain fell on the production, moreover, the audience was treated to an all-female "pretty picture" – Madge Kendal and Frances Burnett holding hands, each "patting the hand" of Vera Beringer, who played the role of the little lord in the play.

Although no text of Seebohm's play seems to have survived, it is certain that the disastrous final act undermined the emphasis in Burnett's work upon women's feeling and female heroism. A review of Seebohm's play, for example, refers to Mrs. Errol becoming "the nurse of her own child," apparently entering the earl's household in disguise sooner than separate from her son. Lost in this treatment of Mrs. Errol, the reviewer points out, is the "truth, heroism, and self-sacrifice" that distinguish the heroine of Frances Burnett's novel. He adds:

There was only one way to dramatise "Little Lord Fauntleroy" successfully, and that was to sympathise with the grace and tenderness of the tale and to understand the style of the authoress. Mr. Seebohm apparently has pounced upon the work merely to show how little he comprehends it.[63]

The reviewer for *The Sunday Times* also complained of Seebohm's final act, which he said degraded Burnett's "idyll" into material for "the low comedian."[64] Once he had had the opportunity to see Burnett's own dramatization of her novel, the *Sunday Times* reviewer was even less sympathetic to Seebohm's version, which he looked back on with contempt. "Those who knew and valued the book could never quite forgive Mr. Seebohm for his treatment of Mrs. Errol," he wrote. "He dealt with her theatrically," he noted, "but Mrs. Burnett has kept her as she originally conceived her," in particular retaining the novel's emphasis on "the idea of the mother sacrificing her selfish comforts for the child's ultimate good."[65] She gives him up to his grandfather the Earl of Dorincourt for the boy's own benefit, thus initiating the process by which – as the critic for the *Theatre* pointed out – "the old nobleman's nature thaws under the gentle influence and bright honesty and pluck of his little grandson."[66] Another reviewer remarked of Burnett's own dramatization of the novel that "we need hardly say that no attempt is made to degrade the beautiful character of the little lord's mother by representing her as capable of an elaborate deception practised upon the old earl."[67] It was the self-sacrificing heroism of the mother, therefore, that seems to have been most noticeably absent in Seebohm's dramatization of *Little Lord Fauntleroy*.

But we may never know the full extent of Seebohm's attempt to erase Burnett's fiction, turning her own language against herself. Not only did Burnett become the first woman novelist to repel this textual violence with a play of her own – it opened at Terry's Theatre in May 1888, where it was a spectacular success – but she became the first also to erase, quite literally, the male playwright's adaptation. Burnett and her lawyers persuaded the Court of Chancery that Seebohm had violated the Copyright Act by "multiplying copies" of her novel – that is, extracting significant portions of it in the four manuscripts of Seebohm's play, one deposited as required by law with the Lord Chamberlain, the other three used in production of the play at the Prince of Wales's. Seebohm, then, was guilty of unauthorized republication of a book, not of staging a play from a novel without the author's permission. In delivering judgment in the case Mr. Justice Stirling considered himself bound by the precedent established in the lawsuit brought almost twenty-five years before on behalf of another woman novelist, Mary Elizabeth Braddon, in *Tinsley* v. *Lacy*. In that case the publication of an adaptation of Braddon's fiction, although not its performance on stage, was held to be an infringement of copyright because it contained passages of description and dialogue more or less the same as those in the original work.

Seebohm's dramatization of *Little Lord Fauntleroy* had not been and never would be published, but Frances Burnett and her lawyers argued that it had never been decided "that where copies of a work were made for the purpose of representation on the stage that that was not multiplication."[68] Finally, Mr. Justice Stirling ruled in favor of Frances Burnett, granting, as he said, "a perpetual injunction to restrain the defendant from printing or otherwise multiplying copies of his play, containing any passages copied, taken, or colourably altered from the plaintiffs' book, so as to infringe the plaintiffs' copyright in the novel or tale entitled 'Little Lord Fauntleroy.'"[69] Burnett asked, and the court ordered, that all existing manuscript copies of Seebohm's *Little Lord Fauntleroy* be delivered up "for cancellation."

That order was apparently carried out, for today the manuscript of Seebohm's drama is missing from the Lord Chamberlain's file of plays licensed in 1888. Indeed, Burnett and her lawyers succeeded in stopping further performances of Seebohm's play by asking the Lord Chamberlain to "revoke his license for the performance of the play" on the grounds that there would be no licensing manscript on file since the court had ordered it to be "given up" for cancellation. "In these circumstances," Burnett's lawyers wrote to the Examiner of Plays, E. F. S. Pigott, "in order to bring your office into conformity with the order of the court, and as we believe a play cannot be continued to be performed without your retaining a copy of it, it seems obvious that your present license must be withdrawn, and if Mr. Seebohm intends hereafter to continue to perform any version of the...work it will be for him to apply to you for a fresh license and deposit with you a fresh copy." *The Times* reported that in reply to this letter "the Examiner of Plays has agreed to move the Lord Chamberlain to return the copy deposited with him...and to revoke the license for the performance of the play."[70] Four days after judgment against Seebohm had been delivered, Burnett's *The Real Little Lord Fauntleroy* opened at Terry's Theatre on 14 May 1888.

Several months later, in New York City, police discovered the bloated corpse of a well-dressed young Englishman who had swallowed poison and shot himself in the mouth, according to the *New York Times*.[71] He was identified as E. V. Seebohm only by the name that police found under the tailor's tag of his overcoat in his room at the Hoffmann House. Seebohm reportedly had left London on a world tour after the injunction taking his play off the stage in London, and was in New York just when news arrived there of the great success of the opening night in Boston of *The Real Little Lord Fauntleroy*.

"From my brief acquaintance," Burnett told newspaper reporters who asked her reaction to Edward Seebohm's death, "I should not imagine that he was a man to commit suicide." He was, though, and playwrights thereafter became less reckless in plundering the texts of novelists, thanks in large measure to lawsuits brought by Frances Hodgson Burnett in 1888 and Mary Elizabeth Braddon a quarter-century earlier. The importance of Burnett's singlehanded action to retain control over her own text has never been recognized. After her victory in the Court of Chancery, unauthorized adaptations of novels could no longer be lodged safely with the Lord Chamberlain's office for the required licensing. The ruling in Burnett's favor was indeed, as the *Era* pointed out a few months later, "a rude rebuff to pirates," all the more so because it "was followed by a catastrophe in the suicide of the unauthorised adaptor."[72] Burnett's lawsuit against Seebohm "practically secures to a novelist," *The Sunday Times* declared, "the right of dramatising his own story" – a right that would finally become official with the passage of the Copyright Act of 1911.[73]

CHAPTER 6

Victorian plays by women

You make character and exigency all circle about women. Consider the man's view [and] let men dominate.

(Elizabeth Robins, in a note scrawled to herself on the manuscript of *Discretion*, a play she was writing that would never be produced)

Despite arguments that playwriting was beyond their intellectual and linguistic capabilities, women are identifiable as the authors of hundreds of plays staged in London theatres in Victoria's reign.[1] Most of these dramas were never published, however, and none has penetrated the literary or dramatic canon; none of their titles and few of their authors are familiar today. It seems certain, moreover, that a vast, additional number of plays by women was never produced at all, often because their works failed to serve the interests of managers, usually men, who controlled the selection and casting of works for the stage.

Many dramas written by women will always be veiled in anonymity, or disguised by a male pseudonym. As Virginia Woolf speculated about an imagined "sister" of Shakespeare in *A Room of One's Own*: "Undoubtedly, I thought, looking at the shelf where there are no plays by women, her work would have gone unsigned. That refuge she would have sought certainly."[2] Even near the end of the Victorian period, Florence Bell and Elizabeth Robins kept their joint authorship of *Alan's Wife*, staged by the Independent Theatre, a closely guarded secret; the talented Harriett Jay wrote as "Charles Marlowe"; Constance Fletcher renamed herself "George Fleming," and Pearl Marie Craigie was known as "John Oliver Hobbes." Cicely Hamilton recalls having learned early that for a woman writer of a play "it was advisable to conceal the sex of its author until after the notices were out, as plays which were known to be written by women were apt to get a bad press."

Her first play, therefore, she signed in the "indeterminate, abbreviated form, C. Hamilton."[3]

Except for those occasions when their dramas were passed for the work of men, Victorian women who wrote plays competed against male dramatists on an equal basis on only two occasions. Both were open playwriting competitions sponsored by actor-managers in the face of a popular impression that the managers' self-interested choice of dramas had led to the suppression of some excellent writing for the stage. Unknown, untried women playwrights won both of these open playwriting competitions, one near the beginning of the Victorian period, the other at the end. In 1844 Ben Webster – the Haymarket manager known for productions of plays by himself, Dion Boucicault, Mark Lemon, Douglas Jerrold, and John Westland Marston – presented a £500 prize to Catherine Gore for her play entitled *Quid Pro Quo: or, The Day of Dupes*, one of ninety-seven dramas sent in anonymously, as the contest required, and judged by a special committee.[4] In 1902 the Playgoers' Club, with George Alexander and Beerbohm Tree leading the way, staged another open playwriting contest in response to grumblings that the cozy association of actor-managers and "certain well-known dramatists" made it difficult for new playwrights to get a fair hearing. One dramatic critic revealed that "many hundreds of manuscript plays came pouring by every post into the club letter-box," and that a special committee read and considered all of them before judging the best to be *The Finding of Nancy* by Netta Syrett, a woman novelist who by her own account was, like most professional women writers, "absolutely ignorant of the stage."[5] *The Finding of Nancy* was staged at a special matinee at the St. James's Theatre, where it failed as miserably as Catherine Gore's prize play had done at its premiere at the Haymarket more than a half-century earlier.

Catherine Gore attributed the hostile reception given her play on its first performance on 18 June 1844 to several factors, including the "vast expectations" arising from her £500 prize and the organized resentment of rival playwrights at opening night. Also, as she explains in the preface, she had felt compelled to attempt a "broader style" in her drama than she employed as a novelist, influenced by the notion that plays were a "very different species of entertainment" from fictions and required a different kind of writing. Indeed, Gore was writing to the prescription of what William Archer would later call the "conventionally dramatic," a prescription for crises, shocks, and – as Gore puts it in the preface – "exaggeration" or "disproportion" in the drawing of character and incident. The play that resulted is built of secret engagements, lovers' disguises, political corruption, and social-climbing imbeciles who produce one comic débâcle after another. The "custom of the stage" demanded no less, yet at the same time ensured the failure of *Quid Pro Quo* by virtue of the author's being a woman writer. Dramatic critics who were in the main playwrights themselves – and nearly always men – would not allow a woman to succeed in playwriting, Gore believed, and thus influenced popular opinion against her even though she had written a play to their own recipe. A similar fate, after all, had befallen recent women dramatists just before the opening of the Victorian era. The animosity of the theatrical establishment, which Gore observes had "succeeded in condemning the very superior plays of Joanna Baillie, Lady Dacree, and Lady Emmeline Wortley, could scarcely fail to crush any attempt of mine." Gore felt herself besieged, that is, by sinister gatekeepers of the theatre – male critics who, as she says, were also, "almost without exception, rival dramatists," determined that an outsider, and especially a woman, would not be allowed to succeed as a playwright. The fact that *Quid Pro Quo* enjoyed some success in later performances did not alter her opinion in the least.[6]

Many Victorian plays by women are the result of an attempt by their authors to write like men, as Catherine Gore did self-consciously in *Quid Pro Quo*. Gore was merely wearing the mask that Elizabeth Robins would later insist was necessary for any woman writer who hoped for success in any literary genre. "She must wear the aspect that shall have the best chance of pleasing her brothers," Robins's essay "Woman's Secret" declares. "Money, reputation – these are vested in men. If a woman would coin a little at their hands, she must walk warily, and not too much displease them." But playwriting, even more than other literary occupations, was under the control of men, and Gore at the beginning of the Victorian period, like Robins at the end, seems alert to the fact that in drama especially it is "*his* game she is trying her hand at."[7] When women playwrights kept this fact always before them, and wrote accordingly, they sometimes found prestigious managers who produced their plays at leading London theatres. Even a revolutionary like Elizabeth Robins could be tempted down this road. "You make character and exigency all circle about women," she chided herself in a marginal note in the manuscript of an aborted play called *Discretion*; "consider the man's view...Let men dominate."[8] Lady Violet Greville's *Justice*, for example, written in collaboration with Arthur Bourchier for production at the Lyric Theatre in 1892, rationalizes male violence against women by tracing through four tedious and incredible acts how a woman who called on God for "justice – justice – justice!" gradually falls in love with, then marries, the aristocrat who raped her.[9]

But it would be presumptuous to offer sweeping conclusions about the work of Victorian women playwrights, especially given the inaccessibility of the plays themselves – some irretrievably lost behind male pseudonyms, most of them unpublished, some missing even from the Lord Chamberlain's file of licensing manuscripts, and virtually all of them ignored by theatre history and literary criticism. Some tentative observations suggest themselves, however. It seems clear, for example, that the number of women playwrights grew remarkably in the later years of the nineteenth century, from the 1870s onward, as the writing of drama became a more profitable enterprise and the number of theatres in London drastically increased. Barred from at least some theatres by men like Beerbohm Tree – powerful actor-managers who were convinced that women could not write plays – the dramas of women were frequently produced by the few Victorian women stage managers. It was Madge Kendal who staged Frances Hodgson Burnett's smash hit *Little Lord Fauntleroy*, Elizabeth Robins who managed Constance Fletcher's *Mrs. Lessingham*, and Sara Lane of the Britannia Theatre who put on many plays by women, including herself, in the 1870s and 1880s before large working-class audiences in Hoxton. Robins, for the most part, and many other Victorian women dramatists wrote against the masculinist grain of Victorian theatre. Their "anxiety of influence" referred not to any strife between poetic father and son, as in Harold Bloom's patriarchal model of literary history, but rather to women's struggle with the male playwriting and theatrical establishment which actively partook of the authority silencing Victorian women. In this kind of play, women answered the male precursor's "reading" of themselves, and in doing so, therefore, sought new ways in which Victorian theatre and the culture itself could enact gender.

Much of Victorian drama reduces women nearly to the level of properties – ancillary images imprisoned in male-written texts, shaped and constrained by male interpretations. A remarkable instance occurs in the last act of Oscar Wilde's *An Ideal Husband*, when Lord Goring offers this sudden revelation to Gertrude Chiltern:

A man's life is of more value than a woman's. It has larger issues, wider scope, greater ambitions. A woman's life revolves in curves of emotions. It is upon lines of intellect that a man's life progresses...A woman who can keep a man's love, and love him in return, has done all the world wants of women, or should want of them.[10]

Lady Chiltern's own convictions about gender are instantly overturned by this speech, which she repeats parrot-like to bring about the happy conclusion of Wilde's piece. Even plays like *Macbeth*, whose bloodthirsty heroine as played by Charlotte Cushman made the Victorians shudder, could be brought into harmony with the official gospel on the nature of women. Articles appeared in late-century newspapers stating that Lady Macbeth was "a most loving, gentle wife" rather than the horrid woman or monster who was usually represented. Indeed the Lady Macbeth portrayed by Ellen Terry was a woman mild and "essentially feminine," as her son Gordon Craig recalls – a woman who "did her best to keep Macbeth straight, and the failure to do so utterly wrecked her, and she died." This kind of woman – a "feminine" heroine who loved the hero and influenced him for the good – was, as Craig points out, a character "in almost every play then being written." It was the story of *The Lady of Lyons* (1838) told and retold, the story of an unworthy or treacherous man redeemed by his love for a "divine" woman.[11]

This tendency in male-written Victorian drama to read women as being contingent on the husband and home helps explain the obsession with the Cinderella story in dozens of extravaganzas, pantomimes, and plays. Whether in a burlesque version such as H. J. Byron's *Cinderella; or, The Lover, the Lackey and the Little Glass Slipper* (1860) or T. W. Robertson's more sophisticated comedy *School* (1869), the dramatist gestures consciously to Cinderella in narratives showing how women find success, fulfillment, and meaning through men. Robertson's play, which opens with a recitation of "Cinderella" among attentive schoolgirls, concludes with the poor and mistreated Bella, "*discovered as gate opens, dressed as a bride; two footmen attending her,*" announced triumphantly as "Lady Beaufoy!", transfigured into the wife of the aristocratic young hero. "Bella is contented and happy," her new husband tells her former oppressors; "she does not fetch or carry like a servant. She rings bells – she does not answer them." From her husband Bella receives not only social distinction but identity – her name as well as her appearance is changed, realizing H. J. Byron's observation in his Cinderella burlesque that "a good husband" is the "best reward" a young woman can hope for.[12] What happens when women forget or ignore this explanation of who they are, and why, is illustrated in plays like *East Lynne*. In the many stage adaptations of Ellen Wood's novel – unlike the novel itself – the only explanation for Isabel Carlyle's leaving her husband and home is "madness." Her features disfigured and her name changed, the heroine apart from her husband is unrecognizable and grotesque. Her disastrous swerve from the Cinderella story leaves Isabel Carlyle with nothing to look forward to but death, the physical evidence of her own self-erasure in abandoning husband and children.

Plays by Victorian women often tell a different story, but one that has been forgotten or suppressed in histories of the drama of the period – and not only in the histories. As the previous chapter made clear, the Victorians made a conscious effort to persuade themselves that women by nature could not and did not write for the stage, barring a few exceptions which only proved the rule. Aspiring women playwrights, therefore, could have felt little or no sense of a women's tradition in drama. They were creating a tradition where none was recognized, engaging almost inevitably in what Harold Bloom has characterized as "the re-writing of the father" by thinking back through the dramas of prior men in order to create their own. If this was an act of "deliberate misinterpretation" of the male precursor, it obviously could not be contained by Bloom's model of literary history in which new work is created when father and son become locked in an Oedipal struggle.[13] As women, these playwrights struggled against cultural codes which pronounced them incapable of writing plays and narrowed the scope of their activities in a thousand other ways. In their "misreading" of previous dramas by men, women playwrights were reacting less to specific precursor-dramas than to the oppressive codes of gender with which those works as a whole were inscribed.

But the female playwriting tradition which was, despite many denials, being formed in the second part of the nineteenth century amounted to much more than the belated rewriting and reversal of male precursors. Dramas by Victorian women were the product, above all, of the social conditions under which they wrote, even when their habits and training made them compromise with the dominant tradition or led them to doubt whether they were equipped to write plays at all. One result was the kind of work that Sandra Gilbert and Susan Gubar have identified in women's fiction of the period, a discourse with dual voices in which a familiar, authorized story overlies, as in a palimpsest, a deeper and "less socially acceptable" subtext.[14] One striking feature of plays by women, for example, is their departure in many instances from the usual recipe for Victorian drama, in which, as Henry Irving once explained it to a young performer, the actress has only to "appear" and charm the audience with her graceful movements and pretty face. When women wrote plays, the plot frequently centered on heroines or female villains who were violent or mad, or who performed strong and unconventional reinterpretations of their conventional roles as mothers, daughters, and wives. These subversive and passionate characters, like the heroine of *Jane Eyre*, act out the female rebellion that was forbidden in life, often dying extravagantly in the last act to bring the drama into outward conformity, at least, with what the theatre and society itself demanded. Dramas by women often were played out in a purely domestic arena, moreover, without the recurring shocks and conflicts and intersecting "moments of crisis" which for William Archer and other critics were fundamental to any working concept of the "dramatic."[15] The plots and characters of these plays remind us of the social disadvantages under which women wrote as well as of the sexual organization of society as such. In women's dramas social determinants such as these are far more documentable than any biologically influenced literary style, or *"l'écriture féminine,"* the nonlinear "writing with the body" that has been proposed as an essentially female style by Hélène Cixous.

While plays by men typically made women contingent, even when providing a role that (as Shaw put it) "uncorks the eye of the emotional actress," plays by women often discovered larger possibilities in female character and gave it more scope in determining the action. This defining characteristic of Victorian women's writing for the stage crosses the boundaries of time, genre, and class – exhibiting itself in East End melodramas and in productions at the most prestigious theatres, in earlier Victorian drama and in the Ibsenite productions of the 1890s. Despite hesitations and conflicts, often discernible in the plays themselves, women writers as a group drew female character with more depth, complexity, and strength than the more conventional interpretations of women found in plays by men. The central characters in plays by women are usually female, and it is women whose heroism determines the outcome of the action. In *The Cruel Kindness*, a blank-verse drama staged at the Haymarket in 1853, dramatist Catherine Crowe presents a heroine, Viola, who rescues an innocent young woman from jail and a decree of death when she exchanges clothing and identities with the prisoner. In a "foul cell" the heroine gives up her cloak to the wrongly accused Florentia, who proceeds safely outside the prison walls while her rescuer remains in the cell to play the part of the condemned woman.[16] Several years before the appearance of *A Tale of Two Cities*, therefore, the play by Catherine Crowe anticipates Dickens's narrative of heroic self-sacrifice in a prison setting, but with women enacting the central roles rather than being the spectators and background figures that they would become in the famous novel.

But the strength of female characters in plays written by women was not always so benign as in Catherine Crowe's *The Cruel Kindness*. In *The Woman of the World* by Clara Cavendish, staged at the Queen's Theatre in 1858, raven-haired, Indian-born Lisa Selby dominates the action by becoming a forger, thief, and accessory to murder to satisfy her ambitions of wealth and control. "I feel that I was born for joy – for power," she exults early in the second act, laying the foundation for her crimes; "– I – I – oh, my brain goes dizzy at the mere thought of such delight." Lisa Selby's quest for pleasure and power is made to conform with social morality, outwardly at least, when the dark-skinned antiheroine declares herself unhappy, bursts a blood vessel, and dies at the final curtain. A benevolent uncle extracts the moral lesson by contrasting the stricken Lisa with her fair and amiable cousin Joanna, "single-minded, truthful, and loving," yet a marginal figure in this play dominated by her energetic and unscrupulous kinswoman.[17]

In a later, more sophisticated play, *A Long Duel* (1901) by Mrs. Lucy Lane Clifford, performed at the Garrick Theatre, the heroine is ageing, selfish, cruel, and ambitious. Before the final curtain, however, she instructs the artist she loves in the inaccuracy of male readings of women – including the idealized portrait he has painted of her:

I am a worldling...and a fool – both...and if I am worldly I am human – if I am old...my heart is young, it is singing for joy now, like a girl's, though the tears force themselves (*dashing them away*) to my eyes – You don't understand, but no man does – the contradictions in a woman.[18]

Among these "contradictions in a woman" is the existence of qualities coded by the dominant culture as masculine – an androgynous mixture that many Victorian plays by women dramatize. In *Nurse!* (1900), a comedy by Clo Graves, the heroine's appropriation of masculine dress and directness in speech and behavior continue unabated to the final curtain, blending easily into the romantic attraction she exerts over a frail, self-indulgent young man whose character she manages to transform. By the end of the play Dorothy Finch and her rehabilitated male patient have met one another halfway on a continuum of gender, in a zone distinctly neither male nor female.

Of the traditionally "masculine" characteristics of Victorian stage heroines drawn by women writers, one of the most striking is the capacity they display for violence – a violence often anchored in their intensity of feeling as wives, mothers, and sisters. In *A Physician* by Clo Graves (1893), a young wife picks up a whip and cuts her would-be seducer "*stingingly across the face*," then cooly breaks the whip across her knee and tosses it into the fireplace.[19] The heroine of *Mabel's Curse!*, a melodrama by Maria Hall, has been driven mad by the murder of her son, a madness which has given her, however, "the sacred power...to bless or curse."[20] Powerful and feared, the heroine of this play staged in 1837 at the St. James's Theatre leads a band of marauders against her enemies and levels a curse against the man who killed her son – with the result that his own sons are doomed to death. Mad Mabel's death at the final curtain allows the playwright to concede something to conventional views about women without cancelling the effects of her heroine's madness and rebellion. In a later melodrama staged at the Standard Theatre, *The Wife's Tragedy* (1870) by a woman playwright known only as Mrs. Edward Thomas, the heroine gleams "like a flame of hell" as she excoriates the Duke of Beauvais for having killed her husband in order to make her his wife. The unhappy duchess has the duke arrested, then leaves in his cell a dagger with which he ultimately commits suicide while she proceeds to the river bank and plunges "headlong in" – thus embracing, like many violent heroines in Victorian plays by women, a death which to some degree neutralizes her unconventional behavior and renders it palatable for the stage.[21]

At theatres such as the Standard, where *The Wife's Tragedy* was produced, audiences composed mainly of working-class people were accustomed to dramas which adopted an adversarial perspective of employers, landlords, and aristocrats. Thousands of spectators jammed into these vast auditoriums for as little as 3 pence each to see productions that often reflected their own experience with problems ranging from urban poverty and homelessness, class antagonism, and industrial strife. The working-class audience could release its pent-up resentments, vicariously at least, through the humiliation and violence inflicted upon the elite. Moreover, the oppositional tone of these entertainments and their audiences made the representation of women's heroism and violence less problematic than it would have been in more exclusive theatres where dominant codes of gender were more rigorously enforced. At playhouses like the Standard and the Britannia, furthermore, playwriting remained to the end of the century far less remunerative than in the West End, and the profession of dramatic authorship less exclusive than in more prestigious venues. Men dominated playwriting everywhere, but women clearly found more success in getting their dramas staged in theatres where the audience was predominantly working-class.

No woman was better at building a successful career on the East End stage than Sara Lane, the impresario of the Britannia Theatre in dingy Hoxton after she succeeded her husband upon his death. The plays in which she acted – many of which she wrote, had a hand in writing, or adapted herself, and all of which were staged in the theatre where she presided as manager – concerned themselves in various ways with the representation of female violence and heroism. None of her plays appears to have been published, but the licensing manuscripts are written in a blunt, breathless style and with a hasty penmanship that left little room for the niceties of punctuation. In *Red Josephine* (1880), for example, she creates a heroine who in the opening scene watches her son being stabbed by robbers, then is assaulted herself as the villain *"drags her about strikes her on forehead."* The assaulted heroine struggles bravely, upsets a chair in her adversary's path, and bites him on the hand, eventually freeing herself to pursue revenge later on. This she accomplishes in the fourth act when she surprises the villain and *"seizes him by shirt collar,"* as the stage directions say, then *"stabs him twice in the breast"* while his own mother looks on, horrified. Roc, the villain, screams "Farewell Mother," and the heroine, calling herself "Red Josephine," shrieks triumphantly. Then she falls and dies – unsurprisingly, although without warning or any apparent medical cause – as the final curtain descends.[22]

The title page of the ms. of another play, *Faithless Wife* (1876), identifies Sara Lane as having "translated and adapted" the play "from the French," although the source drama is not identified.[23] Whether author or dramaturge, Lane was engaged in performing, writing, and producing dramas for which there was no model in the English theatre – dramas with magnetic, heroic women whose depths of character gave the actress a professional opportunity that rarely arose in native drama by men. These dramas credited to Sara Lane often add a wife's infidelity to her appetite for violence and displays of physical heroism, thus creating a sexually raw and physically dangerous heroine of the type rarely if ever seen in West End productions at the time. In *Dolores* (1874) – an adaptation of Victorien Sardou's *La Patrie* – the title character describes how she set fire to a house, burning alive the soldiers who beat her husband and raped her daughter. "I burnt them aye burnt them alive you hear," cries Dolores; "I listened to them...howling and blaspheming through the flames and I laughed." Her only wish, as she tells a tribunal of the dead soldiers' comrades, is that she had been able to kill all of them, "to pull out your hearts with my nails, and tear them with my teeth." Meanwhile Dolores has betrayed the husband she violently avenged, committing adultery with his best friend and thus driving her spouse to suicide. Her lover Karlos, overwhelmed and frightened, curses Dolores before he kills her with his own hands and then commits suicide himself in the final scene.[24]

But when female heroism was less aggressive, more idealized and domesticated, the plays in which it appeared could be staged in prestigious theatres and the leading role enacted by respected actresses such as Mary Anderson and Anna Cora Mowatt. Both of these women, in fact, played the heroine in *Ingomar the Barbarian*, adapted by Maria Lovell from the German and staged at Drury Lane in 1851 before being revived several times through at least the 1880s. Parthenia, whom Anna Cora Mowatt called "one of my favorite embodiments," is a commanding figure among violent men without ever resorting to violence herself.[25] In the first act she rushes off to the mountains to rescue her father when he is kidnapped by the Allemani, a tribe armed with spears and clad in wolf skins. "A woman in heart, a man in courage," Parthenia offers herself as a hostage to Ingomar, leader of the barbaric Allemani, in return for her father's freedom. First, however, she must overcome Ingomar's prejudice that women are "born to bear, and serve," as he says, "to oil their hair, and look at themselves in brooks," mere objects of purchase for a warrior like himself. When Parthenia, however, expounds romantic love to Ingomar – "two souls with but a single thought, two hearts that beat as one" – he begins to undergo a change which results in his giving up the leadership of the Allemani and falling in love with Parthenia. Part of the task of civilizing Ingomar is to temper his rough masculinity with a measure of the feminine, and in the process the heroine takes on some of the accoutrements of the masculine. Thus he casts off his wolf-skin, shaves his beard, and surrenders his sword to Parthenia – "trust me with it now," she says reassuringly as their journey across the mountains nears its conclusion in Act III and Ingomar is about to begin a new life as a Grecian and the husband of Parthenia.

Parthenia may exhibit physical courage and take over the sword and shield of a warrior, but in the end, as Mowatt says herself, this is no "'woman's rights' drama." By arming herself, moving amid scenes of violence, and demonstrating bravery, Parthenia appropriates some traditional masculine properties even as she guides Ingomar's makeover into "a woman," as his fellow barbarians refer to their newly feminized chieftan. "I liked the play," Anna Mowatt explains, "on account of its thorough exemplification of woman's mysterious influence over the sterner sex." Rather than announcing a revolutionary upheaval in gender roles, however, Maria Lovell's play softens male aggression without challenging the traditional definitions of male and female and the social structures which underpin them. In the final act Parthenia acknowledges her inferiority, sinking "down into the dust" before Ingomar, who is made the "Timarch of a new city" and, having learned his lesson well, reminds his new wife that they are not slave and master, but rather "two hearts that beat as one."[26] As Mowatt says in her autobiography, the play finally does little to undermine male supremacy. "Few men," she writes, "would object to the very obvious right of women to *Parthenia-ize* without seriously trenching on their sphere of action."[27] Some did object, however, including the critic of the drama yearbook *Echoes of the Year 1883*, who writes of *Ingomar the Barbarian* as a "preposterous" and "imbecile" drama, offended above all that "the concrete idea which underlies the whole story of 'Ingomar' is that of the subjection of Man to the weaker sex."[28] But Mary Anderson stunned audiences as Parthenia in that revival, her London début, "superb in her beauty, and winning in her childlike loveliness." Thus it was Anderson who won all the praise on that occasion while Maria Lovell's blank-verse drama about the taming, if not exactly the subjection, of the male was "almost unanimously" condemned as romantic and absurd.[29]

The association of women and violence in earlier Victorian plays by women was carried on into the "new" drama by women playwrights in the 1890s, where it tended to be presented within the context of a social problem and, as such, more thoughtfully rationalized. Although the heroines of these late-Victorian plays display on many occasions the power and aggression of female characters in earlier dramas by women, they often resonate with a psychological complexity which is more fully elaborated than in their precursors. They also confront more straightforwardly the social codes which women's plays of an earlier date called into question by implication more than direct challenge. In *The Mirkwater*, for example, written by Elizabeth Robins in the early 1890s, Felicia Vincent assists her sister, incurably ill with breast cancer, in committing suicide by drowning. "I did all I could to dissuade her – and then – all that love could do to help," Felicia Vincent says just before policemen arrive at the final curtain to arrest her for murder. In

Robins's play the suicidal Mary Vincent displayed a beauty before she fell ill that "frightened men rather than attracted them," and her nature was such that women brought their troubles to her and leaned on her. "It was her evil fate," as Felicia Vincent says of her sister, "to hear too much of the sufferings of women, & to see men – only through women's eyes." Her own father sometimes turned pale in her presence, sensing accurately that Mary was capable of killing him for his mistreatment of her mother. Instead of the usual script that called for women loving men, or dying for them, Robins's play presents women who have given up on men and, like Felicia Vincent, "don't believe in the love that through all – in spite of all – stands fast till we die." The love that comes closest to the "perfect thing" that Felicia Vincent imagines in *The Mirkwater* exists only between women, a bond too powerful to be constrained by the law or by the opinions of those who judge them as outcasts from "decent society."[30] Thus abandoning erotic love for a concern with breast cancer and assisted suicide, *The Mirkwater* unsurprisingly found no producer – although George Alexander, before declining, considered staging it in exchange for total rights to the play.[31] It remains unproduced and unpublished, a monument to the difficulties that overwhelmed women playwrights when they placed unconventional heroines at the center of their work.

Also unproduced and unpublished was Florence Bell's *Stella*, written in the early 1890s and focusing on a heroine known as "a type of perfect womanhood" to the magistrate she is engaged to marry. Although one character is repelled by the title character on the grounds that "I don't think women ought to be too intelligent," her husband, as he becomes in due course, believes that in modern times women must be allowed a scope for accomplishment that previously they were denied. "In these days," he remarks, "one must allow a woman to have a future, but she must not have a past." It is the "past" of Stella de Chauvannes that, for all her intelligence, she cannot overcome. Her love-letters to another man have fallen into the hands of a woman determined to send them to Stella's husband, and in an ensuing struggle between the two women Stella stabs her adversary to death with a knife. The curtain speech of the heroine, exposed to her magistrate husband, emphasizes the lack of control that she has been able to exert over her own life in an age which is supposed to allow women a "future." "It is some blind desperate Power," she cries, "that chooses to give one woman happiness, and to another an eternity of despair."[32]

Violence or madness thus become in many of these plays by women a last resort for redressing a conspiracy of the institutions of society to thwart their liberty and happiness. Estelle Burney's *Settled Out of Court*, produced at the Globe in 1897, takes for its main character a woman who in the first act leaves the husband who "never loved me, his heart is on his work." Eventually she becomes the wife of the man she elopes with, only to be overcome within a short time by her daughter's death and her new husband's unfaithfulness. "They don't think of these things in our Courts," reflects Moyra Delacourt, who takes matters into her own hands, appoints herself God's executioner, and with a mad but "almost happy" laugh attacks her husband with a knife at the final curtain.[33] The legal but unscrupulous behavior of men forms the background also for *Mrs. Lessingham*, Constance Fletcher's play of 1894 in which the title character turns her violent impulses against herself. Gladys Lessingham, who suffered at the hands of an abusive husband, left him to live with another man whom she eventually marries. When she learns of his attachment to someone else – a "good woman" who represents for him "the ideal" – Gladys Lessingham takes poison and dies, perceiving that in her world women receive no "second chance."[34] Although a casualty at last, Mrs. Lessingham, like other late-nineteenth century heroines of violent tendencies, interrogated social attitudes toward women and provided an actress with a rare opportunity to represent a character of depth and power. The play ran for thirty-three performances at the Garrick Theatre, making it one of the more successful productions of a woman's play in the late Victorian period.

Like plays written by men, Victorian plays by women are preoccupied with motherhood and domesticity – but in a way that deepens and complicates the vision of maternity presented on stage in *East Lynne* and its many imitators. In the male-authored stage plays based on Ellen Wood's novel, unlike the novel itself, no rational explanation or excuse can be found for the "madness" of a wife and mother who abandons her home. Even in *Lady Windermere's Fan*, in which Oscar Wilde set out to resist a single ideal of motherhood for all women, the views promulgated in *East Lynne* and in society at large prove irresistible. Lady Windermere, on the brink of deserting her husband and child to go away with another man, is advised against it in no uncertain terms by Mrs. Erlynne, her mother, who years ago did the same thing herself:

Back to your house, Lady Windermere – your husband loves you! He has never swerved for a moment from the love he bears you. But even if he had a thousand loves, you must stay with your child. If he was harsh to you, you must stay with your child. If he ill-treated you, you must stay with your child. If he abandoned you, your place is with your child.[35]

Many plays by women, however, avoid the polarized choice between being a "good" or "bad" mother – between living entirely for her family or abandoning it altogether. Women playwrights devise morally ambiguous scenarios in which this patriarchal version of maternity is tested and found wanting. Indeed, plays by Victorian women suggest that circumstances redefine motherhood for every woman, and that even a choice to leave the child, or kill it for that matter, could in some situations be justified or at least imagined without condemnation. These dramatic revisionings of maternity occur especially in plays that were written near the end of the century when conventional ideas of motherhood were coming under increasing scrutiny.

In *Alan's Wife*, the collaborative effort of Florence Bell and Elizabeth Robins staged by the Independent Theatre in 1892, Jean Creyke finds the "courage," as she calls it, to end the life of her "hideous and maimed" infant. "I've had courage just once in my life – just once in my life I've been strong and kind," this woman reflects, " – and it was the night I killed my child."[36] In Aimée (Mrs. Oscar) Beringer's *Tares* (1887), produced at the Prince of Wales's and later at the Opéra-Comique, motherhood is a matter of individual temperament, not biology, and there are women unsuited for it. The action turns on Mrs. Stanhope's recognition that although she gave birth to a son seven years ago, she has no right to take him from the woman who has loved and cared for him since. "He does not love you – you do not love him," points out Margaret Gyde, a "real" mother without having given birth; "my heart is wrapped up in him – he has become part of my life – bone of my bone – flesh of my flesh."[37] The right thing for the biological mother to do in this misprision of *East Lynne* is to turn her back on her child, which she does, although at considerable cost to herself.

Another of Beringer's plays, *Bess* (1891), depicts a woman who confesses to a murder she did not commit in order to protect her son, the actual perpetrator of the crime. To preserve her home and family, the once "model wife and loving mother" leaves them for a prison cell, forgotten by the son for whom she made this sacrifice, scorned by her daughter and husband. By the final curtain, however, the "many tearful eyes" in the audience gave testimony to the fact that Bess had proven herself most a mother when she left her children and husband, assuming for their sakes a guilt not her own.[38] In *Men and Women* (1882), by a woman identified only as Mrs. Reginald Fairburn and staged at the working-class Surrey Theatre, a poverty-stricken young mother, homeless, friendless, and deserted by her husband, determines that to abandon her infant daughter to the care of others is the only way to save her. Sooner than let her infant starve, she bids that it be taken from her "fainting arms, & left it, when, as she thought, she should never see it again."[39]

The actress and title character of *Thyrza Fleming* (1894), a play by Dorothy Leighton staged by the Independent Theatre, left her husband years ago "simply...to be free. He had hideous ideas of woman's duty." In a scene reminiscent of *Lady Windermere's Fan*, Thyrza Fleming is brought into contact with the daughter she abandoned at the same time she left her husband. The mother who absconded, as in Wilde's play, tries to persuade the daughter not to leave her own family, having reversed her position that a mother owes a higher duty to herself than to her child. "I suppose it was all a mistaken view of duty," Thyrza Fleming announces tentatively in the fourth act. "I begin to see that the true self of a woman never can be developed at the expense of those who look to her for love and tenderness, and that self-development is generally an excuse for self-indulgence." But the daughter, who has been ignorant of her true relation to Thyrza Fleming, learns in the last scene that the actress is her mother. Distraught at the revelation of her "fearful secret," the actress seizes a pistol with the intent of killing herself, but is stopped when her daughter rushes forward, flings her arms round her, and speaks the last word of the play with the wild cry of "MOTHER!"[40] Although the title character has renounced her own, supposedly unmotherly, behavior of years past, the emotional reconciliation at the final curtain stands in marked contrast to the conclusion of Oscar Wilde's play about a similar set of characters and circumstances. In *Lady Windermere's Fan* the daughter is left unaware that the older woman who has befriended her, and persuaded her not to leave her family, is in fact the mother who years ago left her own child and husband for a lover. Dorothy Leighton, in laying out a similar narrative, has the daughter recognize her mother's behavior and forgive it, thus charting a course between Wilde's narrative, in which the mother's secret is kept, and that of older, male-authored melodramas such as *East Lynne* in which it is disclosed but with terrible results.

A woman revises conventional ideas of motherhood even more emphatically in Blanche Crackanthorpe's *The Turn of the Wheel* (1901), a play banned from the stage by the Lord Chamberlain's office. Its central character, Isabel Broadwood, can find compassion only from another woman when her child is born out of wedlock. "A woman's measure is not the same as a man's," says a friend; "by a woman's measure Isabel needs little forgiveness." By contrast a "man's measure" is exemplified by Isabel Broadwood's father: "I can't breathe in the same room with her," he exclaims; "– take her out of my sight – and when I know the man, by God, I'll deal with *him*!" What accounted for the Lord Chamberlain's banning of *The Turn of the Wheel*, however, was probably the central character's lack of repentance and, above all, her unwillingness to play the role of a mother, even after the birth of her son. "I care nothing for the child," she remarks in the second act of Crackanthorpe's play; "– I don't even care enough for it to hate it. Let it live, let it die, what does it signify to me? It's not me – it's not part of me, I tell you – I've done with it."[41] Although Isabel Broadwood experiences some change of heart in the last act, the representation of a woman with such iconoclastic views of motherhood was still impossible on the English stage at the conclusion of the Victorian period.

Although they differ from one another radically, these dramatizations of motherhood by women playwrights share to varying degrees a flexibility and openness that resist both law and custom. Heroines such as these – women who aspire to a vocation or mode of life that lies outside the roles of wife and mother – are increasingly common toward the end of the nineteenth century. "A woman should learn to be a good wife, a good mother even," says a character in Florence Bell's drama of 1895, *The Dean of St. Patrick's*, "and let her leave the rest to Providence and her husband." But the heroine of this unpublished, unproduced play on Esther Vanhomrigh, the friend of Jonathan Swift, is determined to become a scholar – "to learn things that a woman's mind was never constructed to understand."[42] In a different register, but with a similar emphasis on expanded choices of life for women, a dramatist known only as Mrs. Musgrave creates as her central character in another unpublished play, *Cerise and Co.* (1890), a female shopkeeper, "a woman of superior ability – independent and capable." She is precisely "the sort of woman I can't bear," says the male lead in this comedy produced at the Prince of Wales's Theatre, who prefers "fine ladies who are helpless."[43] The central character of *Nurse!*, a comedy by Clo Graves staged at the Globe Theatre in 1900, is a career woman "with great self-possession and an air of professional coolness and resolution." Wearing a masculine Inverness cap, Dorothy Finch defines herself in terms of her profession rather than her gender in order to escape the limitations imposed upon "nice" ladies at the turn of the century. "I don't call myself a lady," she declares, "– I call myself a nurse."[44]

In another unpublished comedy called *The Masterpiece* (1893) the main character is an aspiring playwright, Lucy Bromley, whose writing astonishes the husband who imagines she has "no desires, no ambitions beyond the household groove." When he learns of Lucy's playwriting, the husband, himself an aspiring but unproduced dramatic author, reacts incredulously:

BROMLEY – You, Lucy, have written a play?
MRS. BROMLEY – And why not?
BROMLEY – What do you know about it?
MRS. BROMLEY – Everything.
BROMLEY – That's a great deal, certainly.
MRS. BROMLEY – Besides, if you come to that, what do you know about it?
BROMLEY – I? I'm a man. That's different.

The Masterpiece concludes with the heroine made over, through her own efforts, into a collaborator in playwriting with her husband, who follows her lead in drafting the scenario for their first joint effort and sighs for the old days "when my wife was humdrum & domestic."[45]

In addition to these plays in which women dramatize their own lives rather than allowing men to make them into what they are or will become, many other late-century plays by women function in some way to critique the Cinderella story head-on, illuminating the limitations of the marriage-plot for women. In *Cinders* (1899), a one-act play by Lily Tinsley that apparently was never produced professionally, the heroine is a maid of all work who declines the hero's spontaneous offer to "marry you and educate you up to my standard." But the idea of his marrying a work girl and making her into a "lady," she tells him before the curtain, "would be a bit too rediclous. [*little laugh*] Jest as if I didn't know yer was only a-jokin'!"[46] There will be no transformation scene for Cinders, no benevolent prince to translate her mean existence into one of dependent ease – and this by her own choice, however hesitant.

Another woman's play in which the heroine declines a transformation in the mode of Cinderella is *The Showman's Daughter*, by Frances Hodgson Burnett, staged at the Royalty Theatre on 6 January 1892. The title character decides not to be a lady in the usual sense once she understands that the sacrifices of her father, a common showman, have made it possible for her to live in good society. When she meets her father after a long separation, she acts out a reversal of the Cinderella transformation, taking off her finery for the simple dress of a common girl. "Not a lady!" cries the showman's daughter. "Look at my clothes! I put all my fine things away! What right had I to be a lady and spend whole years away from you! I don't want to be a lady – I want to be your girl & stay here with you & show you how I love you – the girl who is your daughter *is* a lady!" She becomes engaged in the final act, but only after redefining herself, and what it means to be a "lady."[47]

Janet Achurch, who caused a sensation in her performance as Nora in *A Doll's House*, created her own anti-Cinderella in *Mrs. Daintree's Daughter*, written at about the same time as Shaw's *Mrs. Warren's Profession* and with a heroine who, as in Shaw's play, learns that the source of her mother's money is prostitution. Instead of feeling revulsion, like Vivie in Shaw's play, the less fastidious Violet in *Mrs. Daintree's Daughter* eagerly embraces the business herself as her own entree to wealth and fashion. She will do so under the sponsorship of the unscrupulous Howarth, the Crofts of Janet Achurch's play, who sneeringly refers to the ambitious Violet as "quite a Cinderella."[48] This surprising conjunction of prostitution and Cinderella in Achurch's play – produced only once, in Manchester – looms ominously as well in other dramas written by women. "I ought to be happy," says an unhappy wife in Clo Graves and Gertrude Kingston's *A Matchmaker* (1896), staged at the Shaftesbury Theatre, but "these princely pearls for which I sold myself lie cold upon my heart – like frozen tears. I seem to the world a woman smiling in a paradise of rich possessions, and all the while I'm a soul in hell."[49] One reviewer found *A Matchmaker* "nothing short of offensive," regretting especially that some of its more disturbing lines, presumably those equating marriage to prostitution, "have been written by women."[50]

Despite their tendency to assert a more various and powerful femininity than was customary in Victorian drama, plays by women in this period are often full of hesitations, second-guessing, and self-betrayal. *The Ambassador* (1898), by Pearl Marie Craigie – or John Oliver Hobbes, as she signed herself – enjoyed a long run at the St. James Theatre with its story of a 19-year-old heroine, "a little thing without a shilling" and without social position.[51] Juliet Gainsborough, however, fascinates the aristocratic St. Orbyn, played by George Alexander, and, after a series of misunderstandings that tests her "innocence" and sincerity, walks away with him in the fourth act. Finding happiness, wealth, and meaning through a man, dissolving herself into his life, the heroine of *The Ambassador* re-enacts the motif of transformation through marriage which is at the heart of the Cinderella story. This uncritical rescripting of the marriage-plot in a polite setting also reified the attitudes of the exclusive audience before which it was performed. The reviewer for the *Era*, for example, wrote of this society drama that it turned the stage of the St. James's Theatre into "an idealised and improved reflection of the stalls," and moreover that the likeness was a flattering one. In dramatizing her audience rather than writing with her own voice, creating a heroine without a self, Pearl Marie Craigie wrote a typical Victorian drama which was staged in one of London's most prestigious theatres with the certainty, as the *Era* said after its opening night, of having a "long run."[52]

It was predictable that Pearl Craigie, who once expressed doubt in a published interview that women could write good plays, should turn out a popular success for the stage by imitating the work of her male precursors. More surprising is the fact that Mary Elizabeth Braddon, author of *Lady Audley's Secret*, could have written the appallingly conventional blank-verse drama *Griselda; or, the Patient Wife*, produced at the Princess's Theatre in 1873. This insipid, unpublished script belongs to a genre of "copy texts" that has been said to re-enact male writing and male readings of the feminine.[53] Its heroine, a peasant's daughter, endures a series of torments at the hands of her husband the Marquis of Saluzzo, indignities more or less similar to those figuring in the traditional medieval stories of Griselda. Announcing its theme with the question "What should a woman bear?", Braddon's play answers, in effect, "everything" – even the wife's expulsion from her home and the kidnaping of her child. Griselda expresses her willingness, after the kidnaping, to visit the woman whom she believes her husband is about to marry and bring into the palace as his new wife. Griselda's incredible "patience," her unwavering loyalty to the man who tortured her throughout three interminable acts, is rewarded in the fourth when he reveals that these trials have been only a test to prove the heroine "that most angelic mortal, a perfect woman."[54] In *Griselda* there is no trace of the violence – acts of murder, arson, and the like – that women perpetrate in Braddon's fictional texts when they are silenced and confined. Equally surprising is that the New Woman novelist Sarah Grand could have co-authored *The Fear of Robert Clive*, a hymn to colonialism staged with an all-male cast at the Lyceum Theatre in 1896. With a quarrelsome ensign pointing a handgun at him, the young Robert Clive displays a bravery and "fear" of dishonor that, as one character exclaims, "might give us India!"[55]

Even such a delightful, although forgotten, play as Clo Graves's *A Mother of Three* (1896) introduces a heroine who assumes masculine dress

6. A production photograph from *A Mother of Three*, 1893, with Fanny Brough as the title character crossdressed as her own husband in the hit play by Clotilde Graves.

and authority – masquerading as her own husband – but at the end of the play longs to "cast these awful responsibilities from me, and be my dear old self again." From the opening scene, wrote the critic for the *Sketch*, the question was whether a woman playwright could do justice to a story in which a mother takes on the identity of her vanished husband in order to advance the fortunes of herself and the three daughters he left behind. "Is the rest of the play," he asked after Fanny Brough first appeared in trousers, "merely to be a 'Charley's Aunt' with sexes reversed...[or] has Miss Clo Graves the constructive skill to build up a plot on the well-worn theme of the troubles of a human being disguised in the clothes of the other sex?" Although this critic ultimately answered his own question in the negative, the press in general was enthusiastic about the "clever and well-written play" which drew large crowds to the Comedy Theatre night after night.[56] The scenes which drew the loudest laughter were those in which Fanny Brough, as Mrs. Murgatroyd, wore wig and trousers to pass herself off as the father of her three marriageable daughters – thus providing them with a "certificate of respectability." The return of the real father in the final act, however, not only throws matters into confusion, but awakens him belatedly to his own "neglected responsibilities." Recognizing his duty to assist his wife at last "in the discharge of her domestic duties," the absent father takes on a feminized aspect just as his wife had earlier put on the clothing as well as the responsibilities of a man. Clo Graves's farcical comedy thus concludes with a collaboration of masculine and feminine, an elision worked out in the masculinized dress and behavior of Mrs. Murgatroyd and, in the final scenes, the feminization of her long-absent spouse.

A Mother of Three was the work of a woman who, as *The Times* reported in its obituary of Clo Graves, "quite early...adopted an almost masculine appearance and dress."[57] In general women who wrote for the Victorian stage were casting *themselves* in a transvestite role in effect, so it is not surprising that their work sometimes reflects the same nostalgia for "petticoats" and "Woman's true sphere" that haunts the heroine of *A Mother of Three*.[58] Clo Graves's witty farce about a strong mother who claims as her own the rights and responsibilities of Victorian fatherhood may be conflicted and even compromised at the final curtain, but in its transgression of "the boundaries of Woman's true sphere," as the heroine puts it, this play and others by women form a notable, although forgotten disruption of Victorian theatre.

That disruption was exemplified at the close of the Victorian period with the production of a play by Netta Syrett, a novelist who entered a playwriting competition "open to the whole of Great Britain."[59] Sponsored by the Playgoers' Club, some of whose members had complained that actor-managers invariably went to established dramatists for their plays, this contest ended with the same result as its predecessor conducted by Ben Webster of the Haymarket Theatre almost sixty years earlier – it was won by a woman. Like Catherine Gore when she wrote the prize play of 1844, Netta Syrett had never before written a full-length play, but was an experienced novelist. Like Gore, moreover, Syrett's play was given a production with an all-star cast in a distinguished theatre – the St. James's in this case – but with results that were dismaying to the playwright. Her play, *The Finding of Nancy* (1902), concerns the cramped life of Nancy Thistleton, a lonely single woman who works as a secretary in a business office. "Or do we and thousands of women like us live at all?" the title character asks a friend, who answers "you are right; it isn't life ... nothing happens...nothing ever *will* happen." Wanting to live, wanting "anything but just *nothing* – blankness," Nancy Thistleton becomes involved with a married man who is separated from an alcoholic wife. Although, as she says, "I haven't kept the rules of the game," the final curtain finds the heroine in the arms of her ineligible lover, looking forward to a lifetime of happiness.[60] A narrative such as this was not only unfamiliar to the powers that ruled Victorian theatre, but certain to offend their sense of propriety and notions of good playwriting. Clement Scott, the influential critic of the *Daily Telegraph* and devotee of Ellen Terry and Henry Irving, wrote in almost hysterical terms of what he regarded as the play's immorality and the culpability of the woman who wrote it. In the ensuing uproar, and as a result of Scott's diatribe – or so Netta Syrett believed – the first-time playwright was fired from a teaching position she held to supplement her work as a writer. During the production itself, the morality of the play was a contentious issue between Syrett and George Alexander, the manager of the St. James's who had agreed to produce the prize play and act in it along with Beerbohm Tree. "He wanted me to cut out some gossip about the heroine in one of the parts, on the ground that no nice woman would say such things," recalls Syrett in her autobiography. "But she isn't meant to be a nice woman," the playwright responded. "Then," said Alexander, "I don't think Miss So-and-So can play the part," sounding the words with a note of righteous rebuke, according to Syrett. Faced with the loss of a leading lady because she refused to alter the play to Alexander's specifications, Netta Syrett was left to find her own actress, who turned out to be Lilian

Braithwaite. After the single matinee performance that *The Finding of Nancy* was promised, Alexander, impressed despite his misgivings, intended to put the play on for a run of afternoon performances. At the last moment, recalls Syrett, he was dissuaded, on the ground that to do so would be to "sully the purity of the St. James's Theatre."[61]

As for the critics, with the exception of Max Beerbohm they found the play to be not only offensive but flawed as drama by virtue of its female perspective. Beerbohm, writing in the *Saturday Review*, was effusive, at least about the opening of the play with its dramatization of the plight of an unattached working woman:

> I do not hesitate to say that in my time there has been nothing so interesting, so impressive, so poignant, as the first act of Miss Syrett's play...that first act, in its simple strength, is enough to make her in my eyes a more important person than a score of ordinary fashionable dramatists rolled into one.

The Finding of Nancy, he explains, "gives the impression (so rare in the theatre) of something that really matters."[62] Other reviewers, however, could only perceive that Syrett's play failed to observe the prescribed formulas, above all by adopting a woman's point of view. "The play is written not only by a lady – Miss Netta Syrett – but for ladies," *The Times* complained. "That is to say, it assumes as a matter of course that the great interest for all of us in life, the thing we want most to hear about, and that we go to the play to see, is the career of woman, or rather, to adopt Flaubert's phrase, her 'sentimental education.'" *The Times* admitted that it is natural – "perhaps almost inevitable" – that a woman writer should take this outlook, "but it is a mistake nevertheless." Such an approach to narrative, the critic adds, sounding a prominent theme in Victorian dramatic criticism, has all the usual characteristics of "feminine fiction."[63] The *Era* likewise found that Syrett's play violated the generic necessities of drama, "however interesting the vagaries of the winning but wayward heroine might have been to the readers of a novel."[64] *The Finding of Nancy* proved to the *Era*, if nothing else, that actor-managers were the best judges of "dramatic effect," and that there were not, in fact, any significant number of unacted masterpieces or unproduced dramatists of genius, female or male, whose merits no manager had yet recognized.

How was it possible, in any case, the *Era* wondered, to approve a play in which the lesson is that "on the whole, a young woman who feels that her existence is tame and dull had better become somebody's mistress?"[65] Even though the audience might feel some affection for the heroine, chimed in the *Athenaeum*, it can hardly do anything but withhold its "consideration or respect."[66] Fired from her teaching position amid the uproar surrounding *The Finding of Nancy*, opposed and then abandoned by George Alexander when he dropped plans for further performances, and overwhelmed by hostile criticism, "I couldn't go on writing for the stage," Syrett explains in her autobiography. She had made no money out of the play, and novel-writing was, as she said, for herself as for many other women, "a sure thing." Still, Netta Syrett was confident that if given the chance she could have gone on writing for the stage, and succeeded, for she had not forgotten how *The Finding of Nancy*, at its sole performance one afternoon in 1902, had held the rapt attention "of a theatre full of people," whatever the critics and producers thought of it. Had she continued as a playwright Netta Syrett, like many women before her in the Victorian period, would have been a different kind of dramatist from the men who dominated the profession.

"You women have courage," said a young actor who played a small role in *The Finding of Nancy*. "You say things we men wouldn't dare to say!"[67]

PART THREE

Revolution

CHAPTER 7

Elizabeth Robins, Oscar Wilde, and the "Theatre of the Future"

> We are on the verge of something like a struggle between the sexes for the dominion of the London theatres.
>
> (George Bernard Shaw, 1895)

In a decisive moment of the 1890s it appeared that masculine control of the theatre as an institution might be overthrown by the efforts of women and a few male allies. The key figure in this struggle for control of the London stage was Elizabeth Robins, an American actress whose importance has been vastly underestimated. She wanted to make a new career for herself in England – a career which, it turned out, would epitomize the obstacles that Victorian women encountered whenever they performed on stage, wrote plays, or aspired to become "actress-manageresses."

Frustrated by the limits placed on her own theatrical ambitions, and those of other women in the profession, Robins envisioned a radical "Theatre of the Future" in which biases of gender would be set aside. Freeing women to realize their potential in the profession would raise the level of English drama as a whole and increase its value to society, which itself would be rejuvenated by the standard of equality under which Robins's "Theatre of the Future" would operate. For a time in the early to middle 1890s Robins's ideas of reform, and the complementary work of other late-Victorian women, seemed in a position to challenge seriously the theatrical establishment. But, encountering resistance everywhere, Robins became convinced that she could not manage so ambitious a task alone, or even in combination with other women. Her revolutionary aims could only be achieved with the help of a man, she came to believe – a man with the influence, charm, and theatrical genius of Oscar Wilde.

The story of Oscar Wilde's friendship with Elizabeth Robins occupies a few paragraphs in many biographies – of Wilde, that is, for despite her historical importance Robins had no biographers until 1994.[1] Richard Ellmann's account of their relationship is typical, portraying Wilde as a wise mentor to the young actress newly arrived from Boston in 1888 with hopes of success on the London stage. "His practical advice," Ellmann writes, "was that she should give a matinee performance, and he promised to speak to Beerbohm Tree about her." Wilde's advocacy is represented as a professional turning-point for Robins, who, writes Ellmann, "always regarded Wilde as her benevolent pilot through theatrical shoals."[2] Although this narrative relies upon Robins's own memoir of her early years in London, *Both Sides of the Curtain*, it nevertheless provides a distorted, radically incomplete interpretation of Wilde's relationship with the American actress. It functions to illustrate Wilde's expertise and influence in the London theatre, his high standards for the drama, and not least his kindly nature.

But Wilde's "practical advice" that Robins give a matinee performance to launch her career in London ignored her poverty and the hundreds of pounds a matinee would cost her. His introduction of Robins to Beerbohm Tree produced great hopes that ended in disappointment – nothing more than an understudy's role and Robins's dawning realization that Tree himself represented everything she wanted to change in the Victorian theatre. Warning her away from a part in *A Fair Bigamist*, Wilde killed her enthusiasm for a woman-centered play written by a woman playwright, a production of the kind that would become the mission of Robins's professional life. Finally, and most glaringly, Ellmann's claim that Wilde was her "benevolent pilot through theatrical shoals" conceals the more complicated truth – not only that he steered her into those shoals instead of through them, but that in the end Robins sought to take the wheel herself and become Wilde's pilot to what she thought of as "a theatre we could worship" – the "Theatre of the Future."

Elizabeth Robins arrived in London in 1888 as something more than a novice of the stage, having already played some three hundred roles on tour with the Boston Museum and other companies over a period of several years, sometimes to rave reviews. She had already experienced many of the difficulties with which women of the nineteenth-century stage had to struggle – unchallenging roles, low pay, large outlays for expensive stage gowns, and by 1885 the unique problems of married actresses. When the manager of the Boston Museum learned of her marriage to another performer in the company, George Parks, he voided her three-year contract and dropped her from the company at the end of the season. Robins then toured separately from her husband, whose letters became punctuated with demands that she give up her career and live with him full-time. Parks was also offended by his wife's voracious reading and her thoughts of taking up writing, cautioning her that "the writing of a book was the alienation of a mother from her children & finally a separation of husband and wife – the ruin of the home." But women of the theatre were allowed to lead independent and public lives, their success measured by the extent to which they surpassed the liits of patriarchal marriage and motherhood. Experiencing a mixed love and dread of the actress that was symptomatic of men at the time, Parks became frenzied when Robins resisted his demands that she give up her work. He hurled himself into the Charles River with a suit of chain-mail armor strapped to his side.[3]

Thus when she arrived in London, a widow and veteran actress, Robins had bitter experience of the ambivalent and limited position that women occupied in the theatre. Her "Theatre of the Future" was as yet undreamt of, but the need for it had been told and retold already in the events of her own life. Other voices for theatrical reform were audible, or soon would be – among them Matthew Arnold's, pleading for a subsidized and "irresistible" national theatre of literary merit, and Henry James's, espousing a similar project in *The Tragic Muse*. William Archer and J. T. Grein pursued in print and action their own hopes for a serious and artistic English drama for which the West End venues had shown little or no sympathy. Robins's "Theatre of the Future," as she would call it, deserves not only to be redeemed from oblivion, but distinguished from these and other men's proposals for theatrical reform.[4] Robins's analysis was marked by her insight that inequities of gender conspired with self-interested economic motives to weaken the theatre as an artistic institution. Reform would come about through the efforts of women playwrights and managers, along with their male sympathizers, who would inaugurate a noncommercial theatre in which self-interest played no part and drama was more than a commodity. The struggle for a theatre of the future was a struggle against entwined gender and economic injustices. This was the cause to which she would one day call Oscar Wilde.

In an unpublished memoir of Wilde, however, Robins reflects on the period of their first acquaintance in a manner that encourages a different and more modest conclusion – the familiar one that she was simply the beneficiary of Wilde's theatrical wisdom and good nature:

My debt to Oscar Wilde can be paid in part only, by this public acknowledge-
ment of it, and by a picture of the Oscar Wilde I knew many years ago...He
was then at the height of his powers and fame and I was utterly unknown on this
side of the Atlantic. I could do nothing for him; he could and did do everything
in his power for me. He introduced me to Beerbohm Tree and others,
encouraged me to cancel an American engagement and try my fortunes here.
He warned me against a shady theatre manager, advised me about a reliable
agent and solicitor when I needed their help, and suggested plays for matinee
production to introduce the unknown actress to London managers and public.[5]

This fragmentary recollection, even more than *Both Sides of the Curtain*,
not only records Wilde's "personal kindnesses," but virtually credits him
with founding Robins's career on the London stage. The writer is too
polite to mention the dead-ends and disappointments to which Wilde's
counsel led her, and not until near the end of the typescript memoir does
she hint at her regret over the directions that Wilde's own life and work
took in the 1890s.

   Why would Robins misrepresent herself as ancillary to Wilde, the
blessed recipient of his good advice and generous nature, thus prompting biographers to do the same? The answer may lie in Robins's
understanding of the peculiar constraint under which women wrote. As
she says in her essay "Woman's Secret":

Contrary to the popular impression, to say in print what she thinks is the last
thing the woman-novelist or journalist is commonly so rash as to attempt. In
print, even more than elsewhere (unless she is reckless), she must wear the
aspect that shall have the best chance of pleasing her brothers. Her publishers
are not women.[6]

Jane Marcus has pointed out that a characteristic of Robins's own
writing is its "subordination of herself to the men in her life" – to the
heroic figures of Henry James, for example, in *Theatre and Friendship*, to
Wilde and Tree himself in *Both Sides of the Curtain*.[7] "Let men dominate,"
she cautioned in a scribbled note on the manuscript of a play on which
she was working in 1912.[8]

   Robins met Wilde at a reception in 1888, she recalls in *Both Sides of the
Curtain*, and at once he encouraged her to arrange a London appearance. Meeting him by chance in Regent Street some time later, Robins
proudly related how she had received an offer to make her London
debut in a new play called *A Fair Bigamist*. To Robins's surprise, however, Wilde did not congratulate her but launched inquiries about the
play, the manager, and the theatre. The manager was described by
Wilde as declassé, untrustworthy, a "penniless adventurer." The the-

atre, the Royalty, was "unpopular," the cast "unknown," the play "questionable – a vulgar title like that!" For an hour or so, Wilde sat with Robins on a sofa in the hall of her modest lodgings and read with scorn the part that Eleanor Calhoun, another American actress, was surrendering to enable Robins's London debut.

Oh, the poor part! At first he laughed and then he scarified. He read out things that Miss Calhoun made sound beautiful and behold they were cheap, ludicrous, they made your spine twist with shame.

The result was that Robins reluctantly turned down the part, putting aside her "determination," as she called it, "to astonish and delight London with my *Fair Bigamist.*" "There were other managers," Wilde assured her. "He would see one of them."9

In September 1888 Wilde asked Robins not to mention his name to Eleanor Calhoun in any explanation of why she was declining the role that Calhoun had surrendered in *A Fair Bigamist.* "These things get about and make mischief," Wilde said in a note, "but you might ask Miss Calhoun to enquire from any of her theatrical friends, as they will I think speak in the same way as I did."10 Opening at the Royalty Theatre on 20 September, with Rose Murray in the part Robins would have acted, *A Fair Bigamist* received unfriendly reviews and closed within a week. Wilde's estimate of the play seemed to have been confirmed. "I hope you have looked at the criticisms on *A Fair Bigamist,*" he wrote to Robins. "It has been the fiasco I prophesied and no acting could have saved it."11

The review in *The Theatre* noted, however, that Rose Murray "acted with some power as Marion, 'the fair bigamist.'"12 In what sense, then, was the play the "fiasco" that Wilde claimed? The reviewer of *The Times,* at least, believed that no audience could sympathize with the unconventional and transgressive behavior that Rose Murray was called on to enact:

The piece is evidently intended as a protest against the rigidity of the marriage law, which does not allow a woman who has made a disastrous marriage to contract a fresh one before she is released by death or divorce from the husband of whom she would like to get rid. As a rule the dramatist who wishes to interest an audience in a heroine of this kind lets it be understood that at the time of her second wedding she had every reason to suppose, short of absolute proof, that a kind providence had removed for ever the marital obstacle from her path. But this "fair bigamist," whom the ungallant law would sternly regard as a fair felon, marries a second time although she is apparently fully conscious that her

husband is still above ground. This of itself is sufficient to alienate the sympathies of those who have not yet joined the revolt against matrimony as it exists in
its present form, and if sympathy is not enlisted on behalf of the lady the evident
intention of the playwright fails and the play is robbed of its purpose.

Consequently some in the audience "exhibited a ribald disinclination"
to receive *A Fair Bigamist* as the "very serious" play it really was.[13]

   Whether *A Fair Bigamist* was a "very serious" play or an accidental
farce apparently depended upon one's individual perspective of this
drama by a woman. Robins had observed as much, noting in *Both Sides of
the Curtain* that Wilde "laughed" at and made "ludicrous" the very
things in the heroine's part that Eleanor Calhoun had made sound
"beautiful," and that she herself had determined to "astonish and
delight London" with her own part in the play. The author, U. Burford
– identified in *The Times* review as "a lady" – surely aimed at the kind of
response Robins and Calhoun gave her heroine, not the reading shared
by Wilde, the *Times* reviewer, and at least a significant part of the
first-night audience. In its portrait of a self-consciously transgressive
woman, *A Fair Bigamist* was a herald, in outline at least, of the kind of
play that would preoccupy Robins throughout her revolutionary work
to come.

   Indeed Eleanor Calhoun, the woman who offered to launch Robins's
career in London by giving up her own role in *A Fair Bigamist*, was herself
a revolutionary of the stage. Calhoun imagined a theatre which would
produce plays at a level above those ordinarily staged by West End
managers "acting on self-evident economic principles." In due time, she
believed, the theatre could eliminate "that type of exploiter," and with
progressive leadership rise to "a standard of perfection and form."[14]
Calhoun put this vision of a new kind of theatre to the test with her own
production of *As You Like It* in the open air of Coombe Wood in 1885.
Wilde, in his notice for the *Dramatic Review*, said the woodland setting
increased the value of the play "as a picture," but took no notice of the
really revolutionary aspects of this performance – namely, that two
women, Eleanor Calhoun and her protégé Lady Archibald Campbell,
were in charge of the production; that they played both leading roles,
Orlando as well as Rosalind; and that in moving the production out-
doors they were introducing a drama beyond the reach of male actor-
managers and the theatres that they ruled.[15]

   At the time, however, there seemed to be no work at all in England
for Robins, who was preparing to sail immediately for America when a
note arrived from Wilde. It brought with it two stalls for the Haymarket

and a message from Beerbohm Tree saying he would see Elizabeth Robins between the acts of *Captain Swift*. Tree was charming, persuasive, held out hopes, and before the beginning of Act III Robins found herself deciding to cancel her passage home:

He spoke of a play that was being written for him. There was a woman's part that he had foreseen would be difficult to cast. An unconventional part...He was walking about. "There are *plenty* of opportunities," he said, while my heart nearly leapt out of my body. "There are never enough clever people to go round."[16]

So Robins stayed in London, encouraged by Tree to think of herself in the "unconventional woman's part" of a play then being written for him – a play that turned out to be Henry Arthur Jones's *Judah*. This prospect was a continuing theme of the frequent meetings between Tree and Robins in the weeks and months to come, but at last, sitting in her drawing-room one day, Tree suddenly announced that he would not do Jones's play after all – rejected it, Robins later learned, because his own part in it suffered by comparison to the unconventional woman whom Robins would have played. Robins was stunned. "To me," she recalls, "Jones's *Judah* long stood for a disappointment so great that had I foreseen it, the *Cephalonia* would not have sailed without me. Tree never realised the depth of my feeling about the matter; had he done so he would have thought me foolishly unreasonable."[17]

   Tree, losing none of his poise and assurance, could only suggest what Wilde had also recommended – that Robins finance her own London debut in a trial matinee. This being impossible, and suspecting now that Tree was actually "wary" of giving her a foothold at the Haymarket, Robins followed up on another offer of assistance from the American actress Eleanor Calhoun. She put Robins in touch with the playwright Aimée Beringer, whose daughter Esmé was playing the title role in a revival of Frances Hodgson Burnett's dramatization of *Little Lord Fauntleroy*, produced by Madge Kendal. Before long Robins was offered the lead role of Mrs. Errol on Saturdays when Mary Rorke was unavailable to perform. She read the sentimental novel on which the play was based "with laughter and wet eyes," and declared Mrs. Errol "a leading part that I adored." Interestingly, it was the strength of Mrs. Errol's character that Madge Kendal wanted Robins to play up:

Mrs. Kendal thinks Mrs. Errol has great force of character underneath her gentleness, etc., etc. ...I see we agree in many things. She speaks of that scene where Somerset as the old Earl, receives his American daughter-in-law – "not only unlike a nobleman, but unlike any commonly decent character." I began at this point to feel distinctly more at home with my instructor. When she went on to say: "Mrs. Errol is wholly fearless, she meets the rebuff, with well-bred amazement; then with a dignity impregnable as it must be womanly and unostentatious." Hooray, I thought, lifting my crest...[18]

In her unpublished memoir of Wilde, Robins notes with appreciation and some surprise that Wilde came to see her act in *Little Lord Faun-tleroy*, a play "not at all in his line."[19] For the second time Robins was concerned with a play written by a woman dramatist, and for the second time Wilde depreciated it. "The play was second-rate and provincial," he wrote her in January 1889, "but there was nothing but praise and enthusiasm for you. Your future on our stage is assured."[20] This time, however, Robins had not given Wilde the veto of her choice of parts.

Whether Wilde saw Robins play her first Ibsen role, Martha Bernick in *The Pillars of Society*, is uncertain. The production at the Opéra-Comique in June 1889 was organized by Aimée Beringer and Madge Kendal in the wake of Janet Achurch's brilliant showing in the first English staging of *A Doll's House*. In her small part as Martha Bernick, "painted in neutral tones," Robins found "something alive, that called to me." As yet she found some of Ibsen's work disturbing – *Ghosts*, when she first read it, she had "turned from with horror" – but in the comparatively bland *Pillars of Society* Robins discerned only half-consciously "a new kind of play," one with real women in it.[21] Wilde did make a point of returning to the Haymarket later in 1889 to see Robins substitute for Maud Tree, the actor-manager's wife, in the current Haymarket hit *A Man's Shadow*. Tree had continued his friendship with Robins, often inviting her behind the scenes and to his home, giving her the "sense of being in the thick of things" while really, as she calls herself, "the remotest of outsiders." The understudy's job at the Haymarket, however, was the only work that had resulted from the joint efforts of Tree and Wilde – who, Robins recalls, "sat through the play he had seen already – not his sort of play at any time – and cheered me on."[22] Still, *A Man's Shadow* must have been suggestive to Wilde at this time, the fall of 1889, when he was writing *The Picture of Dorian Gray*. The play was a showcase for Tree, who dominated this French-derived melodrama as both the mild hero Laroque and his villainous double Luversan, changing dress, voice, and general bearing at a lightning pace throughout the show. *The Times* applauded Tree's performance as a "*tour de force...*astonishingly successful," and only as an afterthought ascribed a few "pathetic moments" to Madame Laroque, the role played by Robins when she filled in for Maud Tree.[23] The reviewer for *The Theatre* reacted similarly, praising Tree for representing "in a remarkably clever manner" both a noble character and a "crafty *vaurien*," altering his voice and gait at a moment's notice in "a perfect *tour-de-force*." For this reviewer, too, the women were scenic background figures – all that he could say about Maud Tree's performance was that the expression on her face "left nothing to be desired."[24]

A few days after her performance in Tree's *tour de force* Robins played the lead in a matinee of Dr. G. H. Dabbs's *Her Own Witness*. Dabbs's new play belonged to the heroine, and in her big scene Robins enjoyed "that experience, intoxicating to the actor, the realisation of a power to hold all those people beyond the footlights as if they were one." Her press notices were brilliant, but the play closed: "one of those flashes in the pan that seem at the time to leave nothingness behind." Why? "*Her Own Witness* was, fatally, a woman's play," Robins recalls, and as such unappealing to managers who sought the kind of self-advertisement that plays such as *A Man's Shadow* provided. There were many "women's plays" among the vast unacted repertory of the late Victorian theatre, plays which never became even failed matinees. Robins recalls, for example, *Germaine*, adapted from the French by Madame Van de Velde, "which interested me most of all":

But her play, much discussed, much worked over, *Germaine*, too, so far as I am aware, has no epitaph – only an unmarked grave. For awhile, I was still to believe that Madame Van de Velde's heroine might be made into a part for me. As a play, *per se*, the significance of *Germaine* was that she was typical, not only in my experience. There have been millions of her.[25]

It was becoming clear to Elizabeth Robins that only women who ran their own companies could depend on acting in plays with interesting roles for women. The Haymarket – whatever Wilde might say, however brilliant that theatre and its manager – offered little for her.

For the time being Robins continued to act in plays she disliked, precisely because she had no company of her own and thus little or no choice of parts. Wilde again disapproved, visiting her behind the scenes after her first performance in the popular farce *Dr. Bill*, staged by George Alexander shortly after he broke away from Henry Irving to launch his own career as an actor-manager. "He congratulates," Robins recalls, "smiling that queer draw-string smile: 'But you oughtn't, you know. Absurd you should be cast for a part quite out of your line.

The wonder – the *danger* is, you do it so well!'" And on another occasion: "'Bad for you to be making a success of that sort of part.'"[26] Was the choice, then, to play "bad" parts, as Wilde called her role in *Dr. Bill*, or not to act at all?

Not long afterward Robins spoke with Henry Irving himself about the special difficulties women encountered on the Victorian stage – especially finding good parts that would advance their careers. But Irving was unsympathetic:

"Ah," he says rather irrelevantly, "but women have an easy road to travel on the stage. They have but to *appear* and their sweet feminine charm wins the battle–"

Irving, then, shared the perspective of the reviewers of *A Man's Shadow*, a perspective concerned with the *acting* of a man but interested mainly in the *appearance* of a woman – the pathetic expression of her face, her charming features. The exchange concluded with Irving addressing "pretty compliments" to Robins rather than engaging the professional issues she had raised. Robins would later remark:

The brief passage with Henry Irving added gently to the general pressure that would confine women of the stage to the old province outside the stage. The rare exceptions, the great actresses, some of them, had escaped – with the result that lesser women or less fortunate, had been mislead [*sic*]. What was wanted of the women of the stage was, first and mainly, what was wanted of women outside – a knack of pleasing. Much as I myself loved pleasing – (and more than most) – it didn't seem enough. Besides, where did it get you – outside the purely sexual limit?[27]

Soon Robins was contemplating writing a piece for the *Fortnightly*, something that would tell "the strange story…of practical stage experience that no one has yet been bold enough to write." It would, as she wrote the editor John Verschoyle, expose "this latter-day slavery" of women in the theatre, "the unworthy bondage of the *successful* as well as the unsuccessful women of the stage."[28] The article was never written, but thinking about it formed, in a manner of speaking, her response to Oscar Wilde's recurring complaints about her choice of parts. She had no choice – no meaningful one – because women of the theatre were systematically reduced to a condition that could only be compared with slavery. Their economic subjection was institutionalized in the Victorian theatre, limiting the exercise of talent and the development of potential in a career that only seemed on the surface to offer a liberating escape from the gender inequities of Victorian life beyond the footlights. To satisfy Wilde's admonitions about her choice of parts, Robins now realized, would require some fundamental changes in the theatre as an institution.

No such changes could be expected from the engagement Robins was soon to take in the Adelphi production of Robert Buchanan's *The Sixth Commandment*, an adaptation of *Crime and Punishment*. Again dissatisfied with the role she was playing, Robins set about rewriting her part here and there, hoping that Buchanan would allow the emendations to stand. In this way and others, Robins felt herself striving toward self-creation, voracious for a professional and personal identity that the theatre seemed bent upon denying. "I didn't have any self as yet," she explains at the end of *Both Sides of the Curtain*, which concludes with her success in the Buchanan play of 1890 – still at the dawn of her career. Nor was the self she aspired to become very distinct as yet. "What I wanted was to be everybody. I *was* everybody."[29]

It was at about this time that Robins read Wilde's novel, *The Picture of Dorian Gray*, when it appeared in Lippincott's magazine in 1890. Her unpublished diary for the latter half of 1890 records this reaction: "vile & revolting & not interesting in any way – Oh Mr. Wilde! Mr. Wilde!"[30] This vehemently negative reaction to *Dorian Gray* occurred at about the time Robins's published memoir, *Both Sides of the Curtain*, abruptly broke off – that is, during her engagement at the Adelphi in 1890 playing in Buchanan's *The Sixth Commandment* for £10 a week. Wilde's counsel had led to a pleasant and flattering friendship with Tree, but professionally to nothing more than an understudy's role at the Haymarket. Eager to advance the fortunes of a brilliant young actress, he had inadvertently guided her toward a theatre and a manager whose founding premise – profit and fame for the manager – could only work against Robins's ambitions for the free play of her own talents in the theatre. Robins began to see her own situation clearly as *The Sixth Commandment* approached the end of its run. What was required, she notes in her still unpublished sequel to *Both Sides of the Curtain* – a memoir entitled "Whither and How" – was a different kind of theatre, one operated on a different basis entirely from the Haymarket or St. James's. Quoting her own diary, she imagines in "Whither and How" a theatre composed of "an association of workers," not owned by any individual and thus not bound to advance a single person's economic and professional interests. The motivation would be artistic – "Art for Art's sake," as Robins puts it:

Our aim. . .doing work of the highest kind without money and without price –
other than an earnest spirit and a generous love of our calling, & of one another.
We could explore the wide field of classical poetic Drama. We could work the
Marlowe vein, then Ibsen & any other helpful modern. We would get the
practice we lack in these times of long runs. We would quicken our artistic
perceptions by all in turn playing little parts. Lifting higher the standard of
dramatic work, we should help actors, the stage – the world.[31]

Robins set to work with another American actress, Marion Lea, to try to
find a manager in London who would produce Ibsen's *The Lady from the
Sea*. "One after another of London's actor-managers rejected the idea of
offering his theatre for the project," Robins recollects in "Whither and
How," and as a result she and Lea formed what they called the "Joint
Management" for mounting their own productions. It was a first step
toward the theatre that Robins had dreamed for the future – a theatre of
independent management and artistic standards, cooperative rather
than competitive, freed from the economy of self-interest which regulated the theatres and national life as a whole.

In "Whither and How" Robins formed the plan initially of producing
a revival of *Pillars of Society*, but made *Hedda Gabler* the object of their
efforts as soon as they heard of this new "woman's play" from the hand
of Ibsen. This idea met resistance from managers who, already preju-
diced against Ibsen, were reluctant to turn over their theatres for a
matinee staged by a management and performers from the outside. It
was perceived, Robins writes, as "a sign of managerial weakness" and as
being "undignified." A less predictable source of friction was William
Archer, the most visible advocate of Ibsen in England, who was working
behind the scenes with Robins and Archer to get *Hedda Gabler* produced.
But he was worried by the prospect of the play's being produced by the
so-called "Joint Management" of Robins and Lea, preferring "with
unblushing readiness," as Robins puts it, that Lily Langtry perform the
lead role under some long-established manager. Lily Langtry, a woman
whom Wilde had pointed out to Robins in 1888 as an example of how a
woman might take the London theatre by storm, was perhaps the
quintessential example of the actress valued for her background qualities – her appearance – over her acting. Just as Robins had repudiated
Wilde's implied suggestion that she emulate Langtry in 1888, so she and
Lea expressed outrage at the idea of their *Hedda Gabler* production being
hijacked by the West End in the way Archer suggested. "It seemed to
shake the fabric of the Joint Management to its foundation," Robins
says in "Whither and How." Eventually Archer was persuaded, but

continued to regard with apprehension "the necessary instability & lack of prestige of a new management."[32]

Without a backer, Robins trimmed the costs of production to about £300, which she borrowed against the little box of gold that had been her father's wedding present to her. Actors were recruited with great difficulty because many managers insisted that performers working for them should be engaged nowhere else, even in an independent matinee such as *Hedda Gabler*. The English translation of the text was considerably reworked by Robins herself for purposes of production. Other difficulties had to be overcome, not least getting the play licensed by the Examiner of Plays, who had just banned *Ghosts* from public performance.

In all this Robins found "a very inspiring kind of freedom,"[33] and when *Hedda Gabler* was finally staged at the Vaudeville Theatre on 20 April 1891, Oscar Wilde wanted to be among those in the audience. He wrote to ask Robins for a stall – "it is a most interesting play, nor could there be any [better] exponent of its subtlety and tragedy than yourself." To Marion Lea he wrote: "It is most plucky of you and Miss Robins to produce this new and fascinating play, and I feel sure you will have a great success, and you are certain to have the sympathy and admiration of all who are interested in the development of the Drama." On 23 April he wrote to Robins again: "Can I have a box or two stalls for tomorrow? I must see your great performance again. It is a real masterpiece of art."[34] Years later, in her unpublished memoir of Wilde, Elizabeth Robins would reflect with gratitude on the welcome that her production of *Hedda Gabler* received from him. "Above all," she writes there, "I value his encouragement in the exciting and critical days of my first Ibsen production with Marion Lea."[35]

In a letter not published until recently, however, Wilde adopts a different tone toward *Hedda Gabler*. Here, in a letter to Ethel Greenfell, his tone is mocking – not so much of the play itself as of the audience, so unlike Tree's, before which it was performed. To Mrs. Greenfell's suggestion that they see the play together on 3 June, Wilde responds in late April 1891:

I am afraid that by June 3rd poor Hedda will have given up looking for scarlet sensations in a drab-coloured existence. I went there on Thursday night, and the house was dreary – the pit full of sad vegetarians, and the stalls occupied by men in mackintoshes and women in knitted shawls of red wool. So at least it seemed to me. However, we might go to *L'Enfant Prodigue* or *The Dancing Girl*...[36]

Here Wilde returns, at least momentarily, to the theme of his earliest conversations with Robins – the crucial role of a recognized theatre and established management. His admiration for Robins's brilliance existed side by side with his revulsion at the surroundings in which it found expression. He clearly preferred an evening at the Haymarket, where *The Dancing Girl* was now playing, but the thought of Tree opening his theatre to Robins for a production of *Hedda Gabler* was inconceivable.

Much as he was pained by the old blue sofa and faded decor of Robins's cheap boarding-house, Wilde's aesthetic sense recoiled from the kind of theatre that Robins's personal ambitions and experimental productions led her to – the Royalty and the Vaudeville rather than the Haymarket and St. James's. His admiration and affection for the actress struggled against his antipathy for the surroundings, the theatrical ambience, that she seemed always to gravitate to. His own plays, as yet unwritten, would find their place in Tree's theatre itself, or others like it, rich productions enacted before audiences no less elegant and glittering. Robins herself recoiled from this purely aesthetic dimension of Wilde's character, as she understood it, and from any impulse to temper her art in a fashion that would win acceptance from men like Tree. One sign of this came out in her production of *Hedda Gabler*, when against much opposition, including William Archer's, she altered Hedda's famous line "Do it beautifully" to "Do it gracefully." Oscar Wilde, she explained, "had spoiled a lovely word...it was the actress who had to *say* the word and the actress declined to say beautifully."[37] To associate Hedda Gabler's invitation to suicide with Wildean aestheticism was, to her own reading of Ibsen, unacceptable.

Interestingly, Wilde's somewhat mixed reaction to *Hedda Gabler* was not uncommon. E. F. S. Pigott, the Examiner of Plays, wrote to ask for a stall and, Robins remembers, "offered his congratulations on a most striking artistic and magnificent rendering of a most difficult part" but also noted that "to my poor perception, all the characters in it appear to have escaped from a lunatic asylum."[38] Even Tree put himself forward as "one of the platonic supporters of this movement" in a note accompanied by a contribution toward the expenses of staging *Hedda Gabler*. But, he added, "It seems to me strange that *women* should be the pioneers of the Ibsen plays – but so it is."[39] Wilde, Pigott, Tree – each in his own way expressed admiration of Robins and the play, yet noted some striking discrepancy between Robins's and Lea's Joint Management and what they were accustomed to. Wilde noted the difference in the absence of signs of wealth and taste in the audience, Pigott in what he regarded as the "lunatic" excesses of the characters, Tree in his observation that women, of all people, were mainly responsible for this outbreak of a new kind of theatre. Women had indeed been the "pioneers" of this revolutionary new theatre and would continue to be – perhaps would have to be, considering what was being revolted against. They found their work in "women's plays" written by men like Ibsen or by women themselves, and in doing so confronted head-on the centers of power in the theatre as it then existed. No wonder that men as different as Wilde, Pigott, and Tree would look round this new kind of theatre and find little that was familiar or, to them, reassuring.

Any hope that the impact of *Hedda Gabler* would provide Robins with meaningful opportunities in the usual West End venues was soon disappointed. Robins notes in yet another unpublished memoir, "Heights and Depths," that parts were offered to her and Marion Lea, but alas, "not such parts as we had in mind – but pretty little dears however much they were called heroines or 'leading parts'..."[40] Unable to finance now another production by the Joint Management, Robins had no choice but to accept a well-paid role in the Adelphi melodrama *A Woman's Revenge*. In notes written and typed at the end of the manu- script of "Whither and How," Robins added these comments:

Marion Lea and I had started out to do something that hadn't ever been tried before, never realising the peril of this, a peril the more should the first steps show marked success...Offers of engagements under regular managers began to flow in. The first on record I refused to go further with, because I knew to what a blind alley it would lead. All the theatres then were either frankly commercial like the Adelphi, or commercial in disguise, & without exception were under the management of men...Men who wrote plays for women had long been seeing that they simply had little or no chance of being acted.[41]

Naming Tree as an example of the system that opposed her aims, Robins recognized her dilemma, and with that "a helplessness and depression fell upon me, for I saw what I was facing." All she had really gotten from the spectacular achievement with *Hedda Gabler* had been personal and transitory, for the "rational Theatre" of her hopes was no nearer now than it had been before – and this must have struck home with extra force when her collaborator Marion Lea married and re- turned home to America.

It was in the aftermath of *Hedda Gabler* that Robins began to write an autobiographical novel of the theatre, never published, called "The

Coming Woman." The Robins-like title character, Katherine Fleet, is a talented young actress whose life's aim is to resist the "commercialism and dullness" of the regular theatres, managed by men whose "first business is to make money." But her own slender resources make it impossible to found "a theatre of her own," so she approaches her aims indirectly, acting in inferior roles so she can one day afford to inaugurate a different kind of theatre. In this cause she proselytizes others, notably the "famous poet and universal genius Maurice Neill," a thinly disguised Oscar Wilde.[42] In this manuscript one continues to hear, only amplified now, the discord in Robins's relationship with Wilde, a discord that ran below the surface before finding expression from both of them during the run of *Hedda Gabler*. Maurice Neill, the Wilde figure, is indolent – "horribly indolent," as he frankly tells the actress Katherine Fleet; "at the present moment, I'm so engrossed with idleness I'm afraid I can't spare time to work." In any case, he reflects, he likes his art to avoid "the straight-jacket [*sic*] of language." Neill – or Wilde – is a man who could write good plays, but contents himself with merely talking about the theatre, tasking Katherine Fleet for allowing herself to be cast in unsuitable roles and conversing brilliantly about an "ideal Theatre" out of the control of actor-managers.

Katherine Fleet pleads with Neill-Wilde to turn his talk into practical action – "you could absolutely change the face of the Theatre-world."[43] But these speeches produce no effect on her friend, who like Wilde (except for failed efforts of years ago) as yet has no plays to his credit at all. The manuscript reveals in short a complete reversal of the Wilde–Robins relationship as it is always presented; here, it is the young actress who attempts to be the "mentor" and "pilot," not the other way round. Instead of being guided professionally by Neill, the actress attempts to transform him from a theatrical hanger-on, one with insider's connections and unique gifts who only talks about the drama, to a playwright in fact. Not only a playwright, of course – Robins, in the person of her heroine Katherine Fleet, wanted him as a playwright for the kind of "rational Theatre" that she and Marion Lea had dreamed of. Wilde was to be recruited, then, in her war against economic theatre – that state of things, as Katherine Fleet says, in which "every play produced is expected to pay in hard cash."[44] In the present system dominated by actor-managers, Katherine Fleet says, the theatre is merely the manager's "mill or manufactory where he turns out material at the lowest possible cost that he imagines the public will pay a steady price for...He is the frankest of tradesmen."[45] This system itself – rooted in economic, professional, and personal self-interest – is recognized by Katherine Fleet as the cause of women's subjection in the Victorian theatre. It puts her in the power of the manager, often physically as well as professionally, because the satisfaction of his greed, ego, and desires gives shape and direction to the theatre as it is. No wonder, then, that actresses so commodified came to feel, like Katherine Fleet, that their brains were turning to "cotton-wool."[46]

In the theatre as it was, plays that offered the kind of opportunities that Robins sought were rare and their fortunes precarious, but she had no difficulty by 1892 imagining what she wanted. Her unpublished story "A Highly Respectable Heroine" concerns such a play, "at last. . .a magnificent play" written by an English man of letters. "It is true," she says, "[its] heroine like many another, had transgressed a particular social law – but the play was nothing less than her triumphant justification." But an actress approached to play the role turns it down, finding the "splendidly fearless. . .double life" of the heroine unconvincing and, to any audience, unacceptable.[47] At Wilde's urging, Robins herself had turned down the part of a strong, transgressive woman in *A Fair Bigamist* – perhaps not a "magnificent play," yet in outline, at least, the kind of play Robins now hoped for. Plays of this kind – not just plays – are what Katherine Fleet wants the Wilde-figure in "The Coming Woman" to write.

By now Robins was no longer merely the grateful recipient of Wilde's personal kindness and professional advice. Instead of being directed by Wilde in her career, she was attempting to direct him – and not only in the guise of fiction. Her diary entry for 17 May 1892 reveals that she and Wilde still met on occasion at least, talking over professional matters as they had so often in the late 1880s: "Oscar Wilde called. Tea and cigarettes & visions of the Theatre of the Future."[48] The next day she wrote to her friend Florence Bell, describing the "royal good time" she had had talking and listening to Wilde,[49] then drew on this letter, apparently, when she described the meeting in her unpublished memoir of Wilde.

In 1892 I recall his laughing summary of a discussion with me: "Well, we've had a profitable time – we've built a theatre, written several plays and founded a school!" I told him that anyone with all those ideas about the Theatre ought to give them to the world in practical, permanent form. He should sketch a working plan, wake people up to the need and value of a Theatre on non-commercial lines. He promised to "speak for it" at a Dinner, shortly to be held, and then to crystallize the subject in an essay.[50]

Like the "universal genius" in Robins's unpublished theatrical novel, however, Wilde was only to talk about such projects without ever committing them to the "straight-jacket" [*sic*] of print.

One way to deal with the lack of suitable plays was of course to write them herself, which Robins began to do, in collaboration with Florence Bell, when she adapted a story by Elin Ameen under the title *Alan's Wife*, staged in 1893. Here was the narrative of the strong, transgressive woman that for Robins had proved so elusive, a heroine who celebrates her murder of her sick child as the kindest, strongest, and most courageous action of her life. Even Shaw was made uncomfortable by *Alan's Wife*, so remote from the kind of drawing-room comedy in which his own reforming impulse was finding expression. The howling strength of the heroine struck him as manic and "most horribly common," and further to discredit the play he ascribed to its heroine an implausible repentance which in fact never actually occurs.[51] If Shaw's defenses were so fully engaged by *Alan's Wife*, it should not be surprising that Beerbohm Tree, to whom Robins read the play, or a scenario of it, told her that "it would be too horrible, too gruesome" for him to think of staging it, even though he was impressed by the writing. "I can't help a chuckle," wrote Florence Bell in late 1892, "when I hear that he approved of the writing of the piece, and when I think of his maintaining that women can't write."[52] In the end only J. T. Grein's Independent Theatre would agree to produce *Alan's Wife*, and even under Grein's progressive management it closed prematurely after only two matinees.[53]

In 1893 Robins organized a production of Ibsen's *The Master Builder* at the Trafalgar Square Theatre, creating the role of Hilda Wangel in English. Wilde wrote to say he was unable to attend the premiere, but came to a later performance and greeted Robins behind the scenes. Later the same year he was a subscriber when Robins gave a series of twelve performances of Ibsen at the Opéra-Comique, and contributed a modest sum for a gift to the actress-manager. Neither *The Master Builder* nor the Ibsen series was financially successful, but Shaw, for one, took notice of what seemed an extraordinary development: "what is called the Woman Question has begun to agitate the stage." In a preface to William Archer's *The Theatrical 'World' of 1894* Shaw recognizes what had been for a long time the theme of Robins's own theatrical campaigns. "A glance at our theatres will show," he writes, "that the higher artistic career is practically closed to the leading lady." Actresses in the employment of actor-managers – even the most successful like Ellen

Terry, Kate Rorke, Mary Moore – merely "support" the manager and give up any opportunity of creating any of the few good women's parts that come along, from Ibsen or others. He points to Elizabeth Robins, "the creator of Hedda Gabler and Hilda Wangel," and to Janet Achurch, "virtually...actress-manager" of the first production of *A Doll's House*, as the omens of revolutionary change:

> We cannot but see that the time is ripe for the advent of the actress-manageress, and that we are on the verge of something like a struggle between the sexes for the dominion of the London theatres, a struggle which, failing an honourable treaty, or the break-up of the actor-manager system by the competition of new forms of theatrical enterprise, must in the long run end disastrously for the side which is furthest behind the times. And that side is at present the men's side.[54]

Shaw recognizes here that the most important critique of late Victorian theatre was taking place on the grounds of gender, and that that critique, which he associates with Robins first and a few others, holds the potential for radical structural change in the theatre. Robins herself was beginning to doubt that the theatrical apocalypse imagined by Shaw would ever occur, or occur in time to benefit her. She was turning to the writing of fiction, weary by now of a struggle which in her own estimation had produced but little. "My brief experiences of having a theatre, and a company of my own," she writes in *Theatre and Friendship*, "had taught me a number of things. In 'leading lady' leading-strings I found the long fascination of the theatre wearing thin." In fiction, she hoped, it might be possible to transcend the biases of gender, for "I would still be playing a part...under a pseudonym . . .the identity of a man."[55]

While Robins was turning away from the theatre, Oscar Wilde's career was soaring, the "circle of his fame," as Robins says in her memoir, "continually widening." But Robins was not as uncritical as she had been in 1888. Wilde's poems "never touched me," she writes, and she "disliked" *Dorian Gray*, "but I read his Essays, laughed with them, admired and marked them, and they marked me." In the memoir her comment on Wilde's plays is strangely noncommittal: "Like a magnesium light Wilde flashed into the Theatre with 'Salome' in Paris and with 'An Ideal Husband' and 'Lady Windermere's Fan' in London." Once she had great hopes that Wilde would help build the "Theatre of the Future," but his popular successes written for Beerbohm Tree and George Alexander were, in the final analysis, tailored to the theatre as it was. It is not clear whether Robins's final judgment of Wilde's work for the theatre would have been as harsh as that of her

protégé William Archer, the Ibsen critic and translator who viewed
Wilde as a representative of what an advanced theatre would react
against. His plays, Archer wrote, were "in reality mere drawing-room
melodramas, and conventional ones at that...there was no real sub-
stance in his work."[56] Robins herself, committed to ideological work –
effecting structural change in the theatre, ultimately in society as a
whole – was increasingly frustrated by Wilde's tendency to avoid engagement and defer meaning:

> These were the years when I saw him seldom, yet often enough to be reminded
> that we did not always agree. Once by ridiculing someone he liked I annoyed
> him greatly; and almost as much by praising another person for being delight-
> fully natural. Wilde rolled his big shoulders away from me. "Anybody can be
> natural. It is the utmost that the majority can do for themselves." "Well, I like
> people to be real," I said, innocently. "What *is* real?" he demanded with
> sudden sternness. While I was trying to hit on an answer, he continued,"To
> think that you've found something real is the last illusion."[57]

To Robins in the 1890s the theatre of the future was no illusion but a
reality most urgent, even if her own efforts to realize it had not been
decisively successful. Shaw, although unsympathetic to Robins in some
respects, at least recognized by 1894 the existence of a gender crisis in
the theatre and foresaw that structural changes in the institution as such
might be inevitable, "as the result of new forms of theatrical enterprise."
But Shaw was thinking only of actresses who would usurp the powers of
actor-managers, not at all of women playwrights – indeed he had
ridiculed the efforts of Janet Achurch and Robins herself when they had
attempted to write plays of their own.[58] He saw his own plays, and
Ibsen's, as providing all that was needed to address the gender crisis of
the late Victorian theatre. In the drawing-room plays of Shaw and
Wilde, however, Robins did not recognize her ideal of the theatre.
During the early to middle 1890s, finding but few men who cared to risk
their own careers writing the "woman's plays" that figured so largely in
the theatre of the future, Robins joined a growing number of women
who were writing plays themselves. In doing so, however, they strove
against very long odds.

"There was a widespread conviction," Robins recalls in *Theatre and
Friendship*, "that no woman can write a good full-length play." Indeed,
when she mentioned to Henry James the possibility of writing one
herself, he reacted "with a start, and a look of horror."[59] Even William
Archer found it incredible that Robins might write good drama: "To tell

you the truth I don't think you have the power of concentration required for playwriting. Certainly you could find a novel far easier than a play."[60] An Archer-like figure in Robins's novel *The Florentine Frame* discourages the heroine from writing plays as a means to realize an ideal theatre, reminding her that "women aren't capable of the intellectual pressure to the square inch necessary to produce certain results."[61] When Robins herself approached Beerbohm Tree about writing a play for the Haymarket, he was similarly incredulous, telling her in a hastily scrawled note that he had "never...read a good play from a woman's hand."[62] Nevertheless, if the Theatre of the Future was ever to be realized, it seemed clear to Robins that women would not only have to stage their own productions of plays, but write them too.

Robins, for example, persuaded John Hare to produce Constance Fletcher's *Mrs. Lessingham* at the Garrick Theatre in 1894, playing the lead role herself with what one reviewer called "sincerity, simplicity, and penetrating, unconventional pathos." But she also rewrote the play in collaboration with the author and Hare while to some extent overseeing the production itself. Originally entitled *The Other Woman*, the play is remarkable for its sympathetic portrayal of a married woman who elopes with her lover and later comes into conflict with the more conventional heroine to whom the leading man is engaged, and whom he loves. It exhibits few of the concessions to conventional morality that compromise such 1890s plays as *The Notorious Mrs. Ebbsmith*, *The Second Mrs. Tanqueray*, *The Case of Rebellious Susan*, and even *Lady Windermere's Fan*, Wilde's own masculinized version of *East Lynne*. A remarkable play by Robins herself, *The Mirkwater*, was turned down by several actor-managers, George Alexander among them. The play concerns Felicia Vincent, who assists in the suicide of her sister, a young woman stricken with breast cancer who "dominated every one she came near."[63] *The Mirkwater* was never produced or published, nor was another play by Robins, *The Silver Lotus*, written in about the middle of the decade. *The Silver Lotus* focuses on a young mother driven to alcoholism by the death of her children and the shallow grief of her husband. The only play of hers to attract strong interest from a West End actor-manager was the unproduced, unpublished *Benvenuto Cellini*, which Beerbohm Tree hoped to produce with himself in the larger-than-life starring role. "He is a good deal fired by it," wrote Robins to her friend Florence Bell; "he obviously *sees* himself as B[envenuto]." But the project foundered because of Robins's reluctance to provide Tree with the alterations he demanded before placing the play under contract, and Tree's refusal to offer her the kind of financial arrangements that she wanted – perhaps something like 10 percent of gross receipts, a common practice at the time for established dramatists in the West End.

Robins's memoir of Wilde ends with the catastrophic events of the mid-1890s, with her own plays unacted and "with every manager in London clamouring for a Wilde play."[64] It was at this time, while Wilde was shaping *An Ideal Husband* for the Haymarket and *The Importance of Being Earnest* for the St. James's, that he called to pay a final visit to Elizabeth Robins. She was a woman who had lived in cheap rooms for years now, walked long distances to save the price of cab fare, eaten too little at times while reading late into the night and nursing plans for the theatre of the future. The Oscar Wilde who presented himself to her now, the Wilde whose prosperity was being founded in the theatres of Tree and Alexander, seemed almost a stranger:

I forget what led to his coming to see me that last time, but I remember being vaguely miserable at his changed appearance. His skin was dark and unwholesome looking, as if (according to my rather cruel note I have come upon which I am not at all sure would have displeased Wilde) as if he were stuffed with spices and caviar. "Poke him and he would bleed absinthe and clotted truffles." He had grown restless, too. For the first time I felt we really had little to say. When he unfolded himself out of the armchair and stood up to go, I made no protest.[65]

After that, Robins's unpublished memoir of Wilde seems to have nothing to say itself, trailing off in mid-sentence after a futile attempt to deal with Wilde's arrest, trials, and imprisonment. Calling it "difficult even at this long distance of time to look back" at those events, Robins only quotes the reactions of others to Wilde's public disgrace. The subject of her memoir recedes further and further into the background, obscured by a haze of quotations and evasions, before the typescript halts abruptly on page 14, having lost its focus altogether.

Wilde's personal catastrophe coincided with Robins's acknowledgment that the "wild projects" of the Robins–Lea Joint Management had come to an end. On reflection, she writes in *Theatre and Friendship*, a principle had been demonstrated, but "at a cost that did not appear in our audited accounts":

Each new production meant, not as in regular theatres the carrying on of a business of which the framework remained the same, the machinery the same, the heads of Department and, most of all, the company the same. Each new play, given outside the established London managements, meant a new attack and a fresh campaign. It meant canvassing the field for a new theatre (the same one was seldom available); it meant the delicate, vital business of choosing a new cast; it mean 'working in' one's views of stage management often with a new stage-manager and (as a part of the general responsibility) trying to arrive at a business competence under circumstances where artistic competence should have been the main if not the sole concern.[66]

Robins now was moving away from the theatre, giving more of her attention to writing fiction with the disappointment of her hopes for a theatre of the future. Nevertheless, what she had begun with Marion Lea helped show the way for William Archer and others to form the New Century Theatre, a deliberately non-Utopian alternative theatre that sought to cooperate with rather than antagonize existing theatres, putting aside all thought of altering the organization of the theatre as it was. As a member of the provisional committee Robins found herself again concerned in the production of plays that West End theatres would not welcome. But in Robins's estimation nothing changed; the actor-managers controlled the theatres as much at the end of the 1890s as at the beginning, and the "surface harmony" between the New Century Theatre and the managers concealed an irreconcilable opposition of interests, even hostility. "I had been at this particular sort of work longer than the new Society," Robins recalls, "and I had begun to ask myself more insistently: What did it all come to? Didn't it come, or wasn't it coming, to be one of those efforts...doomed to ineffectualness and 'the little day'?"[67]

At the dawn of the twentieth century, Robins at times seemed determined to turn her back on the theatre altogether, as a hopeless cause. In a letter to Millicent Fawcett dated 1 November 1906 she writes that "I am just embarked upon the task of turning a play (which I've written at white heat in the last two months) into a novel, as the indications are that the play is held to be too partisan to be ventured upon by the regular managers...Instead of wearing out my soul in battering at their doors, I shall set to and turn the thing into a book as fast as ever I can."[68] The play was probably *Votes for Women*, which she did turn into a novel but which was also accepted for production by the Vedrenne–Barker management of the Court Theatre – "it was a great moment," writes Robins in *Theatre and Friendship*.[69] The play argues for women's suffrage through a heroine who dominates Act II with a stirring political oration and is revealed in Act III as the former lover of a rising politician, a man from whom she can now extort some "political dynamite" for the good of the Cause.

Robins, weary of "battering at the door" of an institution which had resisted her best efforts at reform, had little to do with the theatre in the twentieth century, *Votes for Women* notwithstanding. In the balmy 1890s it had been different, when she was hatching with Marion Lea the "wild projects" of the Joint Management in a confident assault upon the economic and gender injustices of the British stage. At that time her feminist critique seemed to point toward a theatre of the future in which profit would not be the primary motive, or even a concern – a theatre in which actresses and plays would be judged on an artistic basis rather than on their economic value to a small number of powerful men. She could foresee, as she wrote in a memoir, "a Theatre we can worship" springing up from the ashes of a dying and exploitative "Theatre as it is."[70]

Oscar Wilde certainly could not be blamed for the failure of Robins's vision of a "Theatre of the Future," but he had never followed through on his grand promises to write and speak on behalf of the project. Wilde's conversation with Robins over tea in May 1892 had left Robins with the impression that an important advocate had been been won for her cause. "I felt very delighted," she confided in the letter she wrote to Florence Bell the next day. Still, she suffered "qualms of conscience" that her recruiting of Wilde would be resented by other, less well-known partisans of theatrical reform who might feel they were being pushed aside and ignored. "However," she continued, "it's infinitely better in Oscar's hands."[71] But Wilde – like the aesthete-hero of Robins's novel of the theatre, *The Coming Woman* – never followed through on his good intentions, and the question of how much credit he would or should receive for the founding of the Theatre of the Future never came up.

Like Vida Levering, the heroine of *Votes for Women*, Robins had to face the realization that "winning over the men" – even the best and brightest men – was not enough. The struggle for theatrical reform was basically a woman's cause, and some battles concerning women, as Vida Levering says in the play, "must be fought by women alone."[72] In her own work as manager, playwright, and actress, in bringing forward the work of other women in these areas, Robins led an uprising that challenged the institutional bases of the theatre and that Shaw correctly diagnosed as a "struggle between the sexes for dominion over the London stage." This was the struggle to which she had called Oscar Wilde, and to which he responded in 1892, at the dawn of his own career as a playwright, but only with words. In practice Wilde cast his lot with Beerbohm Tree and George Alexander – thus taking his own advice, the same advice he had given Robins herself as a newcomer to London in 1888. Wilde's plays were staged at the Haymarket and St. James's, not only written to their requirements but revised – mutilated, one might say – at the behest of Tree and Alexander. Within the framework of these drawing-room comedies some of Wilde's own subversive opinions could be discerned – in the witty repartee, for instance, of Lord Darlington in *Lady Windermere's Fan* or Cecil Graham in *An Ideal Husband* – but there would be nothing to threaten the position of the actor-manager in these plays, nothing that worked against the grain of the theatrical institution in the way that Robins advocated.

In setting his aim at making "lots of red gold," Wilde entered fully into the economy of the theatre as it was, seeking to ensure profits for himself and the managers alike, and to do so meant working within the established framework of the theatre rather than outside it.[73] So his plays would be brilliant reenactments of *The Dancing Girl*, *East Lynne*, and popular farces of the day – recognizable vehicles for the stars who ran the theatres, and any assault upon them and all they represented would have to be indirect. The "red gold" came to Wilde as it came to many a successful playwright in this period, and when Elizabeth Robins saw him for the last time she saw a man ruined by excessive gain and overconsumption. Robins, the ascetic, feminist revolutionary of the theatre of the 1890s, had foreseen a different outcome for Wilde, and through him for the theatre itself, and on a rainy afternoon in late 1894 looked at him as at a stranger, having nothing more to say.

Notes

I "THINK OF THE POWER —"

1 Mary Elizabeth Braddon, *A Lost Eden* (London: Hutchinson, 1904), pp. 136–39.
2 Francis Gribble, *Sunlight and Limelight: A Story of the Stage Life and the Real Life* (London: Innes, 1898), pp. 54–55.
3 Letter from Jenny (Mrs. Charles Longuet) to Eleanor Marx, 12–13 April 1882, quoted by Yvonne Knapp, *Eleanor Marx* (2 vols., New York: Pantheon, 1977), I, 42–45, 234–35.
4 Christopher Kent, "Image and Reality: The Actress and Society," in *A Widening Sphere: Changing Roles of Victorian Women*, ed. Martha Vicinus (Bloomington: Indiana University Press, 1977), p. 101.
5 Mary Elizabeth Braddon, *The Doctor's Wife* (London: Simpkin, Marshall, Hamilton, Kent, 1890), pp. 65–66.
6 Florence Nightingale, *Cassandra: An Essay* (Old Westbury, NY: Feminist Press, 1979), pp. 40–41.
7 Ibid., p. 40.
8 Mary Elizabeth Braddon, *Aurora Floyd, A Novel* (1863; New York: Coryell, [1885]), p. 14.
9 Madge Kendal, *Dramatic Opinions* (London: Murray, 1890), p. 47.
10 Geraldine Ensor Jewsbury, *The Half Sisters: A Tale* (2 vols., London: Chapman and Hall, 1848), II, 73.
11 Anon., "A Few Words about Actresses and the Profession of the Stage," *Englishwoman's Journal*, February 1859, pp. 385–98.
12 Florence Marryat, *Facing the Footlights* (2 vols., Leipzig: Tauchnitz, 1883), I, 240.
13 George Moore, *A Mummer's Wife* (New York: Boni and Liveright, 1922), p. 326.
14 John Strange Winter, *Connie, the Actress: A Novel* (London: White, 1902), p. 108.
15 Tracy C. Davis, *Actresses as Working Women: Their Social Identity in Victorian Culture* (London: Routledge, 1991), p. 34.

16 Mrs. Patrick Campbell, *My Life and Some Letters* (New York: Dodd, Mead, 1922), p. 60.

17 Ellaline Terriss, *Just a Little Bit of String* (London: Hutchinson, 1955), p. 92.

18 Mrs. Patrick Campbell, *My Life and Some Letters*, pp. 36–37.

19 Mary Elizabeth Braddon, "Across the Footlights," in *'Under the Red Flag' and Other Tales* (London: Maxwell, n.d.), p. 289.

20 See a letter to the *Era* on this subject, signed "An Actress," in which the "fabulous salaries" of neophyte actresses are said to be "unknown on the real stage," however pleasant to young women in novels (12 October 1895, p. 10).

21 Dion Boucicault, *Grimaldi; or, The Life of an Actress* (New York: n.p., 1856), p. 29.

22 Anna Cora Mowatt, *Autobiograph of an Actress: or, Eight Years on the Stage* (Boston: Ticknor, Reed and Fields, 1854), p. 427.

23 George Moore, "Mummer-Worship," in *Impressions and Opinions* (New York: Scribner's, 1891), p. 176.

24 Mowatt, *Autobiography of an Actress*, p. 426.

25 Mrs. Patrick Campbell, *My Life and Some Letters*, p. 437.

26 Ellaline Terriss, *Just a Little Bit of String*, p. 19.

27 Adelaide Ristori, *Studies and Memories: an Autobiography* (Boston: Roberts, 1888), pp. 16, 40–41.

28 "A Few Words about Actresses," pp. 385–98.

29 Geraldine Jewsbury, *The Half Sisters*, II, 82.

30 John Strange Winter, *Connie, the Actress*, p. 37.

31 The phrase was coined by Sarah Stickney Ellis, author of *The Women of England: Their Social Duties and Domestic Habits* (London: Fisher, 1838) and *The Daughters of England: Their Position in Society, Character, and Responsibilities* (London: Fisher, 1847), and other popular works on femininity.

32 Louis N. Parker, *A Buried Talent: An Original Play in Three Acts*, quoted from the licensing ms. in the Lord Chamberlain's Collection, British Library, p. 44.

33 *Era*, 17 June 1899, p. 17.

34 Arthur Symons, *Plays, Acting, and Music* (New York: Dutton, [1903]), p. 27.

35 Zadel Barnes Gustafson, *Genevieve Ward: A Biographical Sketch from Original Material Derived from Her Family and Friends* (Boston: Osgood, 1882), pp. 248, 250, quoting reviews in *Vanity Fair* and the *Era*.

36 Mrs. Patrick Campbell, *My Life and Some Letters*, p. 436.

37 Henry James, *The Tragic Muse* (New York: Scribner's, 1922), pp. 143–44.

38 Oscar Wilde, *The Picture of Dorian Gray*, ed. Isobel Murray (Oxford: Oxford University Press, 1981), p. 50.

39 *The Life and Love of an Actress*, "By an Actress" (New York: Judge, 1888), pp. 26–27.

40 Wilde, *The Picture of Dorian Gray*, p. 51.

2 MASCULINE PANIC AND THE PANTHERS OF THE STAGE

1 G. H. Lewes, *On Actors and the Art of Acting* (New York: Grove, [1957]), p. 32.
2 From a review of Cushman as Lady Macbeth, quoted by Mary M. Turner, *Forgotten Leading Ladies of the American Theatre* (Jefferson, NC: McFarland, 1990), p. 64.
3 Horace Wyndham, *The Flare of the Footlights* (London: Richards, 1907), p. 3.
4 William Winter, *Other Days; Being Chronicles and Memories of the Stage* (New York: Moffat, Yard, 1908), p. 154.
5 Ibid., p. 157.
6 Max Beerbohm, *Around Theatres* (New York: Knopf, 1930), p. 102.
7 Oscar Wilde, "Phèdre" [originally "To Sarah Bernhardt"], in *Complete Works of Oscar Wilde* (London: Collins, 1966), p. 777.
8 George Bernard Shaw, *Our Theatres in the Nineties* (3 vols., London: Constable, 1931), I, 158–60. A useful interpretation of these actresses appears in John Stokes, Michael R. Booth, and Susan Bassnett, *Bernhardt, Terry, Duse: The Actress in Her Time* (Cambridge: Cambridge University Press, 1988).
9 Arthur Symons, *Plays, Acting, and Music* (New York: Dutton [1903]), pp. 27–30.
10 Ibid., p. 128.
11 Arthur Symons, "Esther Kahn," in *Spiritual Adventures*, 2nd edn. (London: Constable, 1908), pp. 85–88.
12 G.B. Shaw, *Our Theatres in the Nineties*, I, 158–60.
13 Oscar Wilde, "Queen Henrietta Maria," *Complete Works of Oscar Wilde*, p. 788.
14 Ellen Terry, *Story of My Life: Ellen Terry's Memoirs* (Westport, CT: Greenwood, 1970), p. 198.
15 Clement Scott, *Ellen Terry* (New York: Stokes, 1900), p. 226.
16 This characterization of Ellen Terry as more "spiritual essence" than woman is from Shaw Desmond, *London Nights of Long Ago* (London: Duckworth, 1927), p. 183, but other critics praised other actresses in the same terms; for example, William Winter wrote that Adelaide Neilson was "more like a spirit than a woman" (*Other Days*, p. 284).
17 Oscar Wilde, "Olivia at the Lyceum," *Dramatic Review*, 30 May 1885; rpt. in *The First Collected Edition of the Works of Oscar Wilde* (15 vols., London: Methuen, 1908–22), ed. Robert Ross, XIII, 28–32.
18 Peter Raby, *Fair Ophelia: The Life of Harriet Smithson Berlioz* (Cambridge: Cambridge University Press, 1982), pp. 66–67.
19 Ibid., p. 77.
20 William Black, *Macleod of Dare: A Novel* (London: Harper, [1878]), pp. 39, 68, 178.
21 Joseph Fitzgerald Molloy, *Merely Players* (2 vols., London: Tinsley, 1881), I, 242.
22 John Bickerdyke, *Daughters of Thespis: A Story of the Green-Room* (London: Simpkin, 1897), p. 207.

23 Oscar Wilde, *The Picture of Dorian Gray*, ed. Isobel Murray (Oxford: Oxford University Press, 1981), p. 54.

24 Gaston Leroux, *The Phantom of the Opera* (New York: The Mysterious Press, 1988), p. 87.

25 Harriett Jay, *Through the Stage Door: A Novel* (New York: Munro, 1884), pp. 20, 26.

26 William Black, *Macleod of Dare*, p. 309.

27 For accounts of this episode, see Angela John, *Elizabeth Robins: Staging a Life, 1862–1952*, (London: Routledge, 1995), pp. 38–41, and Joanne Gates, *Elizabeth Robins: Actress, Novelist, Feminist* (Tuscaloosa: University of Alabama Press, 1994), pp. 19–22.

28 "Does the Theatre Make for Good?: An Interview with Mr. Clement Scott by Raymond Brathwayt," rpt. from *Great Thoughts*, 1 January 1898 (London: Hall, n.d.), p. 7.

29 George Moore, "Mummer-Worship," in *Impressions and Opinions* (New York: Scribner's, 1891), p. 154; George Eliot, Daniel Deronda (Oxford: Clarendon, 1984), p. 586.

30 Moore, "Mummer-Worship," p. 176.

31 "London's Lady Managers: A Chat with Miss Janette Steer," *Era*, 2 June 1900, p. 13.

32 "Actors' Marriages," *Stage Directory*, 1 March 1880, p. 8.

33 Henry James, *The Tragic Muse* (New York: Scribner's, 1922), pp. 342–43.

34 These same words – "I hate the stage" – are uttered in *The Picture of Dorian Gray* by Sybil Vane, whom Wilde leaves, as Madeline is left in Buchanan's novel, choosing death over being an actress.

35 Robert Buchanan, *The Martyrdom of Madeline* (London: Chatto & Windus, 1907), p. 209.

36 J. F. Molloy, *Merely Players*, II, 223.

37 Mary Anderson, *A Few More Memories* (London: Hutchinson, 1936), pp. 17, 21.

38 Edward Gordon Craig, *Ellen Terry and Her Secret Self* (New York: Dutton, 1932), pp. 52, 57, 63, 65–66.

39 Tom Taylor and Charles Reade, *Masks and Faces; or, Before and Behind the Curtain: A Comedy in Two Acts* (London: Bentley, 1854), p. 55.

40 Wynter F. Knight, *Teresa Marlowe, Actress and Dancer* (3 vols., London: Wyman, 1884), III, 227–37.

41 In Nina Auerbach, *Private Theatricals: The Lives of the Victorians* (Cambridge: Harvard University Press, 1990), pp. 4, 18.

42 Gaston Leroux, *The Phantom of the Opera*, p. 105.

43 Anna Cora Mowatt, *Mimic Life; or, Before and Behind the Curtain* (Boston: Ticknor and Fields, 1856), p. 27.

44 Black, *Macleod of Dare*, pp. 39, 48, 67.

45 Ibid., pp. 76, 99.

46 Francis Gribble, *Sunlight and Limelight: A Story of the Stage Life and the Real Life* (London: Innes, 1898), pp. 54–55, 137.

47 Wilde, *The Picture of Dorian Gray*, p. 86.

48 Francis Gribble, *Sunlight and Limelight*, pp. 47, 341.

49 Mary Anderson, *A Few More Memories*, pp. 17–18.

50 Mary Anderson, *A Few Memories* (London: Osgood, McIlvaine, 1896), pp. 227–28.

51 Black, *Macleod of Dare*, p. 135.

52 George Eliot, *Daniel Deronda* (Oxford: Clarendon, 1984), pp. 583–86.

53 Oscar Wilde, *The Picture of Dorian Gray*, pp. 86, 103.

54 Vesta Tilley (Matilda Alice [Powles], Lady de Freece), *The Recollections of Vesta Tilley* (London: Hutchinson, 1934). p. 208. Good recent analyses of Victorian actresses' playing male roles include those by Laurence Senelick, "The Evolution of the Male Impersonator on the Nineteenth-Century Popular Stage," *Essays in Theatre* 1 (1982), 29–44, and Tracy C. Davis, *Actresses as Working Women: Their Social Identity in Victorian Culture* (London: Routledge, 1991), especially pp. 114–15.

55 Tracy C. Davis, *Actresses as Working Women*, p. 114.

56 William Archer, *English Dramatists of To-Day* (London: Sampson, Low, 1882), p. 12.

57 William Archer, *The Theatrical 'World' of 1894* (London: Scott, 1895), pp. 69–71.

58 Max Beerbohm, *Around Theatres*, pp. 48–49.

59 *Era*, 17 June 1899, p. 13.

60 "Giovanni in London," *Theatrical Inquisitor*, June 1820, p. 394.

61 Elizabeth Robins, "Judith", ms. in the Fales Library, New York University.

62 Horace Wyndham, *The Flare of the Footlights*, p. 76.

63 Ibid., p. 313.

64 Geraldine Jewsbury, *The Half Sisters: A Tale* (2 vols., London: Chapman and Hall, 1848), II, 18–19.

65 Sir Frederick Pollock, ed., *Macready's Reminiscences* (2 vols., New York: Harper, 1875), II, 266.

66 William Black, *Macleod of Dare*, p. 175.

67 Ibid., p. 127.

68 Florence Marryat, *My Sister the Actress* (3 vols., London: White, 1881), III, 105, 113.

69 Harriett Jay, *Through the Stage Door*, pp. 4, 31.

70 Daniel Joseph Kirwan, *Palace and Hovel: or, Phases of London Life* (1870; London: Abelard-Schuman, 1963), p. 52.

71 Michael Ryan, M.D., *Prostitution in London, with a Comparative View of That of Paris and New York* (London: Bailliere, 1839), pp. 239–40.

72 William Archer, "The Drama," in *The Reign of Queen Victoria: A Survey of Fifty Years of Progress*, ed. Thomas H. Ward (2 vols., London: Smith, Elder, 1887), II, 569.

73 "Actress and 'Actress'," *Theatre*, 1 August 1896, pp. 58–61.

74 1892 Select Committee on Theatres and Places of Entertainment, 2 June 1892, questions nos. 5179, 5183.

75 L. Taylor, *Fairy Phoebe; or, Facing the Footlights* (London: Shaw, [1887]), pp. 212–22.

76 Henry Herman, *A Leading Lady: A Story of the Stage* (London: Chatto & Windus, 1891), pp. 218–19.

77 L. Taylor, *Fairy Phoebe*, p. 215.

78 Wynter F. Knight, *Teresa Marlowe, Actress and Dancer*, pp. 184–85.

79 "The Artist's Dream; or, Sen Artysty [*sic*]," in *Complete Works of Oscar Wilde*, pp. 822–24.

80 Richard von Krafft-Ebing, *Psychopathia Sexualis*, trans. Franklin S. Klaf (New York: Bell, 1965), p. 263.

81 Judith Walkowitz, *Prostitution and Victorian Society: Women, Class, and the State* (Cambridge: Cambridge University Press, 1980), p. 180.

82 Elaine Showalter, *The Female Malady: Women, Madness, and English Culture, 1830–1980* (New York: Pantheon, 1985), p. 48, quoting Victorian psychiatrist John Connolly. Michel Foucault's studies of madness emphasize its commitment to "ethical uniformity" and authority, but overlook what Showalter brilliantly captures, namely the possibility that the modern asylum was conceived in large part to limit and confine the feminine. See Foucault, *Madness and Civilization: A History of Insanity in the Age of Reason* (New York: Vintage, 1973), pp. 250–57.

83 Florence Nightingale, *Cassandra: An Essay* (Old Westbury, NY: Feminist Press, 1979), p. 65.

84 See, e.g., Showalter, *The Female Malady*; Phyllis Chesler, *Women and Madness* (Garden City, NY: Doubleday, 1972); Sandra Gilbert and Susan Gubar, *The Madwoman in the Attic: The Woman Writer and the Nineteenth-Century Literary Imagination* (New Haven: Yale University Press, 1979).

85 Peter Raby, *Fair Ophelia*, p. 177.

86 Ellen Terry, *Ellen Terry's Memoirs*, p. 239, referring to her performance in *Ravenswood*, staged at the Lyceum in 1890.

87 E. F. S. Pigott, quoted by Elizabeth Robins in her memoir "Whither and How," ms. in the Fales Library, New York University.

88 A. B. Walkley, *Playhouse Impressions* (London: Unwin, 1892), pp. 59–63.

89 Anna Cora Mowatt, *A Mimic Life*, p. 185.

90 George Moore, *A Mummer's Wife*, (New York: Boni and Liveright, 1922), pp. 363–64.

91 Michel Foucault, *Madness and Civilization*, p. 257.

92 Anna Cora Mowatt, *A Mimic Life*, pp. 184, 191–92.

93 "Miss Hamlet," *Era*, 27 May 1899, p. 13.

94 George du Maurier, *Trilby: A Novel* (New York: Harper, 1894), p. 438.

95 W. E. Suter, *Violette le Grande, or The Life of an Actress: A Drama in Three Acts*, staged in 1853 at the Grecian Theatre and apparently never published, is quoted from the ms. in the Lord Chamberlain's Collection of the British Library, pp. 5, 17, 74.

96 Geraldine Jewsbury, *The Half Sisters*, ii, 35, 50.

97 Eva Ross-Church, *An Actress's Love Story: A Novel* (2 vols., London: White, 1888), ii, 185.
98 *The Life and Love of an Actress*, "By an Actress" (New York: Judge, 1888), pp. 64–66.
99 Gertrude Warden, *The Moth and the Footlights* (London: Digby, Long, 1906), pp. 71–72, 294.
100 Florence Marryat, *Facing the Footlights: A Novel* (2 vols., Leipzig: Tauchnitz, 1883), i, 9.
101 Edith Stewart Drewry, *Only an Actress: A Novel* (3 vols., London: White, 1883), iii, 67.
102 Rita [Eliza Margaret J. Humphreys], *Only an Actress* (London: Paul, [1911]), pp. 83–85.
103 "The Candle's Flame," in Virginia Tracy, *Merely Players: Stories of Stage Life* (New York: Century, 1909), p. 258.
104 Florence Marryat, *My Sister the Actress*, iii, 84.
105 Robert Buchanan, *The Martyrdom of Madeline*, pp. 209, 211.
106 Elizabeth Robins, "Whither and How," pp. 1–2.
107 Harriett Jay, *Through the Stage Door*, pp. 41–43.
108 Robert Buchanan, *The Martyrdom of Madeline*, p. 209.
109 Florence Marryat, *My Sister the Actress*, ii, 82–83.
110 Wilde, *The Picture of Dorian Gray*, p. 103.
111 Fanny Bernard-Beere's "The Tale of a Peacock" and Marie Litton's "Chances! Story of a Young Actress" appeared along with Wilde's early poem on Helena Modjeska in an anthology of theatre writing published in 1881. It was edited by drama critic Clement Scott under the title *The Green Room* (Routledge, 1881).
112 *The Life and Love of an Actress*, pp. 63–65, 261–63.
113 Rita, *Only an Actress*, pp. 86–87.
114 William Suter, *The Life of an Actress*.
115 Wilde, *The Picture of Dorian Gray*, p. 86.
116 Gribble, *Sunlight and Limelight*, pp. 146–47.
117 Florence Marryat, *Facing the Footlights*, i, 225.
118 Mrs. Patrick Campbell, *My Life and Some Letters* (New York: Dodd, Mead, 1922), p. 155.
119 Elizabeth Robins, *Both Sides of the Curtain* (London: Heineman, 1940), p. 204.
120 William Winter, *Other Days*, p. 266.
121 Mary Anderson, *A Few More Memories*, p. 19.
122 Quoted in W. Macqueen-Pope, *Ladies First: The Story of Woman's Conquest of the British Stage* (London: Allen, 1952), p. 300.
123 Elizabeth Robins, *Both Sides of the Curtain*, p. 204.
124 Adelaide Ristori, *Studies and Memories: an Autobiography*, (Boston: Roberts, 1888), p. 12.
125 Ibid., pp. 12–13.
126 Max Nordau, *Degeneration* (New York: Appleton, 1895), pp. 405, 412–13.
127 These developments are especially well detailed in Frank B. Hanson,

"London Theatre Audiences of the Nineteenth Century," Diss., Yale University, 1953.

128 This characterization of Robertson's plays is quoted from *The Stage of 1871: A Review of Plays and Players*, by "Hawk's Eye" (London: Bickers, [1871]), p. 27.

129 Marie and Squire Bancroft, *The Bancrofts: Recollections of Sixty Years* (New York: Dutton, 1909), p. 272. For an interesting and persuasive recent account of how the Bancrofts reproduced the middle-class experience at the Prince of Wales's Theatre, see Mary Jean Corbett, *Representing Femininity: Middle-Class Subjectivity in Victorian and Edwardian Women's Autobiography* (New York: Oxford University Press, 1992).

130 Justin McCarthy, *Portraits of the Sixties* (London: Unwin, 1903), p. 426.

131 Henry James, *The Scenic Art: Notes on Acting and the Drama*, ed. Allan Wade (London: Hart-Davis, 1949), pp. 147–48.

132 William Archer, "The Drama," in *The Reign of Queen Victoria: A Survey of Fifty Years of Progress* (2 vols., London: Smith, Elder, 1887), II, 582.

133 Marie and Squire Bancroft, *The Bancrofts*, pp. 119–20.

134 James, *The Scenic Art*, p. 101.

135 William Archer, *The Theatrical World for 1893* (London: Scott, 1894), p. 292.

136 Quoted in Martha Vicinus, *Independent Women: Work and Community for Single Women, 1850–1920* (Chicago: University of Chicago Press, 1985), p. 146.

137 William Archer develops this argument in *English Dramatists of To-Day* (London: Sampson, Low, 1882).

138 Henry James, *The Scenic Art*, pp. 120, 169.

139 Marguerite Steen, *A Pride of Terrys: Family Saga* (London: Longman, 1962), pp. 162–63.

140 Florence Marryat, *Facing the Footlights*, II, 82.

141 Mary Elizabeth Braddon, *Dead-Sea Fruit, A Novel* (New York: Harper, 1868), p. 75.

142 A. B. Walkley, "Prejudice against Players," *Playhouse Impressions* (London: Unwin, 1892), p. 236.

143 George Moore, "Mummer-Worship,", pp. 164, 179.

144 Charles Reade and Tom Taylor, *Masks and Faces*, p. 59.

145 Herbert Blau, *Audience* (Baltimore: Johns Hopkins University Press, 1990), pp. 1–4.

146 Marie Bancroft, *Gleanings from 'On and Off the Stage'* (London: Routledge, 1892), pp. 56–58.

147 Macqueen-Pope, *Ladies First*, pp. 327–29.

148 Gordon Craig, *Ellen Terry and Her Secret Self*, p. 157.

149 *Referee*, 12 June 1887.

150 *Theatre*, 1 August 1887, p. 97.

151 Nina Auerbach, *Ellen Terry: Player in Her Time* (New York: Norton, 1987), p. 203.

152 *Ellen Terry's Memoirs*, p. 128.

153 Kate Terry Gielgud, *An Autobiography* (London: Reinhardt, n.d.), p. 104.

154 Geraldine Jewsbury, *The Half Sisters*, II, 135.
155 Nina Auerbach, *Ellen Terry*, pp. 213–14.
156 *Illustrated London News*, 10 February 1855, p. 132.
157 H. Chance Newton, "My Fourscore Hamlets," in *Cues and Curtain Calls* (London: Lane, n.d.), pp. 186–243.
158 Clement Scott, *Some Notable Hamlets of the Present Time* (London: Greening, 1900), p. 50.
159 *Ellen Terry's Memoirs*, p. 235.
160 Shaw Desmond, *London Nights of Long Ago* (London: Duckworth, 1927), p. 183.
161 Gordon Craig, *Ellen Terry and Her Secret Self*, p. 157.
162 Clement Scott, *Ellen Terry* (New York: Stokes, 1900), p. 226.
163 Shaw Desmond, *London Nights of Long Ago*, p. 183.
164 George Bernard Shaw, *Our Theatres in the Nineties*, I, 246.
165 Sheila Stowell, in *A Stage of their Own: Feminist Playwrights of the Suffrage Era* (Ann Arbor: University of Michigan Press, 1992), pp. 33–34, makes the point that even the author of *A Doll's House* is "too much of a man" – making self-realization and maternity into mutually exclusive concepts.
166 Micheline Wandor, *Carry on, Understudies: Theatre and Sexual Politics* (London: Routledge, 1986), p. 32.
167 Tracy C. Davis, *Actresses as Working Women*; Mary Jean Corbett, *Representing Femininity*; Irene Vanbrugh, *To Tell My Story* (London: Hutchinson, n.d.), pp. 90–91, 102–03.
168 *Diary of an Actress: or Realities of Stage Life*, ed. H. C. Shuttleworth (London: Griffith, Farran, 1885), pp. 58, 64.
169 Geraldine Jewsbury, *The Half Sisters*, II, 23.
170 Florence Farr, *Modern Woman: Her Intentions* (London: Palmer, [1910]), p. 25.
171 Lena Ashwell, *Myself a Player* (London: Joseph, 1936), p. 132.
172 While attacking the idea that it was humiliating or degrading for women to work, handbooks like Mercy Grogan's *How Women May Earn a Living* (London: Cassell, 1880) usually fail to mention acting as a suitable profession for women, while recommending careers requiring "really skilled labour" – teaching at £2 or less a week to start, telegraphy at less than £1, and even making false teeth for dentists at 18 shillings a week. The "fairy world of the stage," as one Victorian called it, seemed unrelated to the campaign for more opportunities for women in work generally, and in any case a typical actress's prospects – even if she were regularly employed – were not much better than those of women in what was termed "practical categories" of labor.
173 Sue-Ellen Case, *Feminism and Theatre* (London: Methuen, 1988), p. 120.
174 W. Macqueen-Pope, *Ladies First*, p. 368.
175 Sir Theodore Martin, *Helen Faucit (Lady Martin)* (Edinburgh: Blackwood, 1900), p. 166.
176 Mrs. C. Baron Wilson, *Our Actresses; or, Glances at Stage Favourites, Past and Present* (2 vols., London: Smith, Elder, 1844), II, 13.

177 Sir Theodore Martin, *Helen Faucit*, pp. 294, 301, 306, 341, 394. Thus the actress becomes involved in what Teresa de Lauretis has called a "technology of gender" – representing gender in a particular fashion, absorbing that representation subjectively, and disseminating it as a measure of social control (*Technologies of Gender: Essays on Theory, Film, and Fiction* [Bloomington: Indiana University Press, 1987]). The force behind this representation of the female, as Laura Mulvey points out in relation to cinematic narrative, is ultimately masculine, whether in the form of a monitory protagonist, director, spectator, etc., whose "gaze" determines the shape of the story ("Visual Pleasure and Narrative Cinema," *Screen*, 16 [1975], 6–18).

178 Mrs. C. Baron Wilson, *Our Actresses*, II, 20.

179 Gordon Craig, *Ellen Terry and Her Secret Self*, p. 157.

180 Madge Kendal, *Dramatic Opinions* (London: Murray, 1890), pp. 78–79, 82.

181 See, for example, Mary Anderson, *A Few Memories* (London: Osgood, McIlvaine, 1896), p. 242.

182 Helen Faucit, *Some of Shakespeare's Female Characters* (Edinburgh: Blackwood, 1885), pp. 25, 52, 411, 433.

183 William Winter, *The Stage Life of Mary Anderson* (New York: Coombes, 1886), pp. 76, 90, 114, 125.

184 Mrs. C. Baron Wilson, *Our Actresses*, I, 71.

185 Marie and Squire Bancroft, *The Bancrofts*, pp. 147–49.

186 Ibid., p. 153.

187 Lillah McCarthy, *Myself and My Friends* (London: Butterworth, 1933), pp. 44–45.

188 Anna Cora Mowatt, *Autobiography of an Actress: or, Eight Years on the Stage* (Boston: Ticknor, Reed and Fields, 1854), p. 427.

189 Madge Kendal, *Dame Madge Kendal by Herself* (London: Murray, 1933), p. 187. The gradually increasing respectability of the actress, and actor, in the Victorian period has been a theme in theatre histories; see, for example, Michael Baker, *The Rise of the Victorian Actor* (London: Croom Helm, 1978).

190 Jessie Millward, *Myself and Others* (Boston: Small, Maynard, 1924), pp. 50–55.

191 Kendal, *Dame Madge Kendal by Herself*, p. 62 .

192 H. Chance Newton, *Cues and Curtain Calls*, p. 68.

193 Gordon Craig, *Ellen Terry and Her Secret Self*, p. 152.

194 W. H. Davenport Adams, *Woman's Work and Worth in Girlhood, Maidenhood, and Wifehood* (New York: Cassell, 1880), p. 283. Such pronouncements worked toward the reconciliation of normative femininity and the theatre, where Victorian understandings of gender had been more blatantly under assault than almost anywhere else.

195 Havelock Ellis, *Man and Woman: A Study of Secondary Sexual Characters* (London: Scott, 1894), p. 7.

196 Sarah Bernhardt, *The Art of the Theatre*, trans. H. J. Stenning (London: Bles, n.d.), p. 144.

197 Tom Robertson, *Caste*, in *Nineteenth Century Plays*, ed. George Rowell, 2nd edn. (London: Oxford University Press, 1972), p. 373.
198 "Does the Theatre Make for Good?: An Interview with Mr. Clement Scott by Raymond Brathwayt," p. 15.

3 ACTRESSES, MANAGERS, AND FEMINIZED THEATRE

1 Cicely Hamilton, *Life Errant* (London: Dent, 1935), p. 47.
2 Charlotte Morland, "Woman and the Stage," *Era*, 23 January 1892, p. 9.
3 Lena Ashwell, *Myself a Player* (London: Joseph, 1936), pp. 52, 81.
4 Lena Ashwell, *The Stage* (London: Bles, 1929), p. 71.
5 Violet Vanbrugh, *Dare To Be Wise* (London: Hodder & Stoughton, n.d.), p. 31.
6 Mary Elizabeth Braddon, *A Lost Eden* (London: Hutchinson, 1904), p. 164.
7 Shaw is quoted among the "replies" included in "Does the Theatre Make for Good? An Interview with Mr. Clement Scott by Raymond Brathwayt," rpt. from *Great Thoughts*, 1 January 1898 (London: Hall, n.d.), p. 14.
8 *Story of My Life: Ellen Terry's Memoirs* (Westport, CT: Greenwood, 1970), p. 132; Ellaline Terriss, *Just a Little Bit of String* (London: Hutchinson, 1955), pp. 64, 285.
9 Genevieve Ward and Richard Whiteing, *Both Sides of the Curtain* (London: Cassell, 1918), p. 238.
10 *Illustrated Sporting and Dramatic News*, 2 January 1889.
11 Ellaline Terriss, *Just a Little Bit of String*, p. 285.
12 Horace Wyndham, *The Flare of the Footlights* (London: Richards, 1907), p. 322.
13 Sir Frederick Pollock, ed., *Macready's Reminiscences* (2 vols., New York: Harper, 1875), II, 266.
14 H. Chance Newton, *Cues and Curtain Calls* (London: Lane, n.d.), p. 125.
15 Marie and Squire Bancroft, *The Bancrofts: Recollections of Sixty Years* (New York: Dutton, 1909), p. 327.
16 Ward and Whiteing, *Both Sides of the Curtain*, p. 220.
17 Mary Elizabeth Braddon, *Dead-Sea Fruit: A Novel* (New York: Harper, 1868), pp. 60, 76.
18 Marie and Squire Bancroft, *The Bancrofts*, p. 55.
19 "London's Lady Managers: A Chat with Miss Janette Steer," *Era*, 2 June 1900, p. 13.
20 Princess Lazarovich-Hrebelianovich [Eleanor Calhoun], *Pleasures and Palaces: The Memoirs of Princess Lazarovich-Hrebelianovich* (London: Nash, 1916), pp. 193–94.
21 Alfred L. Crauford, *Sam and Sallie: A Romance of the Stage* (London: Cranley & Day, 1933), p. 318.
22 Mary Anderson, *A Few Memories* (London: Osgood, McIlvaine, 1896), pp. 246–49.
23 Lena Ashwell, *The Stage*, pp. 109, 173–76.
24 Lena Ashwell, *Myself a Player*, pp. 145–52.

25 *Ellen Terry's Memoirs*, p. 32.
26 Violet Vanbrugh, *Dare To Be Wise*, pp. 50–55.
27 A. E. Wilson, *East End Entertainment* (London: Barker, 1954), pp. 58, 191–92.
28 Alfred L. Crauford, *Sam and Sallie*, pp. 309, 318.
29 Madge Kendal, *Dramatic Opinions* (London: Murray, 1890), pp. 98–99.
30 Ibid., p. 40.
31 Violet Vanbrugh, *Dare to Be Wise*, pp. 54–55.
32 Marie Bancroft, *Gleanings from 'On and Off the Stage'* (London: Routledge, 1892), p. 305.
33 Marie and Squire Bancroft, *The Bancrofts*, p. 125.
34 *The Stage of 1871: A Review of Plays and Players*, by "Hawk's Eye" (London: Bickers, [1871]), pp. 40–41.
35 Charles E. Pearce, *Madame Vestris and Her Times* (London: Paul, 1923), p. 168.
36 *Playgoer*, August 1889, p. 1.
37 From a review by A.B. Walkley, quoted by Mrs. Patrick Campbell in *My Life and Some Letters* (New York: Dodd, Mead, 1922), p. 306.
38 Walter Besant, *The Revolt of Man* (London: Collins, 1882), pp. 82–83.
39 Clement Scott, *The Wheel of Life: A Few Memories and Recollections* (London : Greening, 1897), p. 20.
40 Tom Robertson, *Society: A Comedy in Three Acts*, in *Plays by Tom Robertson* (Cambridge: Cambridge University Press, 1982), Act II, scene 1, pp. 51–58.
41 For a history of Victorian playwriting as a profession, with an emphasis on its economic growth, see John Russell Stephens, *The Profession of the Playwright, British Theatre 1800-1900* (Cambridge: Cambridge University Press, 1992).

4 THE IMPOSSIBILITY OF WOMEN PLAYWRIGHTS

1 Virginia Woolf, *"A Room of One's Own" and "Three Guineas"* (London: Hogarth, 1984), pp. 43–47.
2 William Archer, *The Old Drama and the New* (Boston: Small, Maynard, 1923).
3 Micheline Wandor, *Carry On, Understudies: Theatre and Sexual Politics* (London: Routledge, 1986), pp. 126–28.
4 Sue-Ellen Case, *Feminism and Theatre* (New York: Methuen, 1988), pp. 37, 44.
5 Cicely Hamilton, *Life Errant* (London: Dent, 1935), p. 60.
6 Mrs. Musgrave, *Our Flat: Farcical Comedy in Three Acts*, is quoted from the unpaginated licensing ms. in the Lord Chamberlain's Collection. The play was first performed in London at the Prince of Wales's Theatre and was apparently never published.
7 Letter from Bell to Robins, possibly from November or December 1892, in the Fales Library, New York University.
8 These figures are derived from J. P. Wearing, *The London Stage, 1890–1899: A Calendar of Plays and Players* (Metuchen, NJ: Scarecrow, 1976).
9 "Women as Dramatists," *All the Year Round*, 29 September 1894, p. 299.
10 *Era*, 10 June 1894, p. 10.

11 Hélène Cixous, "Aller à la Mer," *Modern Drama*, 27 (1984), 546-48. See also Jill Dolan, *The Feminist Spectator as Critic* (Ann Arbor: UMI Research Press, 1988), pp. 86–87, for a discussion, indebted to Cixous, of a women's drama that would be "fluid, irrational, body-centered, fragmentary, nonlinear, openly female," abandoning the structure of male narratives of desire.

12 Frank Archer, *How To Write a Good Play* (London: French, 1892), p. 71.

13 Leon Edel, ed., *The Complete Tales of Henry James*, (12 vols., London: Hart-Davis, 1963), VIII, 157.

14 William Archer, *The Theatrical 'World' of 1894* (London: Scott, 1895), p. 97.

15 Mrs. Musgrave, *Our Flat*.

16 "Women as Dramatists," *All the Year Round*, 29 September 1894, p. 300.

17 "The Finance of the Drama," *Era*, 26 March 1892, p. 15.

18 W. H. Davenport Adams, *Women of Fashion and Representative Women in Letters and Society* (2 vols., London: Tinsley, 1878), II, 165–66.

19 Except as noted, this information on the income of playwrights is drawn from J. R. Stephens, *The Profession of the Playwright: British Theatre, 1800–1900* (Cambridge: Cambridge University Press, 1992), *passim*. I am indebted to him for sharing the proofs of his book with me prior to its publication.

20 Robert Lee Wolff, "Devoted Disciple: The Letters of Mary Elizabeth Braddon to Sir E. Bulwer-Lytton, 1862–73," *Huntington Library Bulletin*, April 1974, p. 151.

21 The manuscript of this play, and correspondence related to it, is in the Humanities Research Center of the University of Texas.

22 *Era*, 12 October 1895, p. 10.

23 Stephens, *The Profession of the Playwright*, provides an excellent and detailed survey of the professional environments of playwriting in the Victorian period.

24 "A Chat with Miss Clo Graves," *Sketch*, 21 February 1900, p. 218.

25 Anna Cora Mowatt, *Autobiography of an Actress: or, Eight Years on the Stage* (Boston: Ticknor, Reed, and Fields, 1854), p. 296.

26 Constance Fenimore Woolson, "Miss Grief," in *Women Artists, Women Exiles: 'Miss Grief' and Other Stories*, ed. Joan Myers Weimer (New Brunswick, NJ: Rutgers University Press, 1988), p. 256.

27 Elizabeth Robins, letter to Florence Bell, 24 February 1900, Fales Library, New York University.

28 Tree expressed himself on women playwrights in a note to Robins in the Fales Library of New York University. In that note he counts her play on Benvenuto Cellini as an exception to the rule.

29 This claim is based on entries in Gwenn Davis and Beverly A. Joyce, *Drama by Women to 1900: A Bibliography of American and British Writers* (Toronto: University of Toronto Press, 1992); *"The Stage" Cyclopaedia* (London: The Stage, 1909); Donald Mullin, *Victorian Plays: A Record of Significant Productions on the London Stage, 1837–1901* (New York: Greenwood, 1987); Allardyce Nicoll, *A History of English Drama, 1660–1900* (6 vols., Cambridge: Cambridge University Press, 1952–59); J. P. Wearing, *The London Stage, 1890–1899*, among other sources.

30 John Pick, *The West End: Mismanagement and Snobbery* (Eastbourne: Offord, 1983), pp. 17–34.

31 William Archer, *The Theatrical 'World' of 1894*, pp. 355–56.

32 See Frank Archer, *How To Write a Good Play*, pp. 18, 20.

33 *The Stage of 1871*, p. 15.

34 Quoted by Olive Logan, *Before the Footlights and Behind the Scenes: A Book about the "Show Business" in All Its Branches* (Philadelphia: Parmelee, 1870), p. 391.

35 William Archer, *English Dramatists of To-Day* (London: Sampson, Low, 1882), p. 76.

36 "Female Dramatists of the Past," *Era*, 23 May 1896, p. 18.

37 Gail Finney, among others, makes this point; see *Women in Modern Drama* (Ithaca: Cornell University Press, 1989), pp. 17–18.

38 *Illustrated Sporting and Dramatic News*, 29 June 1889.

39 *The Stage of 1871: A Review of Plays and Players*, by "Hawk's Eye" (London: Bickers, 1871), p. 15.

40 *The Times*, 7 June 1853, p. 8.

41 William Archer, *Play-Making: A Manual of Craftsmanship* (Boston: Small, Maynard, 1912), pp. 37, 48–49.

42 Ibid., pp. 134–39, 189–91.

43 Frank Archer, *How To Write a Good Play*, p. 202.

44 Max Beerbohm, "Mr. Shaw's Profession," 1898; rpt. *Shaw Review*, 5 (1962), p. 7.

45 Henry James, *The Tragic Muse* (New York: Scribner's, 1922), p. 293.

46 *The Times*, 20 March 1882, p. 7.

47 William Archer, *Real Conversations* (London: Heinemann, 1904), pp. 67–68.

48 *Story of My Life: Ellen Terry's Memoirs* (Westport, CT: Greenwood, 1970), p. 244.

49 Frances Ann Kemble, *Records of a Girlhood* (New York: Holt, 1879), pp. 446–47.

50 William Archer, *The Theatrical 'World' of 1894*, p. 96.

51 *The Life and Love of an Actress*, "By an Actress" (New York: Judge, 1888), pp. 88–89, 230.

52 Constance Fenimore Woolson, "Miss Grief," in *Women Artists, Women Exiles*, p. 259.

53 Anna Cora Mowatt, *Autobiography of an Actress*, p. 297.

54 Braddon plays the role of humble petitioner in the correspondence between herself and Jerome (mss. in the Humanities Research Center, University of Texas).

55 Oscar Wilde, *The Picture of Dorian Gray*, ed. Isobel Murray (Oxford: Oxford University Press, 1981), pp. 101–02.

56 *The Sunday Times*, 5 November 1933.

57 H. Chance Newton, *Cues and Curtain Calls* (London: Lane, n.d.), p. 158.

58 Clement Scott, *The Stage and the Age: A Lecture Delivered at the Playgoers' Club on March 17, 1885* (London: French, n.d.), p. 16.

59 H. Chance Newton, *Crime and the Drama; or, Dark Deeds Dramatized* (1927; rpt. Port Washington, NY: Kennikat Press, 1970), pp. 203–04.

60 Max Beerbohm, "The Advantage of Writing Plays," *Around Theatres* (New York: Knopf, 1930), pp. 258–62.
61 Quoted from Ellen Terry's promptbook of *Olivia*, in the collection of the Ellen Terry Museum, Tenterden, Sussex.
62 Madge Kendal, *Dramatic Opinions* (London: Murray, 1890), p. 65.
63 Anna Maria Hall [Mrs. S.C. Hall], *A Woman's Story* (3 vols., London: Hurst & Blackett, 1857), I, 309; II, 6,101.
64 Dorothy Leighton [Dorothy Forsyth], *Disillusion: A Story with a Preface* (3 vols., London: Henry, 1894), I, 22.
65 Mrs. Musgrave, *Our Flat.*
66 Olive Logan, *Before the Footlights and Behind the Scenes*, pp. 412–13.
67 Anna Maria Hall, *A Woman's Story*, II, 240.
68 Michel Foucault, *Madness and Civilization: A History of Insanity in the Age of Reason* (New York: Vintage, 1973), p. 250.
69 Elizabeth Robins, *George Mandeville's Husband* (New York: Appleton, 1894).
70 Elizabeth Jordan, *Mary Iverson's Career* (New York: Harper, 1914), pp. 277–78.
71 George Colman the Younger, *The Female Dramatist: A Farce in Two Acts*, unpaginated ms. in the Larpent Collection of the Lord Chamberlain's Collection of plays.
72 Mrs. Musgrave, *Our Flat.*
73 Rita (Eliza Margaret J. Humphreys), *A Husband of No Importance* (London: Unwin, 1894), pp. 223, 229.

5   TEXTUAL ASSAULTS: WOMEN'S NOVELS ON STAGE

1 Gaye Tuchman, *Edging Women Out: Victorian Novelists, Publishers, and Social Change* (New Haven: Yale University Press, 1989), pp. 52, 54. Tuchman uses the files of Macmillan as the sample for this study.
2 Susan Morgan, *Sisters in Time: Imagining Gender in Nineteenth-Century British Fiction* (New York: Oxford University Press, 1989), pp. 3–4.
3 Nancy Armstrong, *Desire and Domestic Fiction: A Political History of the Novel* (New York: Oxford University Press, 1987), p. 48.
4 Nancy Armstrong, "Literature as Women's History: A Necessary Transgression of Genres," *Genre*, 19 (1986), 347–70.
5 Mary Poovey, *The Proper Lady and the Woman Writer* (Chicago: University of Chicago Press, 1984), p. xv.
6 Sandra Gilbert and Susan Gubar, *The Madwoman in the Attic: The Woman Writer and the Nineteenth-Century Literary Imagination* (New Haven: Yale University Press, 1979); Elaine Showalter, *A Literature of Their Own: British Women Novelists from Brontë to Lessing* (Princeton: Princeton University Press, 1977); and Showalter, "Feminist Criticism in the Wilderness," in *Writing and Sexual Difference*, ed. Elizabeth Abel (Chicago: University of Chicago Press, 1982).
7 For helpful accounts of dramatic copyright in the nineteenth century, see Victor Bonham-Carter, *Authors by Profession* (Los Altos, CA: Kaufmann, 1978), and John Russell Stephens, *The Profession of the Playwright: British Theatre, 1800–1900* (Cambridge: Cambridge University Press, 1992).

8 Quoted by Bonham-Carter, *Authors by Profession*, I, 139.

9 Robert Lee Wolff, *Sensational Victorian: The Life and Fiction of Mary Elizabeth Braddon* (New York: Garland, 1979), p. 142.

10 *The Times*, 3 March 1882, p. 10.

11 Ibid., 6 March 1882, p. 6.

12 Ibid., 24 March 1882, p. 4.

13 Ibid., 27 March 1882, p. 7.

14 Allardyce Nicoll, *A History of English Drama 1660–1900*, v: *Later Nineteenth-Century Drama*, 2nd edn. (6 vols., Cambridge: Cambridge University Press, 1952–59), 79–81.

15 George Augustus Sala, *Echoes of the Year 1883* (London: Remington, 1884), p. 392.

16 George Rowell, *The Victorian Theatre, '1792–1914': A Survey*, 2nd edn. (Cambridge: Cambridge University Press, 1978), pp. 50–51.

17 Robertson Davies, "Plays and Playwrights," in *Revels History of Drama in English*, vi: 1750–1850 (London: Methuen, 1975), p. 240.

18 I base this estimate on entries in Gwenn Davis and Beverly A. Joyce, *Drama by Women to 1900: A Bibliography of American and British Writers* (Toronto: University of Toronto Press, 1992); *"The Stage" Cyclopaedia* (London: The Stage, 1909); Donald Mullin, *Victorian Plays: A Record of Significant Productions on the London Stage, 1837–1901* (New York: Greenwood, 1987); Allardyce Nicoll, *A History of English Drama, 1660–1900*; J. P. Wearing, *The London Stage, 1890–1899: A Calendar of Plays and Players* (Metuchen, NJ: Scarecrow, 1976).

19 Harold Bloom's theories of literary influence are elaborated in *The Anxiety of Influence* (New York: Oxford University Press, 1973) and *A Map of Misreading* (New York: Oxford Univesity Press, 1975).

20 Robertson Davies, "Plays and Playwrights," in *Revels History of Drama in English*, vi: 1750–1850, 242.

21 *Jane Eyre: A Drama in Two Acts* is quoted from the licensing ms. in the Lord Chamberlain's Collection at the British Library, pp. 1–16.

22 Charlotte Brontë, *Jane Eyre (New York: Norton, 1971), pp. 384–97.*

23 Terry Eagleton, *Myths of Power: A Marxist Study of the Brontës* (London: Macmillan, 1975), pp. 15–32.

24 *Daily News*, 25 December 1882.

25 *Jane Eyre* by W. G. Wills, apparently never published, is quoted from the licensing ms. in the British Library.

26 Quoted from an unidentified review in the Theatre Museum.

27 *Daily News*, 25 December 1882.

28 John Brougham's *Jane Eyre: A Drama, in Five Acts* (New York: French, n.d.) is the source of these quotations.

29 James Willing and Leonard Rae, *Jane Eyre, or Poor Relations: Drama in 4 Acts* (1879), apparently never published, is quoted from the licensing ms. in the Lord Chamberlain's Collection of the British Library, pp. 41, 61.

30 Elizabeth Gaskell, *Mary Barton* (London: Oxford University Press, [1906]), pp. 306, 456.

31 Poster advertisement for *The Long Strike* in the Theatre Museum.

32 Ellen Moers, *Literary Women* (New York: Doubleday, 1976), p. 28.

33 Thompson Townsend, *Mary Barton: A Drama in Three Acts*, has apparently not been published and is quoted from the licensing ms. in the British Library.

34 George Eliot, *Adam Bede* (Boston: Houghton Mifflin, 1968), p. 376.

35 Ibid., p. 386.

36 The play *Adam Bede* by J. E. Carpenter, staged at the Surrey Theatre in 1862 and evidently never published, is quoted from the licensing ms. in the British Library, pp. 22–24.

37 Eliot, *Adam Bede*, p. 446.

38 Jane Tompkins, *Sensational Designs: The Cultural Work of American Fiction, 1790–1860* (New York: Oxford University Press, 1985), p.125.

39 Harriet Beecher Stowe, *Uncle Tom's Cabin* (Boston: Houghton Mifflin, n.d.), p. 495.

40 Ibid., pp. 308–09.

41 H. Chance Newton, *Crime and the Drama: or Dark Deeds Dramatized* (1927; rpt. Port Washington, NY: Kennikat, 1970), pp. 194–95.

42 This scene ends the first act of *Uncle Tom's Cabin: A Drama in Two Acts*, quoted from the licensing ms. in the British Library.

43 The scene occurs near the end of Act i in the licensing ms. of *Uncle Tom's Cabin or The Negro Slave, a Drama in 2 Acts*, by Edward Fitzball.

44 George F. Rowe, *Uncle Tom's Cabin* (n.p.: "printed for private circulation only," 1878), pp. 12, 49.

45 Mark Lemon and Tom Taylor, *Slave Life; or, Uncle Tom's Cabin. A Drama, in Three Acts* (London: Webster, n.d.), pp. 9–10.

46 *Uncle Tom's Cabin: A Drama in Two Acts*, p. 65.

47 Stowe, *Uncle Tom's Cabin*, p. 484.

48 Mary Elizabeth Braddon, *Lady Audley's Secret* (New York: Dover, 1974), pp. 227, 231, 248–51.

49 C. H. Hazlewood, *Lady Audley's Secret*, in George Rowell, ed., *Nineteenth Century Plays* (London: Oxford University Press, 1972), p. 266.

50 Quoted from the licensing manuscript of William Suter's apparently unpublished play, *Lady Audley's Secret*, Act ii, scene iii.

51 George Roberts, *Lady Audley's Secret: A Drama, in Two Acts* (n.p.: "privately printed – not published," n.d.), pp. 39–40.

52 H. Chance Newton, *Cues and Curtain Calls* (London: Lane, n.d.), p. 177.

53 Ellen Wood, *East Lynne* (New Brunswick, NJ: Rutgers University Press, 1984), pp. 517–19.

54 John Oxenford, *East Lynne*, in *The Golden Age of Melodrama: Twelve Nineteenth Century Melodramas*, ed. Michael Kilgarriff (London: Wolfe, 1974), pp. 293, 304.

55 Quoted here is the anonymous licensing ms. of a version of *East Lynne* submitted in 1875.

56 Edmund Gurney, *The New East Lynne*, apparently never published, is quoted from the licensing ms. of 1898.

57 The International Copyright Act, validating in Great Britain the Berne Convention of 1885, gave dramatists and novelists protection over their own work, except in the United States, but did not specifically protect novelists from having their works adapted for the stage. The American Copyright Act of 1891 extended this protection to the U.S. But "full protection" of dramatic copyright was delayed until the 1911 Copyright Act, as pointed out by J. R. Stephens in *The Profession of the Playwright*.

58 *The Times*, 25 April 1888, p. 11.

59 Frances Hodgson Burnett, *Little Lord Fauntleroy* (New York: Scribner's, 1947), pp. 173, 179.

60 Frances Hodgson Burnett, *The Real Little Lord Fauntleroy*, licensing ms. in the British Library, p. 21. A somewhat different version was published in the Samuel French series of acting texts (New York, 1889).

61 Quoted from an unidentified clipping in the Theatre Museum.

62 Review of *The Real Little Lord Fauntleroy*, in *Illustrated Sporting and Dramatic News*, 14 July 1888, p. 546.

63 Unidentified review of Seebohm's *Little Lord Fauntleroy* in the Theatre Museum.

64 Undated review in the Theatre Museum of Seebohm, *Little Lord Fauntleroy*, from *The Sunday Times*.

65 "The Playhouses," *The Sunday Times*, 19 May 1888.

66 Review of Burnett, *The Real Little Lord Fauntleroy*, in *Theatre*, 1 June 1888, pp. 321–22.

67 Unidentified review of *The Real Little Lord Fauntleroy* in the Theatre Museum.

68 Law Report, *The Times*, 25 April 1888, p. 11.

69 Ibid., 11 May 1888, p. 3.

70 Ibid., p. 10.

71 "A Hoffmann House Mystery," *New York Times*, 12 September 1888, p. 5; "His Identity Unknown," *New York Times*, 13 September 1888, p. 3; and "The Mystery Still Unsolved," *New York Times*, 14 September 1888, p. 2.

72 "The Dramatic Year," in the *Era*, 29 December 1888, p. 16.

73 Quoted from an undated clipping in *The Sunday Times* in the Theatre Museum.

6   VICTORIAN PLAYS BY WOMEN

1 This estimate is based on entries of plays and authors listed in Gwenn Davis and Beverly A. Joyce, *Drama by Women to 1900: A Bibliography of American and British Writers* (Toronto: University of Toronto Press, 1992); *"The Stage" Cyclopaedia* (London: The Stage, 1909); Donald Mullin, *Victorian Plays: A Record of Significant Productions on the London Stage, 1837–1901* (New York: Greenwood, 1987); Allardyce Nicoll, *A History of English Drama, 1660–1900* (6 vols., Cambridge: Cambridge University Press, 1952–59); J. P. Wearing, *The London Stage, 1890–1899: A Calendar of Plays and Players* (Metuchen, NJ: Scarecrow, 1976).

2 Virginia Woolf, *"A Room of One's Own" and "Three Guineas"* (London: Hogarth, 1984), p. 47.

3 Cicely Hamilton, *Life Errant* (London: Dent, 1935), p. 60.

4 This is the account given by Catherine Gore in the "Preface" to *Quid Pro Quo; or, the Day of Dupes* (London: National Acting Drama Office, n.d.), p. iii.

5 *The Times*, 9 May 1902, p. 8; Netta Syrett, *The Sheltering Tree* (London: Bles, 1939), p. 118.

6 Catherine Gore, "Preface" to *Quid Pro Quo*, p. v.

7 Elizabeth Robins, "Woman's Secret," in *Way Stations* (New York: Dodd, Mead, 1913), p. 6.

8 Quoted from the ms. of *Discretion* in the Fales Library, New York University.

9 Lady Violet Greville and Arthur Bourchier, *Justice, A Play in Four Acts*, is quoted from the licensing ms. in the Lord Chamberlain's Collection of the British Library, Act i, p. 16. The play appears never to have been published.

10 Oscar Wilde, *An Ideal Husband*, in *Two Society Comedies*, ed. Ian Small and Russell Jackson (London: Benn, 1983), p. 264.

11 Gordon Craig, *Ellen Terry and Her Secret Self* (London: Low, Marston [1931]), pp. 158–59.

12 T. W. Robertson, *School*, in *Plays by Tom Robertson*, ed. William Tydeman (Cambridge: Cambridge University Press, 1982), pp. 224–25; H. J. Byron, *Cinderella; or, The Lover, the Lackey, and the Little Glass Slipper* (London: Hailes, n.d.), p. 6.

13 Harold Bloom, *The Anxiety of Influence: A Theory of Poetry* (New York: Oxford University Press, 1973), p. 43.

14 Sandra Gilbert and Susan Gubar, *The Madwoman in the Attic: The Woman Writer and the Nineteenth-Century Literary Imagination* (New Haven: Yale University Press, 1979).

15 William Archer, *Play-Making: A Manual of Craftsmanship* (Boston: Small, Maynard, 1912), pp. 29–33.

16 Catherine Crowe, *The Cruel Kindness: A Romantic Play, in Five Acts* (London: Routledge, 1853), pp. 43–49.

17 Clara Cavendish, *The Woman of the World: A Drama in Two Acts* (London: Lacy, n.d.), pp. 22, 57.

18 Lucy Lane (Mrs. W. K.) Clifford, *A Long Duel: A Serious Comedy in Four Acts*, was evidently never published. It is quoted from the ms. in the Lord Chamberlain's Collection, British Library, Act iv, p. 25.

19 Clotilde Graves, *A Physician: A Play in Three Acts*, was performed at the Lyric Theatre in 1893 but apparently never published. It is quoted from the licensing ms. in the Lord Chamberlain's Collection, British Library, p. 56.

20 Maria Hall, *Mabel's Curse: A Musical Drama in Two Acts* (London: Duncombe, n.d.), p. 14.

21 Mrs. Edward Thomas, *The Wife's Tragedy: An Emotional Drama in 5 Acts*, apparently never published, is quoted from the Lord Chamberlain's licensing ms. in the British Library.

22 Sara Lane, *Red Josephine, or A Woman's Vengeance, in 4 Acts*, is quoted from the licensing ms. in the Lord Chamberlain's Collection of the British Library, pp. 43–44, 52.

23 Sara Lane, *Faithless Wife*, licensing ms. in the Lord Chamberlain's Collection, British Library.

24 Sara Lane, *Dolores*, is quoted from the licensing ms. in the Lord Chamberlain's Collection, British Library, p. 14.

25 Anna Cora Mowatt, *Autobiography of an Actress* (Boston: Ticknor, Reed, and Fields, 1854), p. 409.

26 Maria Lovell, *Ingomar the Barbarian: A Play, in Five Acts* (London: French, n.d.), pp. 20, 28, 30, 31, 49, 60–61.

27 Anna Cora Mowatt, *Autobiography of an Actress*, p. 409.

28 G. A. Sala, *Echoes of the Year 1883* (London: Remington, 1884), p. 388.

29 William Winter, *Other Days; Being Chronicles and Memories of the Stage* (New York: Moffatt, Yard, 1908), p. 261.

30 Elizabeth Robins, *The Mirkwater*, quoted from the ms. in the Fales Library, New York University.

31 Joanne Gates, *Elizabeth Robins, 1862–1951: Actress, Novelist, Feminist* (Tuscaloosa: University of Alabama Press, 1994), p. 86.

32 Florence Bell, *Stella: A Play in Three Acts*, is quoted from the ms. in the Fales Library, New York University, pp. 3, 22.

33 Estelle Burney, *Settled Out of Court: Play in Four Acts*, apparently never published, is quoted from the licensing ms. in the Lord Chamberlain's Collection, British Library, pp. 84–91.

34 Constance Fletcher ["George Fleming"], *Mrs. Lessingham* (London: Miles, 1894), "printed as manuscript," pp. 41, 55.

35 Oscar Wilde, *Lady Windermere's Fan: A Play about a Good Woman*, ed. Ian Small (London: Benn, 1980), pp. 57–58.

36 [Elizabeth Robins and Florence Bell], *Alan's Wife: A Dramatic Study in Three Scenes* (London: Henry, 1893), p. 47.

37 Aimée (Mrs. Oscar) Beringer, *Tares: A Social Problem: Printed as Manuscript for Private Circulation Only* (London: Miles, 1887), p. 55.

38 Aimée Beringer, *Bess: A Play in Three Acts*, apparently unpublished, was performed at the Novelty Theatre in 1891. It is quoted from the licensing ms. in the Lord Chamberlain's Collection at the British Library, Act II, p. 17. The description of the audience's strong reaction to the play comes from a review in the *Era*, 17 June 1893, p. 9, on the occasion of a charity performance put on by George Alexander at which Aimée Beringer was "summoned to the footlights and was cordially cheered." Genevieve Ward was said to act the part of Bess with a great "power to compel sympathy."

39 Mrs. Reginald Fairburn, *Men and Women: An Entirely New and Original Drama in 7 Tableaux*, apparently never published, is quoted from the licensing ms. in the Lord Chamberlain's Collection, British Library, p. 140.

40 Dorothy Leighton [Dorothy Forsyth], *Thyrza Fleming. A Drama in Four Acts*,

was apparently never published. It is quoted from the licensing ms. in the Lord Chamberlain's Collection, British Library, pp. 33, 63, 67.

41 Blanche Crackanthorpe, *The Turn of the Wheel*, never produced or published, is quoted from the ms. in the file of plays in the British Library that were denied a license by the Lord Chamberlain; Act I, p. 11; Act II, pp. 14, 20.

42 Florence Bell, *The Dean of St. Patrick's, or Vanessa*, quoted from the typescript in the Fales Library, New York University, Act I, pp. 3, 7.

43 Mrs. Musgrave, *Cerise and Co.: A Farcical Comedy in Three Acts*, apparently never published, is quoted from the ms. in the Lord Chamberlain's Collection, British Library.

44 Clotilde Graves, *Nurse! An Original Farce in Two Acts and One Scene*, Act I, p. 6; Act II, p. 5, quoted from the licensing ms. in the Lord Chamberlain's Collection, British Library. There is no record of the play having been published.

45 *The Masterpiece: Comedietta in One Act*, was performed at the Royalty Theatre in 1893. It is quoted from the ms. in the Lord Chamberlain's Collection, British Library, pp. 2, 4, 10.

46 Lily Tinsley, *Cinders* (London: French, 1899), pp. 16, 19.

47 Frances Hodgson Burnett, *The Showman's Daughter*, apparently never published, is quoted from the licensing ms. in the Lord Chamberlain's Collection, British Library, p. 71.

48 *Mrs. Daintree's Daughter* by Janet Achurch has evidently never been published and is quoted from the ms. in the Lord Chamberlain's Collection, British Library, p. 63.

49 Clotilde Graves and Gertrude Kingston, *A Matchmaker*, apparently never published, is quoted from the ms. in the Lord Chamberlain's Collection, British Library; Act II, p. 14.

50 Quoted from an unidentified review in the Theatre Museum.

51 Pearl M. Craigie ("John Oliver Hobbes"), *The Ambassador: A Comedy in Four Acts* (London: Unwin, 1898), p. 67.

52 *Era*, 6 April 1898, p. 13.

53 The term was coined by Sandra Gilbert and Susan Gubar in *The Madwoman in the Attic*.

54 Mary Elizabeth Braddon, *Griselda, in Four Acts*, is quoted from the licensing ms. in the Lord Chamberlain's Collection, British Library, pp. 27, 36.

55 Sarah Grand and Haldane McFall, *The Fear of Robert Clive. A Play in One Act*, apparently never published, is quoted from the licensing ms. in the Lord Chamberlain's Collection, British Library, p. 27.

56 *Sketch*, 15 August 1896.

57 "Miss Clo Graves, Novelist and Dramatist," *The Times*, 5 December 1932, p. 17.

58 Clotilde Graves, *A Mother of Three: An Original Farce in Three Acts* (London: French, n.d.), pp. 18, 63, 65.

59 Netta Syrett, *The Sheltering Tree*, p. 116.

60 Netta Syrett, *The Finding of Nancy*, never published, is quoted from the licens-

ing ms. in the Lord Chamberlain's Collection, British Library, pp. 7, 8, 54.
61 Netta Syrett, *The Sheltering Tree*, pp. 121, 125–26.
62 Max Beerbohm, review of *The Finding of Nancy* in *Saturday Review*, 17 May 1902, pp. 633–34.
63 *The Times*, 9 May 1902, p. 8.
64 *Era*, 10 May 1902, p. 19.
65 Ibid., p. 14.
66 *Athenaeum*, 17 May 1902, pp. 635–36.
67 Netta Syrett, *The Sheltering Tree*, pp. 119, 126.

7 ELIZABETH ROBINS, OSCAR WILDE, AND THE "THEATRE OF THE FUTURE"

1 Two biographies have appeared recently: Angela John, *Elizabeth Robins: Staging a Life, 1862–1952* (London: Routledge, 1995), and Joanne Gates, *Elizabeth Robins, 1862–1952: Actress, Novelist, Feminist* (Tuscaloosa: University of Alabama Press, 1994).
2 Richard Ellmann, *Oscar Wilde* (New York: Knopf, 1988), pp. 330–31.
3 These events were described for the first time by Angela John, *Elizabeth Robins: Staging a Life*, pp. 38–41, and Joanne Gates, *Elizabeth Robins, 1862–1952*, pp. 19–22.
4 Even recent histories such as John Elsom and Nicholas Tomalin's *The History of the National Theatre* (London: Cape, 1978) make no mention of Robins's crucial role in envisioning a noncommercial national theatre. The contributions of other women such as Eleanor Calhoun are ignored as well. It needs to be recognized that discrimination against women in the Victorian theatre was what made it obvious to progressive actresses that the English drama needed a new, more equitable institutional framework.
5 Elizabeth Robins, "Oscar Wilde: An Appreciation," unpublished ms. in Fales Library, New York University, p. 1.
6 Elizabeth Robins, "Woman's Secret," in *Way Stations* (New York: Dodd, Mead, 1913), p. 6.
7 Jane Marcus, "Elizabeth Robins," diss. Northwestern University, 1973, p. 5.
8 Elizabeth Robins, *Discretion: A Play in 3 Acts*, ms. in Fales Library, New York University. The play was never performed or published.
9 Robins, *Both Sides of the Curtain* (London: Heineman, 1940), p. 16.
10 Rupert Hart-Davis, ed., *The Letters of Oscar Wilde* (New York: Harcourt, Brace, 1962), p. 223.
11 Ibid.
12 *The Theatre*, review of *A Fair Bigamist*, 1 October 1888, pp. 220–21.
13 *The Times*, review of *A Fair Bigamist*, 21 September 1888, p. 3.
14 Princess Lazarovich-Hrebelianovich [Eleanor Calhoun], *Pleasures and Palaces: The Memoirs of Princess Lazarovich-Hrebelianovich* (London: Nash, 1916), pp. 193–94.

15 Oscar Wilde, *"As You Like It* at Coombe House," in *Dramatic Review*, 6 June 1885; rpt. in *The First Collected Edition of the Works of Oscar Wilde* (15 vols., London: Methuen, 1908–22), ed. Robert Ross, XIII, 32–36.

16 Robins, *Both Sides of the Curtain*, pp. 27–28.

17 Ibid., p. 51.

18 Ibid., pp. 132, 144–45.

19 Robins, "Oscar Wilde: An Appreciation," ms. in Fales Library, New York University, insert for p. 1.

20 Hart-Davis, ed., *Letters of Oscar Wilde*, p. 79.

21 Robins, *Both Sides of the Curtain*, pp. 208–09.

22 Ibid., pp. 201, 215.

23 *The Times*, review of *A Man's Shadow*, 13 September 1889, p. 3.

24 *The Theatre*, review of *A Man's Shadow*, 1 October 1889, p. 206.

25 Robins, *Both Sides of the Curtain*, pp. 217, 220.

26 Ibid., p. 223.

27 Ibid., p. 242.

28 Ibid., p. 252.

29 Ibid., p. 328.

30 Elizabeth Robins, diary for 8 July to 4 December 1890, ms. in Fales Library, New York University.

31 Robins, "Whither and How", ms. in Fales Library, New York University, chapter II, p. 11.

32 "Whither and How," chapters VII–VIII.

33 Robins, *Ibsen and the Actress* (London: Hogarth, 1928), pp. 16–17.

34 Hart-Davis, ed., *Letters of Oscar Wilde*, pp. 290–91.

35 Robins, "Oscar Wilde: An Appreciation," p. 2.

36 Rupert Hart-Davis, ed., *More Letters of Oscar Wilde* (New York: Vanguard, 1985), pp. 95–96.

37 Robins, "Whither and How," chapter XV, p. 5.

38 Ibid., from a handwritten note on the typed ms., and chapter XIV, p. 7.

39 Herbert-Beerbohm Tree, letter to Robins, 24 April 1891, ms. in Fales Library, New York University.

40 Robins, "Heights and Depths," ms. in Fales Library, New York University.

41 Robins, "Whither and How," handwritten and typed notes under the title "Odd Bits" at the end of the manuscript.

42 Robins, "The Coming Woman," ms. in Fales Library, New York University, pp. 3, 7.

43 Ibid., pp. 35, 36, 38, 48.

44 Ibid., p. 51.

45 Ibid., p. 108.

46 Ibid., p. 51.

47 Robins, "A Highly Respectable Heroine," ms. in Fales Library, New York University, p. 2.

48 Robins, ms. diary, in Fales Library, New York University.

49 Robins, letter to Bell, 18 May 1892, ms. in Fales Library, New York University.
50 Robins, "Oscar Wilde: An Appreciation," p. 9.
51 George Bernard Shaw, *Collected Letters, 1874–1897*, ed. Dan H. Laurence (New York: Dodd, Mead, 1965), pp. 393–95.
52 Letter from Bell to Robins (1892), ms. in Fales Library, New York University.
53 *Alan's Wife* was published with an introduction by William Archer (London: Henry, 1893).
54 Shaw, preface to William Archer, *The Theatrical "World" of 1894*, (London: Scott, 1895), pp. xiv–xxv, xxviii–xxx.
55 Robins, *Theatre and Friendship* (New York: Putnam's, 1932), pp. 149–50.
56 William Archer *The Old Drama and the New: An Essay in Re-Valuation* (Boston: Small, Maynard, 1923), pp. 303–04.
57 Robins, "Oscar Wilde: An Appreciation," p. 5.
58 G. B. Shaw, *Collected Letters, 1874–1897*, pp. 393–94, 478–79.
59 Robins, *Theatre and Friendship*, pp. 144–45.
60 Letter from Archer to Robins, quoted by Gates in *Elizabeth Robins, 1862–1952*.
61 Robins, *The Florentine Frame* (New York: Moffat, Yard, 1909), p. 260.
62 Letter from Tree to Robins, 23 February 1900, ms. in Fales Library, New York University.
63 Robins, *The Mirkwater*, ms. in Fales Library, New York University, Act III, p. 8; see also chapter 6, pp. 133–34.
64 Robins, "Oscar Wilde: An Appreciation," p. 6.
65 Ibid.
66 Robins, *Theatre and Friendship*, p. 185.
67 Ibid., p. 196.
68 Robins, letter to Millicent Fawcett, 1 November 1906, ms. in Fales Library, New York University.
69 Robins, *Theatre and Friendship*, p. 260.
70 Robins, "Whither and How," chapter II, p. 9.
71 Robins, letter to Bell, 18 May 1892, ms. in Fales Library.
72 Robins, *Votes for Women: A Dramatic Tract in Three Acts* (Chicago: Dramatic Publishing, 1907), pp. 122–23.
73 Hart-Davis, ed., *Letters of Oscar Wilde*, p. 364.

Index